Team, It's Only Radio!

John Myers

Life, laughs and the radio business

Published by KENTON PUBLISHING
The Granary, Hatham Green Lane, Stansted
SEVENOAKS TN15 7PL
www.kentonpublishing.co.uk

The right of John Myers to be identified as the Author of the Work has been asserted
by him in accordance with the Copyright, Designs and Patents Act 1988
First published in 2012 by KENTON PUBLISHING
ISBN 978-0-9546223-9-8
eISBN 978-0-9546223-4-3
2 4 6 8 10 9 7 5 3 1

Typeset by Decent Typesetting, www.decenttypesetting.co.uk
Printed and bound by CPI Group (UK) Ltd, Croydon, CR0 4YY
Every effort has been made to contact copyright holders but some were untraceable.
We would be grateful if relevant owners could contact us.
www.myersmedia.co.uk
Book@myersmedia.co.uk
twitter.com/johnmyersteam

In memory of my amazing parents, Jimmy and Helen Myers, and with thanks for the support and love of all my eight brothers and sisters.

To my children, Kerry and Scott, my lovely grandchildren, Marcus and Mia, but most of all to my wonderful wife, Linda. Every single thing that is good in my life has come through being with this kind and inspirational woman.

All profits from this book will go to three charities:

- ***The Radio Academy Benevolent*** *fund to help and assist those who have spent time in the radio industry and have fallen on difficult times.*

- ***Radio Tyneside****, my local hospital radio station where I am the proud chairman*

- ***British Lung Foundation****, in memory of my lovely mum.*

CONTENTS

FOREWORD
by Jeremy Vine

In the film *Radio Days,* Woody Allen is portrayed as a young boy whose mother catches him listening to the wireless. She is furious. 'STOP LISTENING TO THE RADIO!' she shouts at him. 'It's going to ruin you.'

The lad responds, 'But Ma, you listen to the radio all the time.'

'That's different,' she tells him. 'My life is ruined already.'

We often think that radio has always been there – has always been the same. But that movie scene reminds us how, less than a century ago, commercial radio was new enough to scare your mother.

Since then it has been through every kind of boom and bust. Survival was never guaranteed. While the BBC is fortified by a licence fee, commercial radio has had to fight like a tiger just to get its next meal.

At this point I would like to introduce you to the biggest tiger in the jungle.

I met John Myers nearly a decade ago. At the time I did not know his first rule in business was: 'Never employ anyone with a weak hand-shake' but I think my grasp must have been just strong enough because we became friends. All I knew was that he had once been a breakfast presenter; now he ran stuff at the Guardian. Above and beyond all of that, this was a lovely guy who wanted to talk endlessly about radio. John was modest enough not to push his CV at me. I was sufficiently incurious not to look it up. I now realise I should have done.

Reading this book has been a revelation and a joy. You will think I am exaggerating if I say that John Myers is probably the most important figure in British commercial radio since Marconi, but who else comes close? He starts as a DJ in clubs. Then he gets on air, fuelled by sheer desperation, initially presenting a Country music show for £25 a time; his hatred of the genre is not diluted when he is hilariously named Country Music Presenter of the Year. Other shows follow, each slot bigger than the last, each new adventure wilder and wackier, a haze of deranged competitions, barking mad callers and crazy promotional stunts. Then, with a head for business, John begins buying radio stations.

The central character in this book is so much larger than most of the people around him that at times it is like watching Motorhead take the stage at the village fête. The tale is not all sweetness and light. When a film crew making the documentary *Trouble At The Top* walked into Nottingham's Century 106 alongside John, the receptionist gulped at the camera, 'Every time Mr Myers comes here, someone gets fired.'

He was later shown in a meeting with the presenter of the station's religious programme. 'Your audience figures are so low,' he told her, 'even God's not listening.'

When I reached the paragraph where John calmly mentions that his combined purchases for the Guardian Media Group totalled a hundred million pounds, I nearly dropped my Kindle in the bath.

Certainly, there is sage advice here for any radio person on the mike or on the make. But actually, this is primarily not a book about big business. It is about the intimate pleasure of working on the wireless. It's a love letter to that uncomplicated box by your toaster, an uproarious but also deeply touching account of what I fear may well have been radio's golden age. I adored reading John's personal tally of disasters and triumphs: when his competitors at Metro Radio festooned the

Tyne Bridge with a huge poster to catch the attention of TV viewers watching the Great North Run, he wrapped a double-decker bus with the name and colours of his own radio station, Century, and successfully bribed the driver to break down 'for a minimum of four hours' in front of the poster.

What makes the whole story special? In broadcasting, precious few can host a show and run the show. The number who become both hugely successful presenters and then make millions as radio entrepreneurs – well, even Marconi didn't do that. The firewall between the broadcaster and the management is the reason all presenters feel misunderstood. 'They could never do this job,' is the regular complaint you hear about the bosses. 'They don't know what it's like.' But John *did* do the job. And he tells us exactly what it's like.

He is honest about the things that possibly should not have happened. The 'live show from the Champs Elysées' that actually came from Preston. The listener who complained and was sent a letter saying: 'Fuck off. You are officially barred from tuning into this radio station in the future and if you continue to write or listen, a stronger letter will follow.' The time he padlocked the doors at BBC Radio Cumbria, leaving a notice on them saying: *FOR SALE due to lack of listeners or entertainment. Any reasonable offer considered.*

John's contempt for regulators is subversively glorious. When Ofcom upbraid him about not playing proper jazz on Jazz FM, they ask him for his definition of the genre. 'Anything with a trumpet', he tells them.

'What, anything with a trumpet?' the regulator replies. 'Are you joking?'

'You started it,' he replies.

I mustn't spoil the stories. They are all here for you to discover. This is a man who has struck deals worth millions and yet never forgets the value of the people around him. Suffice to say, I felt terribly nostalgic reading this book, and then glad. Nostalgic because I'm not sure anyone else will have an adventure like this again. Glad because John did, and he has written it all down.

IMPORTANT CONTINUITY ANNOUNCEMENT

The following pages contains some fruity language from the start. We apologise for any offense this may cause. However, such language is only used where it is necessary to quote directly from the person themselves or if the subject matter requires it. This happens more than once!

Readers are advised not to turn over the pages of this book unless they are prepared to enter into a world where strange personalities ruled the dial, individual owners led the way, localness was important, competititions were won by screaming women on a Friday at 8.15 am, radio presenters played what they wanted and the regulator knew its place. This is a book from the heart, it is not manufactured, there is no playlist and no research was undertaken to determine if it will succeed. Instead, it is all gut feel. A revealing insight into real radio from inside the ropes.

TEAM CALLING

The first pub to be built in Carlisle after the abolition of the city's unique State Management Scheme was called *The Enterprise* and, pleasingly, it was right at the end of the road where I lived. For nearly sixty years all the city's public houses and even the local brewery had been owned by the government, who stepped in at the height of the Great War to take control of the locals' drinking habits, after munitions workers spent all their time boozing instead of making bombs to hurl at the Germans. Until Prime Minister Ted Heath scrapped the State Management Scheme in the early Seventies, every landlord in Carlisle was a government employee. Customers even had to purchase one beer at a time because buying a round of drinks was banned under the No Treating law.

The local newspaper ran a competition to name the city's first free enterprise pub. Its readers came up with *The Enterprise* but the locals simply called it *The Starship*.

This new, modern, building held about two hundred people and was the place to go to before you hit the city for a night out, except on a Sunday when nightclubs didn't open. So, on the Sabbath *The Starship* was the busiest place in town. I knew the owner quite well from often having to go and pick my dad up there after a few beers.

I was eighteen years old and desperately wanted to be in the entertainment business, so I hired the big room at *The Starship* and put on
monthly cabaret nights, booking the stars of the day through a local
agent, Jason Black. I hired artists like musical comedy act The Brother
Lees, impressionist Les Dennis and soul singer Edwin Starr but I came
unstuck when I booked the brilliant Frankie Vaughan for two nights
running. Frankie was my most expensive performer to date, costing
me a thousand pounds a night, so I sold the Saturday night to BBC
Radio Carlisle for their own Listeners' Club. The second night was
my own gig where I hoped to make a few quid. Sadly, there weren't
enough punters to sustain two nights and I'd made the mistake of
allowing BBC Radio Carlisle to advertise their tickets before I sold my
own. They used the power of their own media to sell out before me.
The bottom line was that I was going to end up around five hundred
pounds short, a fortune to lose in 1977. I told the agent, Jason Black,
that I couldn't find the shortfall so I'd have to cancel before Frankie's
contract reached the 'hard date', the day when we could no longer exit
without payment. Jason gave me the cash and told me to pay him back
when I had it. Nothing in writing, just a handshake. If I wanted to
carry on, he'd pick up the difference.

'Oh, and one more thing,' Jason said. 'Frankie is a big football
fan and wants to watch Carlisle United play on the Saturday, can you
arrange it?'

I rang the football club chairman. He couldn't believe it and
arranged for Frankie and me to sit with him in the directors' box. Being
a big Carlisle United fan myself, this was the best day of my year. I did
have to laugh, though, when we came in at half-time. The only food
was pork pies and, being a good Jewish boy, Frankie couldn't eat them!

Back at the hotel, Frankie said he'd heard I was losing out on the
deal and wanted to apologise for not bringing in the crowds. I explained
he wasn't at fault, it was my own stupidity for allowing the local radio
station to sell their tickets before my own. He gave me his card and
said he had a box at White Hart Lane. As a gesture of goodwill he'd

like to invite me to be his guest at Tottenham Hotspur the next time I was in London. The next time I was in London? There had not been a first time as yet. Going to London was like visiting another world – but I loved his style. It was five years before I got in touch. I sent Frankie a personal note asking if he remembered me and, if so, would it be possible to see the Tottenham v Liverpool game? He sent me two tickets back within the week. What a great man!

Thanks to performers like amazing soul singer Edwin Starr, who packed out The Starship on future nights, I was eventually able to pay Jason back, although by then he'd written off the debt, fully expecting never to see the money again.

One thing I noticed when Edwin Starr bounced into the pub was that he called everyone 'Team'.

'TEAM!' he'd shout at the top of his voice. Everyone connected with it and before long he wanted me to call him Team, instead of Edwin.

'Okay, Team, no problem,' I said. He explained that he met so many people in the record business and he just couldn't remember every-one's name. However, they were all working together as a team – so that's what he called them. Edwin is no longer with us but his backing band is still called The Team. After that I started calling people Team, too. It's just stuck and, today, people call me Team right across the board, from the biggest names in the radio industry to those I work with, they just call me Team.

Many people think it stands for Together Everyone Achieves More. That's a nice fit but it's not the reality.

The only people who I don't call Team are my family. I can remember their names – just!

So, if I call you Team it simply means you're part of my life. You are someone I regard highly. It's a genuine term of friendship. Even today, people who I may not have spoken to for some years, ring me up and the first thing they say is … 'Team!'

PROLOGUE

The speakerphone burst into life. The conversation that followed with the legendary former Editor of The Sun, Kelvin MacKenzie, will live with me for ever:

'Kelvin here. Who's with you?'

'Hi Kelvin,' I replied. 'Err me, Bob Phillis and Nick Castro.'

'Right, well let me tell you all. This is the worst fucking day of my bloody life. To have to sell something to you left wing, sandal-wearing arseholes has really pissed me off. Look, I've done the deal, I've signed the forms and, John, I really hope you make a success of it. But, for now, you can all fuck off.'

The phone went dead. All three of us sat there shocked.

Sir Bob Phillis, Chief Executive of Guardian Media Group, a man who I'd never heard utter a swear word and who had certainly never been subjected to that kind of abuse in his entire life, was astounded.

'John,' Bob said, recovering his composure, 'we've just given that man twenty-five and a half million pounds for a radio station that is losing three million pounds a year and he's just told us to fuck off.'

'He loves us,' I replied. 'You should hear what he says to people he doesn't like. We've got what we came for, so let's move on.'

'I can't believe it,' said Bob, shaking his head. 'I just don't believe it.'

Next morning I met with Kelvin for breakfast and explained how his fruity language had really upset Bob and, if he got the chance, he should apologise.

Kelvin really did like Bob and knew he'd overstepped the mark.

I didn't want any bad feeling to overshadow our relationship, so I found myself saying, 'Look, here's the number for Bob's private line. Why not give him a ring tomorrow to clear the air?'

The following day I was with Bob in his office going through the final details of our purchase of Kelvin's loss-making station, Scot FM, when the private phone began to ring.

'Who could that be?' Bob wondered aloud.

I've never understood people who say that. 'Pick the thing up and find out,' I urged.

Bob went white.

'Hi, Bob. Kelvin here.'

'Kelvin, err hi. How did you get this number?'

'C'mon Bob, I'm a journalist. Getting numbers is what I do.'

'Err, okay. What can I do for you?'

'Look,' Kelvin said. 'I'm ringing to apologise for my harsh words yesterday. It was uncalled for and I just wanted to make sure all was good between us.'

'Well, Kelvin, that's really kind of you. It takes a good man to ring up and apologise. I'm delighted to accept your apology.'

Bob relaxed and made a gesture of goodwill. 'Look, Kelvin, why don't you come over to the office some time and have a coffee?'

The voice on the other end of the line suddenly exploded. 'What? Come to The Guardian? You have to be fucking mad. I'm not going in there. You can fuck off!'

The phone crashed down.

Ah well, I tried.

Chapter One

KNICKERS, KNACKERS, KNOCKERS

I grew up listening to the wonderful sound of Radio 1, though at night it was anything but wonderful. The BBC's most popular radio station by a mile played weird music after dark. In those days most stations actually closed down at night thanks to the commercial radio needle time agreement, which limited music to just nine hours a day, or fifty per cent of your total output. Some stations were able to stay on air for longer by playing music from the Canadian Broadcast Library or surprisingly, on tape. However, by adding in DJ chat, news and speech features it was possible to remain on air for up to twenty hours before you ran out of music.

So, listeners like me moved along the Medium Wave dial to 208 Radio Luxembourg, which had great DJs, a mix of new and exciting features and music late into the night. Luxy, as we called it, faded in and out although the station had a jingle that boasted 'a power of one million, three hundred thousand watts'. I had no idea what that actually meant but it sounded impressive. I used this marketing sizzle to great effect in later years at CFM in Carlisle, where I proclaimed we had one million watts from a 'Tower of Power' at Caldbeck on the edge of the Lake District. The fact that in reality we only had 100,000 watts was never mentioned.

Luxy had The Power Play, where the record of the week was played on the hour – every hour. The station's big-name DJs, Kid Jensen, Mike Read and Emperor Rosko were so different to the formulaic sound of our own national offering. My personal hero was not so much a personality but a man with an incredible voice. Bob Stewart not only had his own show but he was also the official station 'sound' and broadcast a range of messages, including the nightly close down announcement. During the week this was 2 am and an hour later at weekends. I'd often wait in my car until he said those final words 'good night, wherever you are'.

I'd reply, 'And goodnight to you, Bob'.

Madness was setting in even then.

One night, Radio Luxembourg announced the station was running a competition to find a new jock. 'This could be YOU!' it proclaimed.

All I heard was 'This could be ME!'

They wanted a tape. Here was my entry into radio.

Further details were in Melody Maker. It was the first time I'd noticed a connected advertising campaign. I bought a copy and read the details. All Luxy wanted was a 'ten-minute demo that showcased my style, voice and personality'. Considering I had none, I wasn't quite sure how I was going to deliver it but alongside Luxy's advert was an ad for Roger Squires Disco Services. This was the second connected advert for the campaign and Roger Squires Disco Services had studios to record these much sought after demo tapes!

The cost was fifty pounds for a minimum three hours in the studio. This was big money and to me three hours seemed a long time to record just ten minutes. However, it was a real studio and I needed to make the tape.

I loved the '70s, especially Parker coats, bell-bottom trousers, high waistbands and tank tops. The music then was great and, even though the country was just out of a three-day week, people somehow managed to find the money to flock to Tiffany's. The club, above a row of rather run-down shops in Carlisle's Botchergate, was not the best in town by any means but what it lacked in class, it made up for in sound, lights, music and its DJs. In those days, Tiffany's ran a two DJ shift system. I would start off the night, another jock would come in for the middle section and then I'd end it. Basically, I was the warm-up guy for the main turn but I convinced myself it was the other way round, even though he was paid more than me.

This highly paid jock was Hugh Mullins, a giant with a God-given voice that came right up from his platform boots. His vocal strength and the noise he created demanded your attention. I envied him. He was everything I wasn't. Smooth, fashionable, tall, trim and talented. In musical terms we could not have been further apart either. He was Blondie while I was Tavares.

Nevertheless, we were a great club double act. He'd walk in, crank up the microphone to his usual pre-set levels and shout 'One, two … one, two'. I've never understood why jocks do that. I had my own way of testing the mic, 'Knickers, knackers, knockers … show us your tits'. I still use that phrase today.

I longed to be part of Hugh's circle of friends but, whenever I saw him with his pals, I thanked God I wasn't. To me they looked like a bunch of Muppets, dressed in clothes that were certainly way out of my price range. I was still shopping at Burton's while Hugh was making regular trips to London's Kings Road. His god-like status was enhanced when he made it onto the UK VIP Jocks list. This secret list contained the names of the most influential nightclub jocks in the country and, as such, they were given free records.

Yes, *free*. The deal was the VIP jocks would play their free records in clubs up and down the country before the single was officially released to whip up demand. Hey presto! When the song came out, it went straight into the charts. Everyone's a winner, except me. I still had to buy my records at the Pink Panther Record shop for forty-five pence each.

One night, Hugh came in clutching a new song by Donna Summer. *I Feel Love* was revolutionary. Everyone wanted that single but only Hugh had it and there was no way he was leaving it behind for me to play. This made him stand out. This made him better than me. This was competition I didn't enjoy.

Although Hugh was a great jock, I always thought he struggled to maintain a full dance floor. When you're a club DJ you get to know what works and what doesn't. It's a combination of skill, experience and gut feel. More than once he'd seem to misjudge the mood and suffer the embarrassment of an empty floor. In reality, he was a victim of his own success, playing new songs before they were well known. It had the girls picking up their handbags and heading either to the bar or the loo. That never happened when I was in the DJ booth. I had two types of boxes. The Guaranteed Floor Fillers and another packed with oldies and Motown. Once I sensed people were drifting, I'd hit them with one from my guaranteed current hits box. It worked every time.

One night, I mentioned to the boss that he should tell Hughie to play more popular songs.

'Not a chance,' he said. 'When Hughie's in the booth we take more money at the bar. That's because he sometimes plays crap songs and I like that. When people walk off the floor, they go for a drink. I wish you'd play some of these songs so we could make more money. Your problem is you keep them dancing for too long.'

I was flabbergasted. There I was thinking I was great and I was now learning that an empty dance floor was good for business. It might be good for business but it wasn't good for my ego.

Then the boss added, 'That's why Hughie's paid more money than you because he makes us more money. The reason we have you is because we need to send the punters home happy so they come back the next night.'

Another lesson in business.

In an attempt to curry favour with Hugh, I told him about the DJ competition on Luxy. It was an error but as he'd never listened to Radio Luxembourg I honestly didn't think he would be interested. Quite the reverse, he was all over me like a rash asking for the details. When, where and what time? I gave him all the information and he begged me to book him into the same studio on the same day.

We left Carlisle together, me in my red Vauxhall Opel and him following behind in his Blue BMW. Yes, a bloody BMW which only underlined his superior status even further in my eyes. Fifty miles down the M6 we lost each other. I slowed to a crawl and eventually pulled into the motorway services. There were no mobile phones then so I had no chance of making any contact. After what seemed like hours, I resolved to make it to London on my own, worried that Hughie been in an accident but more worried I'd been duped.

I arrived in London later than planned, stayed overnight in a cheap B&B and next morning made my way to Roger Squires' studio in St. John's Wood.

Walking in to a real on-air studio for the first time is daunting but one of the staff helped me choose a few songs and showed me how to use the desk. As a bonus, included in my fifty quid, they produced a jingle with my name voiced by someone called Bill Mitchell. I nearly fainted with excitement. It was not long before it became obvious why three hours would be required to record just ten minutes.

I was useless.

Recording the same thing over and over again was not making it any better. I came across very northern at a time when being very northern was anything but good. There was clearly a big difference between the skills required to be a radio jock and working in a nightclub. Hughie turned up thirty minutes before the end of my session claiming he'd had a flat tyre. He sounded convincing but as far as I was concerned the jury was still out. It was my own daft fault and I headed back up the motorway with a tape in my hands and a resolve to get tougher.

A few days later, Hughie played me his demo. It was brilliant. His trademark voice boomed out of the speakers with not a hint of northern charm. Then I played mine and cringed. Chalk and cheese.

There and then, I knew it was a lost cause. It's like a player from the second division trying to compete in the Premiership. If the boss at Luxy heard these tapes side by side I was doomed. Hughie suggested we send our tapes in together but I surprised myself by saying no. I told him I wanted to write a personal note so he should just go ahead on his own. I rushed home, put the letter together and sent it off the next day in the hope I would get first-base advantage.

The following Saturday, I opened up the club and set the warm-up music going. In those days, people came to nightclubs early. The doors opened at eight o'clock and the place was full by half past nine. Appleby Horse Fair was an annual event and the travelling families would pack the club all that week. This was a very different crowd to normal, yet the gypsy girls loved to dance right from the start, so that was good for me. I spotted a girl with the biggest knockers I'd seen in my life. She also wore a low-cut top and these two sights were bouncing around like giant ferrets in a bag. She headed my way. I was transfixed. The closer to the DJ's booth she got, the bigger they became. Then I noticed something quite remarkable. Tattooed on each breast were the words Mild and Bitter. It was hilarious, so I demanded a pint of mixed in return for playing the song she wanted. While I never received payment, the image has never gone.

Hughie was not due on stage until eleven but this night he arrived an hour early. He invented 'just in time' working practices well before the Japanese. Tiffany's was full of ordinary people and Hughie was certainly not in that mould, moving in much classier circles, with the hottest women. They were good looking but not my type. Too skinny, in love with themselves and wore far too much make-up for my liking. In any case, they never seemed to smile much. On the other hand, I preferred the people in Tiffany's. I'd grown up with most of them and I knew many by their first name. I liked their company and I knew the music they loved to dance to.

Hughie bounced up to the booth and asked if I'd heard anything from Luxy.

'Nothing yet, it's still early days,' I said but I could tell he was bursting to tell me different. Luxy had written right back and asked if he could go down to London to quickly record a show. If it was good they'd put it out the following weekend. I was speechless and have never felt such envy before or since. On top of that, he'd been asked to record some commercials. In his words, 'it was all going too fast'. His big break was coming. He was going for a drink. Could he buy me one?

A drink? I needed gas and air. This was a guy who never listened to Radio Luxembourg, a fact he thought irrelevant. To my naive eyes, he was stealing my show and all he was offering me as compensation was a drink that staff got for free anyway. The only way I could get through the weekend was to convince myself it was an error and my own invitation would be in the post soon. I'd sort it on Monday morning.

I called up Radio Luxembourg's London office bang on nine o'clock. They asked me where I was from and when I said Carlisle they sounded excited and delighted. This elation was short-lived, however, as they soon discovered I was not Hughie. It was understandable I guess. The chances of two people from the same tiny city, applying for the same competition at the very same time was remote to say the least. It confirmed I was crap, although they didn't actually use those words. The following week, Hughie recorded his show and it aired across Europe on a transmitter that I knew was blasting out one million, three hundred thousand bloody watts.

Could it get any worse I wondered?

It could. John Gilbertson, the boss of Tiffany's asked if I would be kind enough to do the whole of Saturday night myself as they wanted to join Hughie for a few celebratory drinks. I was delighted. Having to stand in a room where they all said he was brilliant – even though he was – would have been a killer. There is no greater pity than self-pity and I was full of it.

Strangely, Hughie was not offered any more shows. In reality it was just a PR promotion for the station but, even so, Hugh Mullins was famous in Carlisle for being on national radio. The late 1970s was a time when a number of new commercial radio stations were being launched all over the country. Hugh went for a few interviews but always seemed reluctant to leave the city. I've no idea if he was offered any jobs at all but in my mind he had the best radio voice in the business and yet here he was still working with me in Carlisle, population 120,000. It was some years before I realised why this happens to so many potentially great radio jocks.

If Hughie could not make it in radio, what chance did I have? I wondered.

Then one night, local legend David Lamb walked into Tiffany's. He was the sports producer at BBC Radio Carlisle, a great character who followed the mighty Carlisle United. While I knew him only fleetingly, I gave the impression he was a long-lost friend. Over a beer, he casually mentioned the radio station was looking for new freelance staff.

I could have killed him. Why did he have to tell me that in front of Hughie?

Like a double act, Hughie and I asked in unison, 'Brilliant, who's the boss? What do we have to do and is there a chance we might be able to get on air and play records?'

'Yes, there was a chance,' David confided, 'but not straight away.' This was like a girl saying you can take me out but there's no guarantee of sex afterwards. When you're young you never hear the last bit.

*

Mike Gibbons was the Programme Organiser at Radio Carlisle, which very soon afterwards changed its name to BBC Radio Cumbria, and I rang him at ten o'clock on the dot the next morning. He took my call, confirmed he was looking around and asked me in for a cup of tea. Very BBC.

Later that day, I was browsing through the records in the Pink Panther shop when someone I knew from Radio Carlisle wandered in. I blurted out that I was going for an interview at the station and he gave me a valuable tip.

'Mike Gibbons is smart,' he said. 'He won't give a job to anyone who wants to be on the air. He doesn't need jocks he needs tech-ops, people who want to learn how to use the equipment and deal with mountains of paperwork. If you say you want to be on the air, you're finished.'

Confused, I asked if this meant I wouldn't ever get on the air or did it mean I'd have to play along for a while?

'A bit of both,' he replied. 'You'll need to get your feet under the table before they'll trust you anywhere near a microphone.'

That seemed logical.

Back at home I told my dad the great news.

'Right son,' he said. 'Let's get down to Burton's and get you a suit.'

'It's not a bank,' I pleaded.

'You only get one chance to make a good first impression,' he barked. 'It's not about working in a suit, it's about letting your boss know you respect him enough to scrub up. Plus, it's about time you did something else. You're like bloody Dracula. Working all night, sleeping all day.'

I turned up at Radio Carlisle looking like a best man at a wedding and with the certain knowledge I had to be more than a little economical with the truth to pass the test.

I liked Mike Gibbons instantly. He walked quickly and I noticed people had to skip a little to keep up with him. He carried a diary under his arm like a rifle and would often stop just to write something that would be his reminder for later on. Bearded and with an air of authority, I connected with him straight away. We did the usual interview shuffle. I told him I wanted to learn stuff, work with others to help make great programmes. I was willing to start at the bottom, be a quick learner and, best of all, being a Carlisle lad I knew everyone – a slight exaggeration. Furthermore, I could turn up at a moment's notice. I would later learn this is invaluable for any radio boss. The moment came when he asked me if I wanted to be on the air as a presenter.

Confidently, I said, 'Not really.'

I never actually said no and hoped that would suffice. He paused, smiled and seemed content, although I sensed he was unsure.

He rang back the next day and said I'd be given 'a go' for a week or two. My role would involve shadowing some of their producers and I'd be given some small tasks to do.

'Nothing too difficult,' he said. 'We'll just want to see how you fit in.'

'Brilliant.'

As far as I was concerned, I was in. Before he put the phone down, Mike revealed I'd be with friends as he was also giving 'a go' to Hugh Mullins.

'Hugh only wants to be a DJ,' Mike said. 'I've said we'll try and help him if he helps us on some of the basic studio stuff.'

I was fuming. I'd been dishonest and got what I deserved. Hughie was totally open and got the chance anyway. This was another sharp lesson and I vowed not to fall into that trap again.

The following week, I started on the early shift and Hughie was on a later one, which began at nine o'clock.

I'd got the bum end of the deal again, finishing at the nightclub at two in the morning, going home for a wash, up at five am and straight into the studio. Hughie was in bed for one am and came in as fresh as a daisy. Nevertheless, I was determined not to let this opportunity pass and turned up in a jacket and tie. To say the early team thought I was a little overdressed is an understatement. However, Hughie completely misjudged the mood by turning up in jeans. While I might have been amusing, he was sent home to change.

One-nil to Myers.

Well done, Dad.

*

One of my main jobs was typical BBC Local Radio. When reporters and presenters went to record interviews they carried a machine called a UHER. It was heavy and bulky and the microphone was attached to a shoulder strap. Interviews were recorded onto reels of quarter-inch wide tape, housed in five-inch diameter plastic spools. Each tape lasted about twenty minutes but most interviews were much shorter than that. When a reporter came back to base, any spare tape was discarded into a tape bin. I had to collect these batches of tapes and edit them together to make full reels again. When tapes were being prepared for transmission, they'd have yellow tape edited in at the start, green tape between any segments and red tape at the end. You had to be sure to cut out all these coloured segments before the tape went onto another reel.

I would then wipe any previous recording on the recycled tapes, using a bulk-erasing machine, and them put them back into a cupboard to be used later.

The job was boring but an important one. Hughie hated the task and tried his best to avoid doing it. Mike knew this, so was always on the prowl making sure we all did our equal share. If ever we looked like we had nothing much to do, we were told to place our backsides in the corner and salvage tapes. It was good training, he kept saying.

After that first week, our shifts switched around. I'd come in at nine and Hughie would have to get up at five o'clock. Wonderful. Now I might get some sleep. Monday came and Hughie overslept.

Two-nil to Myers.

Worse still, he arrived after the breakfast show had actually begun. This was a cardinal sin because one of most important jobs in the morning was to make sure the news editor and presenters had a good cup of tea. If you were rubbish at tea making, you'd never last. Coming from a family of eleven, making tea was something I could do in my sleep. I also went in armed with treats from my Saturday job at the Fine Fare supermarket. The early team loved me.

At the end of our trial period, Mike couldn't make up his mind on who would get the spare full-time job, so he was going to split the role into two part-time positions. I was thankful but grumpy. It was clear I was going to have to work at Tiffany's for some time to come and my biggest competitor was still right there beside me.

Despite being poor at tea making, tape editing and getting out of bed, Hughie was no worse off than me.

The prize for failure was success, it seemed. I moaned to my dad but he simply told me to work hard and believe in myself. How right he was. The good news was that I was working in a real-life radio station and was determined not to cock it up. Hughie and I often made mistakes but we covered each other's backsides on more than one occasion. There was no doubt Hugh was destined for bigger things but I never saw him working on his voice technique. I'd spend hours reading scripts and talking to myself. I had to rid myself of the northern accent. Saying 'Bath' instead of 'Baath' would not get me a job on the air, I was told. It amazes me how the greatest footballers in the world work on their skill each day. Yet, in radio, presenters appear to work like mad to get into the business and then make it their business not to work very hard at all. It's one reason why so many fail to move up the ladder.

Instead, I was willing to do anything and everything. I was eager to soak up as much information as I could. I even came in on my days off to help out and that's how I got my first experience on air. The duty tech-op or Station Assistants as we were called then, Martin Plenderleith, had lost his voice as a result of a bad cold. He still came in for his shift but any role that involved him talking would have to be given to someone else. That day he had to present the Lamb Bank, a feature that's so famous across the BBC, even staff in London knew about it. The Lamb Bank service is a lifeline for farmers. During the lambing season – remember there were no mobile phones back then and no one had heard of the Internet – farmers across Cumbria would let the radio station know of newborn lambs that needed a surrogate mother. If a surrogate could not be found quickly, the lamb would die and money would be lost. So, the Lamb Bank was born. Three times a day, Radio Carlisle's presenters would read out the names and phone numbers of farmers with a sheep whose lamb had died and would be perfect as a surrogate to any lamb whose mother had died giving birth. The farmers would listen intently to these Lamb Bank broadcasts, which could last up to fifteen minutes, and contact each other by landline to match up mothers and orphans. Outside the farming community it was seen as a bit of a joke. For Cumbria's farmers, it was a godsend.

*

The first rule of being new to radio is never, repeat never, say no to anything. I'd never been near a farm in my life so the Lamb Bank was all double-dutch to me. To be honest, I was a little upset. It was the very first time I was going to be on the air, probably the biggest moment in my whole broadcasting life, and I'd been given nothing more than reading out a list of bloody sheep. It sounded so easy what could possibly go wrong?

I took the information to a spare studio and practised like mad. What I didn't realise was that Lamb Bank information is very fluid. You can't pre-record the slot because, as soon as you do so, it's out of date. It can only be aired live. Sometimes you'd be reading details out and the list would be taken from beneath you as you were speaking and replaced with a new list. You then had to sight-read and, believe me, it's not as easy as it seems. Giving the slot to someone like me was definitely not good news. I struggled to get my head around a subject I had zero knowledge of. I was also deeply concerned about getting my tongue around names of breeds like Texel, Swaledale, Suffolk or black-faced North of England Mule. Dark clouds were forming.

In broadcasting, or any kind of public speaking, you have to 'train the brain'. That means speaking aloud so you can get your tongue and brain used to the words you are about to say. Mumbling under your breath just doesn't work. It's why I insist jocks are left alone in a studio to practise. They become embarrassed if anyone is in there with them.

Just as I was about to start reading the Lamb Bank, the station receptionist came into the studio and took away the information I'd been practising for the past three hours, replacing it with words neither my eyes, nor my brain, had seen before. As she was doing this, in my headphones I heard the start of a jingle, 'and now Lamb Bank with John Myers … Baaa baaa'.

I started reading but it quickly became apparent to everyone listening that all was not going to plan. I'd dropped the papers with names of farmers and their ewes and lambs. What followed was a catalogue of errors. Farmers' telephone numbers became mixed up, lambs were advertised as parents and, at one point, I even offered a farm for sale for a price that turned out to be a phone number!

Calls to the station were less than complimentary. Rosy-cheeked shepherds had come in from their fields to listen to a jibbering idiot broadcasting utter rubbish. The Lamb Bank information had to be read out again fifteen minutes later, properly this time, by someone who knew what they were doing.

It was not my finest hour. Mike Gibbons was kind. He said,

'We all make mistakes. Mine was asking you to do it when you weren't ready.'

There was one consolation. Everyone I knew avoided listening to the Lamb Bank.

Chapter Two

THE PHANTOM PIP NICKER

Luckily, I'm blessed with a sense of humour. Sometimes it's greatly misplaced but most of the time it works. I refuse to take life too seriously and believe that whatever we're doing, it's not life threatening. I have a reputation for being larger-than-life and fun, so people quite like working with me.

I was often the first person the station rang if they were short staffed. Being paid by the hour meant sometimes taking home more than anyone else, though I was working longer hours. I liked doing the things other people loathed but there was one job I hated just as much as everyone else – filling in PRS returns. This was a hand-written form we had to complete for the Performing Rights Society. It logged, among other things, the artist, record label, number, producer, songwriter, and total duration of every record we played at the station. It took ages to write out all this information properly by hand and if you were tempted to rush it, you'd get a call from a BBC robot at Broadcasting House in London asking you to do it again as they couldn't make out your handwriting. When Shalamar brought out their disco hit *Uptown Festival* life got worse. It contained the works of about twelve different artists all mixed together in one song but the BBC demanded that every time it was played each songwriter was given the appropriate credit on the form. Filling in the paperwork for that song alone could take up to twenty minutes, so we'd practically beg presenters **not** to play that record. They never listened, so in the end I ran the wheels of the studio chair over it. By accident, of course!

At one staff meeting, Mike announced he was making a few changes to the output. This was nothing unusual and, in any case, the changes were always minor. The schedule was AM Breakfast, which was all speech; Tommy Thomas, a local superhero at nine o'clock, followed by the popular mid-morning show, which included The Morning Market at ten. The morning shift finished with a twenty-minute news bulletin at one o'clock. Nothing too exciting there. Then Mike revealed the afternoon programme would not begin until two o'clock, leaving a forty-minute gap to be filled. His answer to the missing minutes was electric – a daily request show presented by whichever tech-op was covering the early shift.

It would give us some valuable on-air experience, he explained. You what? Had I heard those words correctly? Whoever was on the early shift would get to present a forty-minute request show! Better still you got on the air, not because you wanted to be a DJ, but because it was simply part of your shift. Plus, if some of the audience could be encouraged to call up for modern songs, you'd naturally be compelled to play them. It was a request show after all.

I looked at the rota. Damn, bloody Hugh Mullins was already scheduled on the early shift for the next week. He'd launch the new programme and set the standard. In my mind, he'd be so good anyone following him would be seen as useless. I had nightmares about callers ringing in to demand I was thrown off the air.

It was a smart move by management. Winter was coming and the early shift was a pain, so it was a nice little incentive for the staff. It struck me some years later that only the BBC could come up with such an idiotic plan. You'd have to be in at five o'clock, work on demanding shows until one pm. Then you'd have to 'drive' the desk for the most complicated news show of the day and, just when you're ready to drop, you had to present a forty-minute **live** request show. The very moment I was supposed to be alive and focused, I was half dead. You could understand why some people turned to stimulants just to get through it. The crazy name they came up with for this slot was Dateline. I'd no idea why and I didn't care. Myers was now a real-life radio presenter.

*

The music the station broadcast was not what we played in the night-clubs. Radio 1 played all that and we were supposed to be the alternative listen. Believe me, I'd have played crap all day if there was the slightest chance of getting behind the microphone. The best way to describe Radio Cumbria's music policy at the time was five steps behind Radio 2. Back then, Radio 2 was a wonderful, sleepy easy-listening station that played Mantovani and had a programme called, Sing Something Simple. We played the more likeable songs from Jim Reeves, Val Doonican, The Carpenters and Glen Campbell. Our most modern songs came from Abba. We were 'more about the things we said between the tunes'. This thought would stay with me forever.

Hughie Mullins was not comfortable **at all** playing this sort of music. He was the God of local nightclubs, a regular visitor to Wigan Casino. He was into new music and had a great reputation for being up-to-date. Yet, here he was being asked to air what was loosely termed the station 'play list'. Like me, this was his first real live show. We picked all our own songs but Pat the record librarian kept a close eye on us. The first day, Hughie was a good boy. He played all the right songs in the right order. His voice was great, although perhaps not sitting that comfortably between The Carpenters and Jim Reeves.

The next day he was still on track but by Wednesday and Thursday the music began to change a little. By Friday, it was all-out disco and soul music. Personally, I loved it but Mike Gibbons did not. Hughie was hauled into the office and given very clear direction at an impressive volume. I know this because Lesley on reception sat outside Mike's office and always knew the gossip. Mike asked what had happened to the music policy. Hughie told him – and you have to admire his honesty – that his mates had pulled him to pieces for playing 'that shit' and he thought he should bring the station up to date.

Brilliant.

Three-nil to Myers.

Hugh convinced Mike it wouldn't happen again and, in any case, he was now 'off-shift' for two weeks and so it was my turn.

During the following two weeks, the listeners had never heard so much Jim Reeves, Perry Como and Daniel O'Donnell in their lives. I asked everyone I knew to ring up to say how much they were enjoying this new presenter. One of my sisters, who I'd not asked to call, blew my credibility by ringing up to say how great she thought her brother was. But there were actually some genuine callers as well.

Four-nil to Myers.

*

The BBC loved signature tunes and all Radio Cumbria's shows had one. You'd begin and end the programme with it. When the show was ending, you started the music with the audio fader down and then slowly brought the music up to its conclusion. Timing was essential, especially if you had to take the pips from Radio 4. If, for example, the signature tune was 3minutes 54 seconds long, you would start it on pre-fade at exactly four minutes to the hour. The signature tune would end with six seconds to go. You'd then have one second of silence followed by the pips. In those days the pips were live on Radio 4, so you prayed the idiots on the network had stopped talking, leaving a clean feed of the sound. It didn't always happen but most of the time it was simple enough to do and you soon got into the swing of things. It was the technique that was important. You'd listen to your own show in one ear and Radio Four in the other. Then, at precisely the right moment, whack up the Radio 4 fader – job done. It was now the early Eighties and all signature tunes were played out on a cartridge machine, similar to the eight-track carts you had in your car. It was impossible to rewind them, so starting on time was essential for a smooth finish.

Sadly, Hugh Mullins could never master the art of back timing. He was intelligent but just couldn't do basic maths. It was the first time I'd been able to do something better than him and I'm disappointed to say I loved him for getting it so wrong. Missing the pips made your presenter sound like a dickhead and resulted in a scowl being thrown your way through the studio glass. Worse still, you knew you'd be slagged off later in the pub. In-house shame was always worse than real life. Hughie knew he had to resolve this so he came up with an ingenious idea and for a few days at least, it worked. Trouble was, it was literally a matter of time before he was found out.

It is a given at the BBC that you don't piss off engineers. You can deal with a few days of sulking from presenters and fellow producers but engineers are like elephants, they never forget and always, absolutely always, get you back. They deal with things we don't understand which means, in their eyes, we are all pond life. Lowest of the low are those who break their lovely equipment. The engineers' most prized possession is the station clock. It's connected to the outside world in some mysterious and magical way only they understand. The second hand goes around the dial at exactly the same time as any other clock in any other radio station anywhere else in the world. Only the hour hand might be different depending on what country you were in. That was the real genius of the clock. You could be on air from Australia and you could still get into a junction with Radio 4 on time. A radio station could be on fire, but if the clocks were out by just one second, the engineers would have to deal with that emergency first. A clock is a regular hourly comfort blanket, designed by engineers for engineers.

✳

One day, all hell broke out. The mid-morning show came to its conclusion, the signature tune ended and the Radio 4 pips were broadcast. The engineers glanced upwards and let out a loud shout. 'The clocks! Oh dear, they're fourteen seconds out! Yes, fourteen seconds. Not one second out, not five but fourteen.'

As many of our local programmes were required to join the BBC network at some point in the day, the station's clocks had to be spot on. Radio Cumbria was about to become the laughing stock of the whole of the BBC if this could not be corrected with some urgency. An immediate investigation took place. First checkpoint was the speaking clock. BT must have earned a fortune over the years just from BBC staff. The engineers listened, looked up then listened and looked up again, followed by some serious beard scratching.

It would appear that, somehow, the station's clocks had corrected themselves. After a while, and without an explanation, it was put down to 'one of those crazy things'. This is a phrase that never sits well with an engineer. In their world everything has a cause and effect. This was weird and it was suggested that pond life might be involved somewhere! The clocks and the presenters were now put under close watch. Over the next few days, every time the Radio 4 pips came to air – at 8am, 1pm and 5pm - the engineers and management stood watching for any sign that something might be wrong. The soldering iron was even warmed up just in case it was needed urgently. After a week, they relaxed. All was well.

The following Tuesday, just before 1pm the station was in full flow. The mid-morning show had been a good one, lots of callers and much debate. As the Radio 4 pips were aired, disaster struck again.

This time the clocks were nineteen seconds out.

Neville, the Chief Engineer, nearly had a heart attack but, once again, it appeared that everything had quickly returned to normal. As this is just the sort of problem that can get management the sack in the BBC, people jumped. A terrible gremlin was in the works that was both unpredictable and elusive. Every time the pips came on, the whole station glanced up to the wall.

Eventually, the mid-morning show ran an Outside Broadcast from Carlisle's historic Market Hall. It involved taking out the radio car. This was fun but dangerous as it had a giant aerial on the back that had to be erected some forty feet or so into the air to get a signal back to the station. You had to be careful because if you hit overhead power lines, you were dead. A slight problem, they said. Where was Health & Safety back then?

On this day, I was in charge of the radio car, providing on-site technical support while Hugh Mullins was the tech-op back at base. He was playing in the news, phone calls and records. In fact, the only input from the Market Hall was the presenters. It was an easy OB, nothing too difficult but it required planning and an ability to hit junctions. There was a producer in the field but another was needed back at base at Hilltop Heights.

Mike Gibbons decided to step back into the real world and help out. He was standing behind Hugh, directing proceedings from the studio. All was going well until the programme entered the final couple of minutes.

'Shit', Hugh cried aloud. 'I've missed the start of the back-timing for the sig tune'.

Without a moment's hesitation, he opened his bag and brought out a cart. When the signature tune ended some twelve seconds late, Hugh simply played in his own cart. On it, he had secretly recorded the Radio 4 pips. The gremlin had been uncovered and Hughie was blissfully unaware of what he'd done, he just marvelled at his brilliance and ingenuity. His view was that no listener cared if the pips were a few seconds out. He was right, of course, but that was not the issue. He was the phantom pip nicker. The engineers sensed blood. Despite Mike having a very soft spot for him, Hugh had to go.

The game was up.

Final score: Myers 5 Mullins 0.

Hugh was not asked back and suddenly I became full time. I missed him a lot and my respect never wavered.

Chapter Three

BARBECUED LAMB

From the moment I told Mike Gibbons I had no ambition to be on the air, I found myself presenting more and more programmes on Radio Cumbria. One day he asked what I knew about Country music?

'Err, I've heard of Billy Jo Spears if that's any good,' I volunteered.

'Great. You're the new presenter of our Country show.'

Remember, I'd been told never to say no to anything so I simply said, 'Thanks a lot'.

When Mike left the room, I sat down and wondered what the hell had come over me. Country music? This was not good. I headed into the record library and asked our librarian, Pat, to pick out some Country music tracks. One was an artist called Boxcar Willie. My idiotic humour loved his name and over the weekend I researched as much as I could.

Being into disco, I thought of Country music as nothing other than crap. I loathed it but the chance of being on the air with my own show was the prize here and I could pretend I loved anything for that. In the end, I became quite fond of Merle Haggard, Willie Nelson and Don Williams. Before the show started, things got worse, or better, depending on your perspective.

Mike told me, 'I've been thinking and I'm not going to give you a weekly show now after all.'

'What? After all that work, all that research I've lost my show?'

'No,' he said, 'I'm giving you three one-hour Country music shows on Monday, Wednesday and Friday between 5 pm and 6 pm. The Tuesday and Thursday slot will be taken by a new soul and pop music show headed up by another local lad, Grant Leighton.'

Grant was DJ at The Cosmo nightclub and an excellent entertainer with style and charisma, yet totally different to me.

I launched into my show with so much gusto that a year later I was awarded the national prize of Country Music Presenter of the Year. Even today it's a little embarrassing because my thought process was just to play anything with a steel guitar. In fact, I made a lame excuse and didn't attend the presentation ceremony at the UK Country Music Awards in London because I was terrified they would rumble my complete lack of knowledge about Country music and its stars.

*

Life was never dull at Radio Cumbria and there was always some naughty fun to be had. On one occasion, I was caught having sex in the BBC Land Rover. The beautiful county of Cumbria is extremely hilly, so any potential outside broadcast needed a site test before we could go ahead. People like me were sent to the area chosen for the OB to check the station could receive a signal. I had a new girlfriend and decided to impress her by taking her out with me for the morning. We arrived at the test location and set up the giant mast while waiting for base to return my call. There was a delay and, being a young lad, I found other things to do. Just as things were getting interesting, the talkback burst into life, 'Have you got it up yet, John?'

Another morning, I arrived at the station straight from my stint at Tiffany's to be greeted by a presenter and a reporter going hard at it on the sick bay bed. They were purple with embarrassment and so was I. For keeping quiet, I was repaid with some great on-air stints and, best of all, freedom from doing PRS logs for a while. As the station consisted of offices and studios off one long, single corridor it often meant I had to pass the woman involved at least a couple of times a day. We glanced at each other; I was always smiling, she was always looking down.

*

Radio Cumbria's programming included a feature called Access where listeners would phone in with items they wanted to swap, sell or donate to a good home. In reality it was just the Morning Market heard on so many stations but this was also well before the days of eBay, so it was hugely popular. The introduction explained no livestock, guns, pets or anything over a hundred pounds could be swapped or sold. Anything else was up for grabs. I always had fun with the callers. It was not unusual for me to be told off for taking things a little too far but we never received any complaints. It was hard not to have a go when a number of what I called friendly nutters tried to fob listeners off with rubbish in return for cash. Later on, I turned this kind of feature into an award-winning art form but at Radio Cumbria we were encouraged to be polite to our callers. On one occasion, a regular caller came on selling a yellow, used, slightly marked but in good condition ... bathroom toilet.

'Who in their right mind would want this?' I asked. The caller wasn't selling it for cash, but would like to exchange it for something useful. He was adamant it would be okay provided the new owner used a little elbow grease and some Domestos.

'What kind of thing would you like in exchange?' I asked.

'A colour television,' came the reply.

A colour telly! I roasted him for being on the drink and if anyone did the deal could he send them straight round to my house as I would like a new car for my old bike. Another bollocking ensued but it was great radio. Remarkably, the swap happened and we used him in a promo to highlight the extraordinary success of the Morning Market.

I also worked regularly with David Lamb, the man I had to thank for originally tipping me off about the job at Radio Cumbria. David had a big voice, a huge talent and, on rare occasions, a bad temper. He presented Sunday Requests, the most popular show on the station, which aired from noon until two o'clock. Amazingly, the show had a seven-minute long signature tune, which David used to play in full at the end of each show. The reason was David liked to have a lunchtime drink but in those days pubs and bars closed at bang on two o'clock on Sundays. Across from the station, the Hilltop Hotel bar had to obey the strict licensing rules. So, David had an agreement that the barman would have three pints ready for him at exactly 1.55 pm. The duty tech-op would have the lift doors wedged open as David hit the signature tune before sprinting out of the building to arrive at the hotel moments before closing time. God knows what listeners thought of this very long nameless tune being on the air every week but I soon discovered that keeping David happy was quite a good thing for all.

*

Cricketing legend Ian Botham was walking from John O'Groats to Lands End for charity and his route south came through Carlisle. As the station's sports producer, David had been promised an interview with the great man but only if he could do it while they walked. England's greatest all-rounder would not stop to talk under any circumstances, so their chat had to be done on the run.

On the run proved to be completely the right expression. After grabbing a tape from the cupboard, David headed out with his heavy UHER recorder around his shoulders. The cricketer's walking pace was relentless and the interview took place with David skipping alongside him. David was small and took two steps to Botham's one. Dripping with sweat, desperately trying to recover his cool, David arrived back with an exclusive, which management decided to trail every half hour. A slice of the interview would be selected for the one o'clock news and a longer version would be played on the afternoon show.

David gave me the tape and asked for a yellow leader to be spliced onto the front of the interview and a red tape to be added to the end. When I got the tape onto the Studer editing machine, I came out in a sweat myself. There was nothing on it.

The station continued to trail their exclusive.

I spooled back and forth. Nothing. Yet there was something there. I could not make it out. I called in an engineer.

'What's the problem here?' I asked.

'Aha.' he said with a smirk. 'Some idiot has placed the tape in the UHER the wrong way round. The shiny side of the tape is next to the recording head. Someone must have put it on the reel that way.'

My heart sank. So, there was nothing on the tape.

'Is there nothing we can do to save it?' I asked desperately.

'No.'

'Will you tell David?' I pleaded.

'Not on your life, I'm getting as far away from this explosion as possible.'

With that, he headed back into his office and locked the door. I looked at the box the tape was in. Whenever you reclaimed a tape and put it back into the box, you wrote the date and your initials on it. I was lucky. It wasn't me but that meant nothing. Someone would have to pay!

Another golden rule was that whoever took a UHER out had to ensure the machine was recording correctly. That person was David. He was responsible. There was nothing for it. I was going to have to tell him about the tape.

I crept into the newsroom, placed my wide backside next to his, and tried to quietly tell him the bad news. Next thing, the room exploded and a table I'd always thought was permanently fixed to the floor clearly wasn't. He just couldn't take in that there was nothing on the tape. His only explanation was that I must have wiped it in some way. I had erased it. That was the only possibility. It was **my** fault.

People started running for cover, even management were strangely absent. After about a minute of this, there was a pause while he got his breath back. Everyone just looked at each other. The silence was deafening, so I tried to be helpful by asking if it was possible he could record the interview again. Bad mistake.

'You what?' he screamed. 'Ian's already twenty miles away, marching through fucking Penrith. I'm not going back to tell him you've fucked up.'

David grabbed his coat and stormed out of the building, still demanding my head on a plate.

'It was *not* my fault,' I kept saying. 'It's not my fault.'

Thankfully, Mike Gibbons knew the score and told me to keep a low profile for a while. That was a good idea but the next day I made the mistake of getting into the lift just as David was arriving.

'Nice morning,' he said. 'So you don't mind being in the lift with an idiot?'

A lovely quote and a measure of the man but I misjudged my response and tried a comic line instead of simply accepting his apology.

'Of course not, just don't let it happen again,' I replied.

Unfortunately, as he stormed out of the lift, David didn't see me smiling.

It's said that great people give you the biggest problems and David was one of the greats. A wonderful commentator, a great sports producer, and a brilliant presenter with a lovely, deep rich voice and style all of his own. He was also slightly mad – but after three decades in the business I've yet to come across anyone who isn't both brilliant and mad.

Chapter Four

ROSES ARE RED, WORDS ARE BLUE

While Radio Cumbria was good, I could only present so many Lamb Banks and Tourist Line information slots with enthusiasm. I was desperate to play hits, so I sent a demo tape to Red Rose, then a fairly new commercial station, in Lancashire. I addressed my package to Keith Macklin. He was the station's Programme Director but was better known for his brilliance as a rugby commentator and broadcaster. I loved listening to Red Rose but their AM signal was not strong enough to reach Carlisle, so I used to drive up onto the eight-hundred-feet-high Caldbeck Common just to pick up the Lancashire station's output.

It was not long before the depressing thud of a returned tape came crashing through my letterbox with the usual 'Thanks but no thanks' letter. By now I'd collected so many of these rejection slips my home was fast becoming a fire hazard. After a few days, I decided to listen back to the tape I'd sent Red Rose to try and figure out where I was going wrong.

What I heard really shocked me.

Nothing.

There was nothing on the tape. I was listening to a completely blank reel. What an idiot I'd been. Somehow I'd sent the great Keith Macklin ten minutes of silence. Then it dawned on me that he couldn't even have listened to it. He'd simply returned it with a standard letter saying I was not what Red Rose were looking for.

Of course, you could argue a presenter who doesn't play any records and stays silent is not the sort of person they'd be looking for. But the more I thought about it, the more my blood started to boil, so I phoned Keith Macklin to be greeted by his PA, a lady with the lovely name of Innes Bracegirdle. I wasn't expecting to be put through to Keith himself but Ms Bracegirdle was clearly not going to carry the can for this mistake. Now I had Keith on the rails as he desperately sought to find comforting words. In an effort to redeem himself, he said there must have been a simple error and he invited me down to Preston to meet him in person. This was what I'd wanted in the first place but in these circumstances I was meeting him only because I'd accidentally sent a blank tape and not because I was talented.

Red Rose is housed in a beautifully redesigned church that over the years has won many architectural awards. I immediately fell in love with the studios. This was the place for me. I waited in reception, listening to Dave Lincoln live on air. He was a real master of his craft.

Keith was very apologetic. It had been a basic error, the result of receiving more than twenty tapes a week. Nevertheless, he had some time right now and suggested we play the tape there and then. There's nothing more nerve-racking than playing a demo to a potential new boss. The tape was only ten minutes long and, thankfully, Keith was kind, positive and offered excellent advice. I told him about my experience, my ambition and how I loved his station. Sadly there was no offer of work, instead just a commitment to keep my name close to his phone in case he needed someone of my talent. You can take that both ways!

Two hours later he was true to his word.

When I returned to Carlisle, my wife Linda said Keith had called and I was to ring him back immediately. It appeared their Country show presenter had just resigned and 'did I want to take over the show'.

Christ, this was Red Rose, a great radio station that played the hits - and all they wanted me to do was the bloody Country show again.

Remembering the golden rule of radio, I said, 'Yes, of course. Thanks a lot, I won't let you down.'

I was so excited he'd called I forgot to ask about the fee but as this was the new and exciting world of commercial radio, it was bound to be as good or better than my daily rate at the BBC. Oh boy, was I wrong. The fee for the programme was just £25 and that included any expenses for petrol. My desire to leap into commercial radio was suddenly a big move backwards financially.

*

I've never worried about money. I always thought I'd be wealthy some day but right then we had no idea how we were going to manage. It cost me twenty pounds in petrol every time I went to Lancashire, so we were coming out with just a fiver a week, less tax. Thankfully, Linda was working at the local hospital and that kept us afloat but money was tight. We used to put all our spare copper change into a giant whisky bottle next to the fireplace. On more than one occasion, we'd have to empty it out just to get a gallon of fuel. Two months later Keith called me up with good news.

'John', he said. 'We like the show and we like you. Two more shows have become available and we wondered if you'd be interested. But I have to warn you, it's not Country music. Would you be OK with that?'

'Not at all, Keith, no problem,' I said, beaming inside.

Later, I learned the weekend breakfast show presenter was 'let go' for a daft comment he'd said on air and they were looking for a replacement. Once again, I was in the right place at the right time.

From doing one show at £25, I was now doing three shows over two days for £75. Better, but still not great. However, I loved it and over time managed to build up quite a following. I discovered the station's Managing Director, David Maker, had a bizarre system for testing a radio presenter's popularity. Sheila, the receptionist would be instructed to count the mail that came in for each jock. The weekly total would then be sent to Maker. The more mail you received, the more popular you were in his eyes.

It was total madness but that was the system, so I got on the phone and put myself on as many mailing lists as I could to ensure my letter count was high. Some weeks I had more mail than any other jock with the exception of Dave Lincoln, who always got hundreds of letters. When Sheila nipped out for a second, I'd pop around her desk and change my total to a bigger one. Still, I listened to the output all day, learned from the other jocks and got to know how to engage with an audience. I was doing my apprenticeship. I learned the art of building a show from Dave Lincoln, personality from Baz Reilly and how to deal with callers from perhaps the greatest late night phone-in jock I've ever heard, Allan Beswick.

By then my Country show had developed a touch of sheer lunacy. One Sunday, a bunch of boozed-up Lancashire cowboys literally rode into town on their horses, tied their steeds up around the gravestones outside the converted church and crapped all over the deceased. This did not go down well with Maker, who shouted that 'I'd encouraged them to come to the station by playing all this bloody Country music'. Nothing could have been further from the truth.

*

Despite the extra shows, I certainly couldn't afford hotel accommodation, so I stayed overnight in Preston with Mrs Millray, a lovely old lady who charged me three pounds a night in cash for board and lodging. More than anything she just wanted company and loved to stay up and chat. I used to watch snooker with her on a black and white television. I repaid her generosity by nicking her biscuits. Yep, even then I couldn't resist. She knew this and one night shamed me by leaving a few on a plate with a note politely explaining it would save me looking for them. God bless her.

*

As presenters took holidays, Red Rose started giving me even more work so I bought a very old caravan and charmed a local farmer to let me to keep it in his field for a pound a night. Linda and I would take our daughter, Kerry, there every weekend and we'd have a great time, while saving cash. I used to run the five miles into work each day. Hard to imagine, I know. We also had free grub from McDonalds. Red Rose used to run a promotion with the fast-food outlet and offered ten-pound gift vouchers as prizes. Many of the jocks just made up the winners' names and then went along to McDonalds themselves to claim burgers and chips. The wages at Red Rose weren't good but neither was a diet of free fast food.

Part of Red Rose's broadcast licence agreement stipulated that the station had to run a weekly outside broadcast. The Independent Broadcasting Authority was much tougher than today's regulator and would often make spot checks. Management didn't want to spend cash on stuff like this so we cheated a little. I had no idea we were cheating, I was simply carrying out a management instruction to do my fourth show of the week in a certain way.

The show, called Saturday Night Out, was described as a live OB from Blackpool Pleasure Beach, although it had loads of music in it, too. I never went anywhere near the Golden Mile with a live OB unit, instead I'd go into Blackpool town centre during the day and record interviews with a range of characters, celebrities and people on holiday, then pretend they were live from the Pleasure Beach. We did such a magnificent job that listeners were constantly calling in from Blackpool complaining that they couldn't find us. Today, a radio station would be vilified for hoodwinking the public and fined thousands of pounds but this was radio Eighties style. On another occasion, a client sponsored what they thought was a live breakfast show from the Champs Elysees in Paris. The cost of putting in a line for a live link-up to the French capital was going to be enormous, so we didn't bother. Instead, a few days beforehand we travelled over to France and recorded links with people we'd set up and then returned to Preston to play the show out from behind the studio blinds.

From a technical perspective it sounded brilliant but clearly it was very wrong. I was told that radio was all about painting pictures in listeners minds, we were just being a little careful about where we were saying these pictures were painted.

It always used to amaze me how listeners never asked why big prizes always seemed to be won three weeks after a promotion started and always around 8.15am on a Friday by a woman screaming her head off in delight. In those days it was all about 'the moment' creating the biggest climax possible to the promotion. Clients would be guaranteed so many weeks on air before their prize was won and every commercial station in the land was doing it. Today, of course, that would never occur. The system is much stricter now and any prize can be won at any time.

*

Keith was always talking positively about me in the corridors of power. However, I had competition for freelance work from a young lad. There's always competition to contend with but this one, Derek Webster, was good. In fact, I'd argue he was slightly better than me. Dave Lincoln really liked him and would never go on holiday unless Derek was available to fill in for him. For some reason, he worried that I might damage his audience with my particular style of presentation. Derek also lived a lot closer to the station than I did and therefore was the first port of call for all the emergency cover but there was still plenty of other work to go around. After some time, we both noticed that we'd been overlooked for the regular daytime shows whenever they became available. When I mentioned this to Keith he explained that many of the daytime presenters were good but were only good for that one slot. We were **so** talented we could do every show going therefore it was important to keep us free. It was easier to find a full-time replacement, he said, for one particular slot than find a whole team of stand-in presenters for all the specialist shows we put out. We could do any style, any time.

'Bloody hell, Derek', I said. 'It's the first time we've ever been called too good to get a full-time gig.'

Keith was wonderful but at the same time frustrating to work with. He was a gifted presenter who could walk into a studio and sight-read without a moment's hesitation. Yet, he was totally disorganised. He called me one morning at home around ten to nine.

When I said 'Hello' all I heard was, 'Oh, hell John, you've picked up the damn phone.'

'Err yes, Keith, that's because you're ringing me,' I replied. 'What's the problem?'

'Well it means, that if you're there, you're not here.'

'Sorry Keith, you've lost me.'

It turned out Keith couldn't remember if he'd asked me to present a show that morning. When I answered the phone I was confirming he'd cocked up. As the show was due to start in ten minutes and I lived eighty miles away, he had to find someone else, fast.

Perhaps the most wonderful conversation I had with him left me in gales of laughter.

'Hi John, Keith here. Do you have your diary with you?'

'I do. Fire away.'

'Okay, I'm looking at next weekend. Can you do Friday night 10pm to 2am?'

'I can.'

'Plus, do your own breakfast show the next day?'

'Right. So I finish at 2am but you want me back on breakfast at six?'

'Correct John. Then, as Baz Reilly is on holiday, can you do the lunchtime show at 12?'

'Errr...okay.'

'Then do the live Saturday evening show at 6pm?'

'Okay, so I do breakfast 'till ten, the lunchtime show at twelve, finish that at 2pm, then start again at six pm. Wow!'

'Then, can you do your own Sunday breakfast show the following day?'

'Yep' I said, starting to laugh.

'And do your own Country show at lunchtime?'

'Okay, Keith,' I replied, chuckling.

'Then, can you do the late night show on Sunday?'

By now, I was laughing so much I could hardly speak. 'Err … yes, of course', I spluttered.

'And finally, as it's a bank holiday, can you also do Monday morning breakfast, too? '

I was now on the floor laughing uncontrollably. 'C'mon Keith. Who's set me up for this?' I begged.

'Is there a problem?' he asked casually

'Keith, I love you, but are you sure you want me to do all these shows? You're asking me to present *eight* shows in just three days. It's wonderful and I could do with the cash, but tell me, when do I sleep?'

'Oh, c'mon you're a young man and this is great exposure', he exclaimed. 'In any case, if you need to kip, get Billy the security man to let you sleep on my couch in the office.'

The Myers Weekend arrived and by the end of it even I was becoming sick of my own voice. A week later, I sent in my bumper invoice only to receive a call from Keith who suggested some of those shows should surely be included in one fee. In Keith's eyes the £25 payment was for an eight-hour shift and therefore it could be argued that some of the shifts covered two programmes. I let him have both barrels down the phone and he quickly backed off. 'Perhaps, you're right, John.'

There was no perhaps about it.

'But we did save you some money from staying overnight in a hotel,' he protested.

In future I made sure each payment was for a single show.

*

David Maker was a brilliant MD who kept a tight ship. He was also quite frightening and good at keeping presenters in their place. We avoided him whenever possible and he certainly avoided us. Keith Macklin once told me Mr Maker never spoke to freelance staff, that's why he, as PD, was there. Eventually, Maker acquired a brand-new

Jag but, instead of parking it in the car park, he insisted on leaving it right outside the front door. He was the first person at the station to get a mobile phone installed and was constantly calling in with traffic reports. One day, I was heading into the toilet and, as the corridors were very narrow, we had no choice but to meet each other entering the loo. He looked at me and shouted, 'Wait there'. It seemed I was not allowed to pee in the bowl next to him.

What I didn't like was the station's attitude to freelance staff like me. While their staff were paid on the same date every month, we freelancers would be paid when the management could be bothered to sign cheques. Sometimes senior people simply went on holiday without bothering to pay us and the freelance team would just have to wait until they came back and sent us our money. When I moved into management, I made sure freelance staff were always paid on time.

Despite this, there were many fun times at Red Rose. In the early days, we picked all of our own songs until one day management decided to introduce a programme clock. Commonplace now, it's a simple idea where you plan out what you're going to do around the hour in minutes. This ensures you have a helicopter view of the whole hour and can ensure a nice balance of music and features. They also introduced a new 'playlist' idea where the big songs of the week or month were placed in a box in the studio.

We picked from the front and replaced the records at the back. This was the first example of music rotation, as we know it today. Some of the team resented this as they argued that the magic of radio was listeners hearing the unpredictability of the jocks' choices. The era of just turning up and playing whatever we liked was about to end.

I was given a programme clock for my breakfast show and I noticed that at 8.10 am it said, and I quote, 'Funny link'. That's right, the clock was planned so I would have to do a funny link straight after the first song following the 8am news bulletin. I did my best but after one show I was called in for a 'feedback meeting' where it was pointed out that I'd failed to follow the clock and say something funny at the allotted time.

I looked at the programme clock, then stared at my boss and told him, 'Listen. You can't deliver comedy to order on a live breakfast show. I just can't do that. I have to believe something's genuinely funny for me to deliver a funny line. What you haven't said,' I screamed in frustration, 'was that at 7.50 I was fucking hilarious and at 8.25 I was more than a little amusing. But you've focused on one area and all you've succeeded in doing is really piss me off. You're right, of course, at ten past eight I failed. The reason I failed was that I couldn't think of anything funny to say. I just can't be funny to order.'

He looked at me and said, 'Please try.' I nearly smacked him.

Derek Webster is funny but in a very dry way. He doesn't tell jokes but instead reflects on the world at large. That works. It's why he's still liked and on a national radio station even today.

Derek was guilty of a wonderful cock-up with a competition called The Holiday Game. The mechanic was easy. We announced on air that we'd booked and paid for a five-star holiday somewhere in the world. To win, all you had to do was just tell us where that holiday destination was. What's easier than that? We used to strip big competitions across the day and, in those days in the late Eighties, this was a big competition so we ran it every single hour of the day, seven days a week. We'd guaranteed the sponsor that the prize wouldn't be won in the first two weeks, so every time a listener had a guess, we wrote their answer down on a sheet of paper in the studio. As fifty-five per cent of the Lancashire population were tuned in each week, it's fair to say the competition soon got momentum.

All our company cars had the names of presenters or Red Rose plastered all over them, and soon the staff were coming into the studio saying people had been shouting their guesses at them at traffic lights or on filling-station forecourts. Two weeks had passed, so we started to give out clues to the mystery location but after three weeks the comp was still going strong, twenty-four times a day, seven days a week, and still we had no winner. In the studio, the list of listeners' guesses looked like a giant toilet roll. When a caller came on we had two carts lined up ready to play. One, was a big 'UH-UHHR!' for the wrong answer, the other was packed with the sounds of bells, whistles and cheers.

The moment arrived when we seemed to have a winning caller. By now I was both a jock and a manager at the station, so I was upstairs in the office listening to Derek on air. He asked the excited caller for their guess and when she answered correctly, I shouted across to the staff, 'Hey, this woman's about to win'.

We turned up the speakers and waited to share in her glory. Even the staff didn't know the answer so they were just as interested as anyone else to know the mystery location. Derek wound the lady up a bit more and then asked her one more time to say the location at the top of her voice. She screamed out the correct answer and then Derek hit the button to launch the jingle.

'UH-UHHR!'

Oh my god, that was not the correct cart. It was the noise for a wrong answer. As soon as Derek went into a record, I legged it down to the studio. He was white, head in hands and just about in tears.

'Oh, shit,' he moaned. 'I've hit that bloody NO cart so often, Team, I just automatically played it again. I've no idea why. What the hell came over me? I'm so sorry. Team, what have I done?'

'Don't panic,' I said, desperately trying to stay calm. 'You just carry on. It's management's job to panic.'

And, boy, did we do just that. We now had a big problem. We couldn't go back and tell the women who'd just lost that actually there'd been a mistake and she'd won, not in the late Eighties we couldn't. We just had to find another location that hadn't been guessed and keep the competition going. I frantically took the list of names and faxed this to the travel agent we were working with. To save their blushes, I won't name them but the boss was killing himself laughing.

After a few minutes, he calmed down and said, 'Don't worry, John, we'll find somewhere else. I'll work through the list of locations guessed so far and come back to you with another choice.'

I told him not to take too long as the listeners were also keeping a list and were coming up with new locations every single hour. It was a race against time. Next morning he called me back with three locations. They'd all been guessed the previous day. He went back to work on it again but soon called me back.

'John, I've had three people on this and we can't find anywhere that hasn't already been guessed unless we fly the winner to an isolated island on a private jet.'

'We can't bloody do that, Team!' I screamed. 'Look, if we don't sort this out we're both in the shit. We need to find somewhere.'

'I'll keep looking,' he said with a heavy sigh.

'Well, hurry up! The listeners are better at this than us.'

*

A hour later, he called me again. 'John, you must have someone on high looking after you, mate. We've just had a telex from our head office saying Judith Chalmers is going to feature a new island in the Bahamas on television tonight and we've just got the details. It's a place called Paradise Island, owned by a guy called Donald Trump, and some of The Beatles movie *Help!* was even recorded there.'

This was absolutely fantastic news. What a result. When we announced the location, I'd be able to say 'only Red Rose takes its listeners to Paradise'. I could have kissed him. I rushed into the studio and told a lovely guy called John Gilmore to announce we were 'freezing' the competition immediately. The line was that management had declared this fantastic prize must be won tomorrow morning and we'd be giving a major clue at eight fifteen in the breakfast show, a programme I presented, by the way.

We went into overdrive promoting the clue. There was no doubt the prize would be won tomorrow. Next morning listeners started calling in from six o'clock. A young reporter named Kay Burley, who now presents Sky News, was complaining about not being able to get a line out to make check calls to the police and fire brigade. I told her there was nothing I could do about it but it would all soon be over. In the meantime, I'd worked out the killer clue for the destination and was rather pleased with it.

'Billy Fury would take you half way there'

Simple!

At 8.15 I read out the clue. Remember, in the Eighties worldwide travel was not as common as it is today. This was a big prize. All I had to do now was get a caller on air, although picking the right one is an art form in itself. When I arrived at the station, I'd been taught how to find the right caller. I went through them all looking for Lucky Line One Hundred, as we used to say, until I found someone who was lively and right on the edge of a vocal climax. We usually made a decision on who to pick within three seconds. If the caller was lively and sounded like great fun, they had a much better chance than a man who could often be downbeat. While the callers were on hold, I'd make sure they were primed even further by telling them a white lie. I used to say that I really hoped they were going to win, but even if they did, the boss had the power to refuse the prize if they didn't sound happy enough. I asked them not to let me down.

'Oh, don't worry John', the caller said. 'I won't. I just hope I win.'

I now had the perfect caller. And then the game music started....

I got the winner's cartridge out, the correct one this time with all the bells and whistles on and placed it into the slot in the machine. To be on the safe side, I threw the loser's cart to the far end of the studio. I didn't want another cock-up. This was going to be a brilliant end to the competition.

Cue music...

'Okay, time to pick a caller ... Let's go to Lucky Line One Hundred ... Hello, Marion.'

'Ooooh. Hi, John, yes it's me. Here I am.'

'Are you ready to win, Marion?'

'I am, John. I just hope I've got the right answer.'

'Do you want this holiday?'

'Of course, John. We'd just love it. My husband lost his job recently so we've been a little bit down. If we can win this, it'll make our year.'

'Okay. Well, let's hope you're right. Have you been trying to get on for some time?'

'John, I've been late for work so many times because of this competition. I've been trying since day one. I'm just amazed I managed to get on at last. Oh, God… this is great!'

'Did you hear the clue this morning, Marion?'

'I did John, yes. A fantastic clue.'

'Do you want me to repeat it to you?'

'Yes. Please, John. Just to make sure.'

'Okay. Here it is. Billy Fury would take you half way there …'

'Oooohhh, John. Brilliant, this is going to be fantastic!'

'Okay, Marion. The whole of Lancashire is waiting to hear your answer. So, at the top of your voice, shout out where the holiday is?'

'The answer is … TULSA!'

After that clue, she'd come up with that. I couldn't take it in.

'TULSA!!!' I screamed. 'How the bloody hell did you get Tulsa?'

'I don't know, John. I just think that's the answer.'

'But I gave you the clue. This does not seem to match a clue that you've just said was a great one. Are you sure that's your answer?'

'Yes John, it is. I think it's a trick question. You're trying to fool us so I'm staying with my original answer.'

All I had in the machine was the winners' cart. The losing 'UH-UHHR' cartridge was somewhere across the studio. Desperately trying to find it, I asked her to explain again to our audience how she got to that guess. Right now, she had no idea she was a loser so I needed to find that cart. Finally, I found it and returned to the mic.

'So, Marion after all these weeks, all those calls you made that were unsuccessful, all those guesses and, even after the giant clue I gave you this morning, tell us again where you think it is and say it loudly.'

With that she shouted at the top of her voice, 'TUUULLLSAAA!!!'

I hit the 'UH-UHHR' button and went straight into the record. I was speechless.

The door burst open. It was Derek with a number of other staff not far behind him. In a total reversal of fortunes it was now me ashen faced with my head in my hands. Derek was laughing so much he could hardly speak.

'Team, that was the funniest piece of radio I've ever heard in my life,' he said.

I looked up and shouted, 'You're on at ten o'clock. You can have the next caller. This competition is going to kill me!'

'Not on your bloody life, Team' he said, waving his hands in the air. 'I'm not chancing that again for anyone. Do it yourself in fifteen minutes.'

And with that, he left sharpish.

The next caller got it right and that was it - or so you would think. All the talk was not about the person who'd won it or the location, Paradise Island. Instead, it was all about the idiot who thought it was Tulsa. The next day on the breakfast show we had ten facts we didn't know about Tulsa. I even had the Mayor of Tulsa on the phone for a bit of fun. After a few days the happy winners came to see me. The lady was wonderful and I was delighted for both her and her husband. This would be some trip, I said, especially as the prize came with £200 to spend, which in those days was also big money.

She then asked me, 'Where is Paradise Island?'

'It's in the Bahamas,' I replied.

'Is it hot there?' she wondered

'Hot? Of course it is.'

'Well, that's a problem for us. You see, John, we don't like the heat.'

'You what? You don't like the heat?'

'Yes, we always go on holiday where it's not too hot.'

'Well it's going to be hot there,' I said. 'The temperature is about ninety degrees. It really *is* paradise. You can sit in the shade can't you?'

She had a better idea. 'John, we've heard that advert for Pontins.'

'Yes, so what?'

'Well, we were wondering if we could swap Paradise Island for Pontins?'

I looked at her in amazement. 'You must be joking. surely?'

'No, we'd be delighted if you could do this for us. We like Pontins and we'd happily pay to take our two kids there with us, too, if we needed to.'

This just underlines the fact that you should *never, ever* predict people.

'Give me ten minutes,' I said. 'I have an idea.'

I knew the boss at Pontins so I called him up. 'Listen Team, I'm going to make your day. You won't believe this but I've got two people in my office who recently won the trip to Paradise Island.' 'Yes, I heard it,' he said. 'Great comp.'

'Well, you might think so but they don't. They'd rather go to Pontins.'

'Yeh. Right. Is this one of your wind-ups?'

'Not at all, I'm deadly serious, it's completely true. You give me an all-expenses fortnight for this couple, plus their two kids, at Pontins near Blackpool and I'll get you some fantastic Press in return. "Couple ditch paradise for Pontins!" It'll make all the nationals.'

'John, this is brilliant!' he said. 'They must be mad!'

Everyone was happy and as we hadn't given away the big prize I still had a five-star holiday to use again. This time, I changed the location for somewhere closer to home and it was won on the second day, just to prove competitions are never fixed.

Chapter Five

DEALING WITH MR ANGRY

On my weekend breakfast show at Red Rose, I inherited a feature called Bride of the Day. Under the previous presenter this had been a fairly easy five-minute chat with a bride who was due to be married that day. To me it was a boring slot, so over a number of weeks I turned it into something much more edgy and fun. I'd ask listeners to send me information that the bride wouldn't want me to know. Or I'd ring up and tell her the groom had decided to elope with another woman from Taiwan. The duel on the air was all great fun and the brides seemed to take this leg pulling in good spirit. I was always careful not to go too far, especially not on their big day.

In one of my chats with the station's Programme Director Keith Macklin, he reminded me that if I ever went too far with the Brides slot, he wouldn't be able save me from the wrath of the MD, Dave Maker. It would be curtains on a lovely career and, as he'd have to find a replacement for four shows each weekend, he certainly didn't want to be doing that.

'Don't worry, Keith,' I said, reassuring him, 'I know what I'm doing, I'd never take things further than necessary.'

'Well, as long as you know,' he'd say, waving a half-eaten pencil in the air.

The very next weekend the worst thing imaginable occurred. All was going well until I dialled up the Bride of the Day, getting ready for my usual five minutes of leg pulling. This time the information have been provided by her future husband and I also had loads of material from friends to send her off to church with a smile and a spring in her step.

As she came on the air, I said, 'Hey Catherine, how are things going so far?' She replied that, considering how nervous she was, it was all going well. Breakfast had been served, her friends and family were around her and all was lovely. She didn't sound one hundred per cent but I put this down to nerves. Then I said that her future husband had been on and he wanted me to let her know that he'd had a final last fling on his stag night with 'that old witch he used to go out with but from this moment on he was committed to her. There'd be no more other women. Now, he only had eyes for her'. Usually the bride would respond saying, 'Well, tell him I've just done the same'.

Or, 'Yeah, right, well he'll be getting my boot up his backside when I see him.'

All fun stuff. Until now.

Suddenly and without warning there was a very nervy silence. 'Hello Catherine, you still there?'

Down the phone came hysterical crying, followed by the sound of the sobbing bride being comforted by her bridesmaids and family. Oh, my God. This was like a laxative. Right now my career at Red Rose was disappearing down the plughole fast.

What had I said? Had I gone too far? Who could I blame? A thousand things were going through my mind. Above all, I was desperate to get out of this situation. I knew the listeners, that's half the people in Lancashire, would be gripped and thinking the worst of me.

I had to do something and fast.

Most important, I wanted to get out of this with a funny link. Surely there must be something?

'Are you okay, Catherine?' I asked hesitantly. I started to say that her future husband and friends had sent me the information. They'd told me to wind her up. I was now desperately trying to lay the blame elsewhere as Keith Macklin's words of warning rang loud in my ears.

'Hello, Catherine? Hello Catherine!'

Struggling to control on-setting hysteria, I was almost shouting down the phone. Then, without warning, a lady came on the line. A lady who clearly had no idea she was live across Lancashire.

'Hello, who's this?'

'Err, it's John Myers,' I said. 'I was just calling to wish Catherine all the best for her big day and she burst into tears, is she okay?'

'Look John, between you and me, it's not your fault,' said the lady who'd picked up the phone. I know I should have closed the fader right there and then. It was unprofessional but this could be my one chance to save my own skin.

'The problem is, John,' she went on.

'Yes,' I said, 'The problem?'

'The problem, John, is that Catherine has had some doubts about this wedding for some time and only now it's hitting home that she might be making a mistake. Please, it's not you, we just need time to sort it out.'

'Err, I'm sorry but what you've just said has gone out live on Red Rose...'

'You what?' she shouted. 'You're joking!'

'No, I'm not, please, I'm really sorry but I hope you can work it all out...'

All I heard was a swear word and the phone hitting the receiver. I banged on a record. I was part delighted, part worried. It could be argued that I'd turned a potential disaster into a moment of great radio magic but inside I knew I was kidding myself.

All hell broke loose. The man she was marrying had been listening in, along with all of his family.

And that was just the start. On top of that Keith was dialling me up on the ex-directory phone in the studio. Only two people knew the number for the secret XD line. One was my wife. The other was Keith Macklin.

'John, have I really bloody heard what I've just heard?'

'Err yes, Keith, I'm afraid so. For God's sake, this isn't good, John, not good.' That was the understatement of the year. 'Call me back the moment you come off air.'

As I finished my show at nine o'clock Nick Risby came in to present the Top 40. He was wondering why all the phone lines were lit up.

'Nick, whatever happens, don't answer those bloody phones,' I warned him. 'Just KEEP OFF THE PHONES!'

'Team, how the hell are you going to get out of this?' he asked.

'Easy. I'll just sod off quickly and come back tonight.' I headed into the newsroom and rang Keith.

'John, I've never heard anything like it,' he said. 'Ring that poor woman up and find out what's happening.'

'You've got to be joking,' I pleaded. 'We need to change our phone number not ring her up.'

'John, you do this before Dave Maker finds out.' Luckily, the MD was on holiday but we desperately needed to contain this potential disaster.

'Okay, okay,' I said. 'Just give me ten minutes to think about what I'm going to say.'

A short while later, I took a deep breath and rang the bride at home. I was the last person she wanted to hear from but thankfully the family weren't blaming me. In fact, they were blaming everyone *except* me, especially her mum for blurting it out on the radio. I asked them to keep me involved and grovelled the most I have ever grovelled in my life. To be fair to the family, they were great. They even apologised for ruining my show. How good was that? I just kept saying that I was worried about them. I just want to make sure everything was okay, I explained.

Later that morning, the bride's brother called to say the couple were still getting married after all. It was just nerves, they said, and had convinced the husband it was all a joke back on him. Some joke. I rang Keith with the glorious news. He was not as pleased as I was. He said, 'It's very bad John, very bad'. He demanded that I personally took the couple some flowers around to their reception to ensure that Red Rose was going to be okay in all this.

On Monday morning I sat in Keith's office thinking this was it. It was clear that I had been saved due to the fact he couldn't be bothered to find someone else for *four* weekend shows. I was put on warning. I was walking a thin line, he kept saying. He also concluded that if a formal complaint did come in, he could not save me. I ditched the bride calls after that. Time for a pause and I went back to being a generic boring jock for a few weeks.

At the same time I could sense management were losing faith in me. I certainly tested that to the extreme one weekend when I arrived for my Saturday breakfast show. In those days there was a paper log left for each day that outlined in detail the adverts to be placed one by one into a cart machine and the order they were to be played in. How we ever created engaging radio back then is beyond me. We used to line up vinyl records onto record decks, put them back into their sleeves while writing down the details on a PRS log, line up a caller and get the adverts out and put them back again. All that between songs that were much shorter than they are today. In however many seconds were left we used to try and think of something to say. One Saturday morning I came in and all was going well until Nick Risby arrived for the Red Rose Top 40. He came in to check all the records were in their place and suddenly asked me why I was playing all the adverts for a Sunday on a Saturday. I went white. Oh my God, this was not good. I had picked up the wrong log and, as this was soon after the Bride of the Day disaster, I knew I had to act quickly. I came up with what I thought was the perfect solution. Play all of the adverts I should have played from 6 am between now and 9 am. I played them non-stop with just the occasional 'this is Red Rose Radio' in between. Nick pulled them out and I banged them in. I was so elated that I had come up with this brilliant idea I was sure all would be well. Sadly, I had forgotten – well to be more truthful I had no idea – that there was a golden IBA rule that stipulated there must be no more than nine minutes of commercials an hour. This rule remained in place until the

1990 Broadcasting Act. I had just given Red Rose a very big problem because I'd just played out twenty-six minutes of non-stop adverts.

I was suspended for four weeks so I thought it best to find more work on other stations just in case David Maker decided he'd had enough of this Cumbrian idiot. I called Donald Cline at Radio Tees in Stockton and he asked if I could go along and record a live demo. After working in the beautiful Red Rose building, this place was a big shock to the system. The kindest thing I could say about it was that it was a dump. Old, terrible studios in cramped working conditions. I was not that excited to be honest but it was radio. I met up with Donald and a lad with a beard called John Simons or 'Simo' to his friends – spelled with only one 'm' I noticed. John took me into the studio and got me started but I kept cocking it up. Unfortunately, the bosses were listening upstairs but they seemed to like what they heard. And, in any case, it was obvious Simo wanted to start the breakfast show later than his current 5am start. So they created a new slot for me from 5 am to 7 am. I was to do my show then work on traffic reports and leave around nine o'clock. John Simons had taken over from a character called Mark Page, a bit of a superstar on Teesside with the nickname 'Me Mark Page'. He later found a slot on Radio 1. The station also had a madman on the air at night called Graham Robb. It was a show ahead of its time with crazy characters and a phone-in. I loved it. I used to lie in my bedsit in Stockton listening to this artistic fool before getting up at 4am for my own attempt to entertain, and then head off to Red Rose. It was a ridiculous lifestyle by any measure. My workload was such that there was no way I could hang around to do the traffic reports for Simo. So I would just tell him all was fine, make him a cup of tea and leg it out of the door. He used to protect me from the boss who often wondered where I was. We've been great friends ever since. In the end the management were forced to get someone else for the traffic reports. One morning I was asked to go to the local airfield because they were starting a feature called the Eye in the Sky. Radio Tees had found a sponsor prepared to pay the cost of putting a plane into the air allowing a presenter to report into the breakfast show from high above traffic hold ups. But as the plane looked like a flying Robin Reliant, I was not keen. As luck would have it, when I turned up at the airport, the pilot took one look at me and flatly refused to take me up. He said I was far too big to be flown around in reasonable comfort and safety in such a tiny aircraft. Once again, my size came to my rescue and I was allowed to head out of the door bang on seven o'clock.

I like people and the more eccentric they are the better. I would spend hours just watching them at work, learning from the way they go about things and the manner in which they deal with their fellow human beings. In particular, I am facinated by self-made millionaires and would marvel at how they became successful by just doing things slightly differently. In the Eighties and Nineties there were a number of people who either owned a large slice of a radio station or they believed they controlled it. A man I know well was sitting at his desk when one of these eccentric millionaires came past his office door and asked how things were going. At the time he was deep in thought, wrestling with how to a reply to a woman who kept complaining about the station. The millionaire took the letter and said, 'Leave this complaint to me.'

A day later a stencil copy of his letter to the complainer appeared on his desk. He read it, then read it again and laughed out loud. It offered up a style of correspondence he'd not seen before:

Dear Mrs Browning,

I have been handed a letter from you that contains a complaint about our station's output. I also understand we have tried to deal with this complaint professionally without much success.

We have listened to you, offered our view and replied with sincerity. That appears not to be working. I have now come to the conclusion that you should just fuck off. You are officially barred from tuning into this radio station in the future and if you continue to write or listen, a stronger letter will follow.

Yours sincerely

Strangely, he never heard from that woman again.

A local hero of mine was Allan Beswick. I first met him at Radio Cumbria when the boss brought him in to present a new series of The Sunday Phone-in and I was his tech-op. Allan had a way with words, was intelligent and wonderful with callers. He was learning his trade but the guy had talent. At Red Rose, he presented the afternoon show. He was totally professional but being on in the afternoon didn't work for some reason, so he was moved to what management regarded as a safe slot late at night. Allan asked if he could take callers to air and the bosses agreed. From that moment, a star was born and in 1985 he won the prestigious Sony Radio Academy Award for Local Radio Person-ality of the Year. More people tuned in to Allan Beswick than any other jock. At one time, he had double the audience of the breakfast show and that was big. Beswick's late-night phone-in was off the graph in terms of popularity. It was the way he dealt with callers that was the key, he took the mickey, he cut callers off, took them on and just made them look silly.

*

Unpredictability is the key for a great phone-in. If you always know how a presenter is going to react to a particular topic, then after a time the show becomes predictable. Allan would have his fun but occasionally he'd have an intelligent conversation with someone for half an hour, yet with the very next caller go back to cutting them off. It was great radio and because of his intelligence and his love of theatre he knew which buttons to press. This underlines my belief that every radio presenter has a perfect time for being on the air, a slot that suits their own personality and style. Late-night radio was definitely Allan's. He was, and still is, the best I've ever heard on a phone-in. He needs careful managing but that is the problem for management, not a problem for Allan. In my opinion he's wasted in his present slot on BBC Radio Manchester. Here we have probably the best there is with phones and they don't allow him to do the morning phone-in. I'm told management believe Allan is too much of a risk and yet if any station needed to take a risk to build their audience share, it is this one. The people who make these decisions drive me mad. Suits are ten a penny, while gifted broadcasters are as rare as a Salford virgin.

Late night phone-ins were quite new at the time and not all stations had a delay facility. This is now so common it's used all the time when a caller is put to air. The sound is delayed by seven seconds so if the caller says anything they shouldn't, the presenter can cut it out by hitting what was termed the 'dump switch'. This returned you back to real time in an instant, but you had to talk for about two minutes before the machine could build up your seven-second delay again. One night, a radio presenter without this delay facility went on air and asked the audience to ring in with the answer to the question.

If you only had one wish in the world, what would that be?

This is a bad question to ask. It's a green light for every drunken nutter to call in and try to take part. We were all less experienced back then. It was trial and error. There's something in the ears of most broadcasters that can sense when 'the nutter' comes on the air. For instance, most tend to always laugh right at the start of the conversation.

'Hellllloooooo' followed by a chuckle is a *big* warning sign. This presenter did not take heed.

'Hi, Brian, thanks for calling. Now tell me, if you had one wish in the world what would it be?'

Quick as a flash the caller said, 'I'd love to fuck your wife!'

Oh my God, this was very, very bad. The station was now in deep trouble with a guaranteed fine in the offing. The caller was immediately cut off. The damage had to be minimised. The station began playing music, followed at the end of each record by an announcement.

'From the Chairman, we're very sorry for the caller earlier.'

Another record.

'From the Managing Director, we are so very sorry.'

This went on for forty minutes.

'From the cleaner we are very sorry for that earlier caller. Please accept our apologies.'

Jeezus, he thought. Let's hope we all don't get fired.

After about an hour, they decided to go back to the phones. All would be fine by now and, in any case, listeners were calling in asking for the phone-in show to get back on the air. So, with a heavy heart, he opened the lines again and repeated the earlier question.

If you only had one wish in the world, what would that be?

First caller up was Dave from Liverpool. He'd sounded okay before he went on air but, as soon as he was put through, he turned into a nutter.

'Hi Dave … How's it going?'

'Helllllllooooooo, hhhhhhhaaarrhhhr.'

Oh God, the presenter thought.

'First of all Dave, let me apologise for that earlier caller and we very much hope you weren't offended in any way.'

'Not at all, think nothing of it.'

'Okay, well, thanks for that. Now, let's get back to the subject. If you only had one wish in the world, what would it be?'

Without missing a beat, the caller said, 'I'd love to watch that guy fucking your wife!'

He played records for the rest of the show.

＊

While our listeners loved the music and presenters they absolutely adored competitions. Red Rose had made a name for itself coming up with big prizes attached to simple mechanics. The Holiday Game was followed by equally thrilling ideas such as The Currency Game, The Breakfast Gamble, Who's In It To Win It? and many others. Not all of these competitions were original by the way. I used to pinch some of these great ideas from Chris Tarrant's breakfast show on Capital. In his prime, Chris was an absolute genius who was great with callers. It was real end-of-the-pier showbiz stuff that our listeners loved and audiences were building every year. Other stations did similar things to us but we were one of the first to 'strip' a competition across the whole day. This meant we dumped all smaller competitions and the whole station got behind one big idea. This had the benefit of driving the audience to one particular theme and, provided you didn't overdo it, the result could be enormous in delivering more street chat for your station. Too often radio stations make things far too complicated. You have to be able to play along in your car. You can't ask listeners to work things out requiring pen and paper, for example.

All around us radio stations were competing for great ideas. One was a promotion to give away a Renault Clio. The idea behind the competition was good. A local Renault dealership would fill the car with onions – French ones, of course – and all you had to do was guess how many were in the vehicle. There was a further clue on the car windscreen at the garage. This certainly increased footfall in the showroom and the dealer loved that a lot. Each hour of the day, callers went on the air guessing how many onions were in the car.

Each time, their own version of the 'UH-UHHR' sound blasted out.

After a couple of weeks, their boss received a call from the MD at the dealership. They were becoming concerned about the smell.

'What smell?' he was asked. 'Why are you calling my radio station about a smell in your dealership?'

The car dealer explained the stink was coming from the car the station was giving away, customers were complaining like hell and it had to be sorted out. It appeared some dithering idiot had actually put real onions in the car instead of plastic ones. Now, down at the dealership the stench of rotting onions was unreal. It was the middle of summer. The showroom staff had tears in their eyes as the door was opened and hundreds of ripe onions started to roll across the floor. In the end, they pushed the car round the back and emptied the contents into a skip. It cost around two thousand pounds to have the car put right and took more than a month for the smell to disappear.

Another PD really does own the badge of stupidity. He acquired a car for a competition, which he named Star in the Car. To win, all you had to do was name the fictitious celebrity in the car. He came up with a simple competition mechanic and crazily guaranteed the car would not be won for at least three weeks, even though the contest was running on the air every hour of the day.

After the three weeks were up he came into the studio to help find the winner. As PD, he wanted to ensure the jock wouldn't cock this up, so he took sole charge. First task was to go through all the listeners' guesses of the mystery star's name that had been diligently written down on sheets of paper in the studio file. Once he had the list, he waited until a caller came on air with a name that had not yet been chosen. In his view of the world, he wasn't cheating, as the car was always won. The 'winning' caller was put to air and, to be fair, she was a great winner. Fantastic emotion. A perfect end to a perfect competition, he gloated.

Two hours later, the PD received a phone call from a listener who claimed they'd given that same star's name on air just the week previously. How come they hadn't won the car? An hour later, another caller said exactly the same thing. If this proved to be true, it would surely be the end of the PD's job. He'd taken personal charge of this competition and had gone through all of the guesses. The name they were claiming they'd guessed the previous week was not on that list. He went back into the studio and grabbed the file. He went through it in fine detail again and as he did so, came across two pages that somehow had stuck together. He had missed them. Bad news. Sure enough, there they were. Two listeners had named the Star In The Car correctly. He came out of the studio and headed into the engineering room to ask for the audio tapes of the past week's output. It's a condition of any radio station's licence that you keep a copy of everything that's gone to air for a minimum of forty-two days. There was no mistake. The callers were on the tapes. The PD hit the loo and sat there for an hour thinking through his next move. There was no way around this problem. He now had to tell the MD.

'You fucking idiotic pile of shit' was one phrase heard through the door by the Managing Director's PA. As you can imagine that confidential discussion went around the building within thirty seconds. The whole staff knew the PD was getting his arse kicked big time but the reason was still unclear.

'How the hell could this happen?' the boss kept asking. If he had called me I could have told him the answer in a second. The PD was a dickhead. He'd tried to be clever but in the end he was just too clever. There was only one solution. The two people saying they had already guessed the correct name also had to have a free car.

A promotion that should have been a good revenue earner was now the complete opposite. Worse still, the Press soon discovered something was amiss so they had to announce, that due to an error, three people would now win a car. Rival stations loved this and so did I although the biggest winner was the car dealership. They'd started off giving away one car but ended up selling the station two more.

We all make mistakes. The trick is never to repeat the same one twice.

Mind you, even I was fortunate on one occasion. A great lady caller won a big prize one day and when I called to congratulate her she told me that she had been asked to fill in some sort of a diary to record her listening habits. I nearly fainted. This was brilliant. I told her it was hugely important to fill it in correctly while also telling her I was going to take the sound of her winning the prize that morning and would then be playing it out a lot over the coming week. In fact, I played it out every hour on the hour, I knew she would never tune out and would tell everyone she knew to tune in and listen. We had a great result that quarter because the diary she had been given came from RAJAR – JICRAR as it was known then – and was used to compile our listening figures!

Chapter Six

IT'S THE MUPPET SHOW

I was sat at home in Carlisle watching Border Television who at the time employed in-vision continuity announcers. For some reason, Border did not have an auto-cue so all their presenters were nick-named The Nodding Dogs because they continually looked up and down, like those irritating toy animals you used to find on car parcel shelves. It dawned on me that this must be one of the easiest jobs on the planet and, besides, TV looked quite exciting. It was 1985 and at the time I was doing four shows a weekend at Red Rose, along with extra fill-in work in Lancashire plus a shift at Radio Tees in Stockton. So, working for Border TV could be a great way of earning more cash without having to commute hundreds of miles to work.

I put in a call to Border TV's Head of Programmes, Eric Hadwin, who explained there was very little chance of me getting a job and, in any case, I had to be a member of the broadcasters' union, Equity. When I rang Equity, I was told I had to have a job before I could get a union card, yet I couldn't get a job until I had a card. It was a typical Catch 22. Eventually, I found a way of getting entry into the union by asking a few showbiz friends to sign my application form and I was given a year's provisional card. I had twelve months to find a job

otherwise the card would be taken off me. I decided to lobby Border
hard, so every Monday for six months I called Eric Hadwin. I was like
a wart he could not get rid of. I struck up a great relationship with his
PA, Maureen, who was always fun but each chat with Eric was short
and professional. It was always the same.

'Nothing yet, John, but keep calling.'

I phoned week after week until finally one day Eric said, 'I might
have a few days work. When can you come and see me?'

'Any time you want,' I replied.

'Are you free this weekend?'

Remembering the golden rule, I quickly said, 'Yes, of course, Eric.'
'Right, come and see me Friday afternoon.'

I called Red Rose, took a weekend off and then on Friday afternoon, as I entered Border's smart studios on an industrial estate on
the city ring road, it struck me I'd had no screen test, nothing! Just a
relationship struck up on the phone.

I'd asked for this chance so often but Eric Hadwin had no idea
who I was. Thankfully, we got on immediately and he asked if I'd be
willing to have a three-day contract. My first role would be a live six-
minute slot on Sunday morning, reading The Border Diary.

'Can you handle it?' he asked.

That was it. All he wanted to know.

'Of course, Eric, I've been doing radio shows for years and a live
six-minute TV appearance will be no problem,' I said confidently.
Inside, I was bricking it.

'Okay, come in at eight o'clock on Sunday morning. We'll have
someone to look after you. Now, go downstairs, meet Clive Champney,
the duty announcer, and he'll walk you through the plan.' Clive turned
out to be someone I trusted a great deal, he taught me so much and he's
still a wonderful friend today.

That was my induction into Border. A three-day test and if I
passed, who knows?

I went straight to see a local hi-fi dealer, hired a video camera and
stand, then went home and practised speaking into it for hours on

end. I managed to get hold of the previous week's Border Diary script, which was just like a radio What's-On guide but with pictures, and practised when to lift my head, when to breathe and when to smile. Lifting your head at the end of a sentence allows the viewer to think you are looking at them a little more. Seeing the top of your head was never a good look.

On Sunday morning George Jackson, the transmission controller – TC in the trade – was there to greet me. He was the team leader, a great guy, very funny with a formidable reputation for being strict. He told me straight, 'TV works like this. We have a slot for Border Diary today that lasts six minutes and twenty seconds. You go live at 09.30 exactly and you have to finish talking at 09.36.20 exactly so I can hit the network junction. Now, here's the deal. If you finish reading your script early I have nowhere to go. I can't go to someone else because, as continuity announcer, you are that someone else. You're supposed to be the person we go to when I have nothing else to go to. So, as you're actually on the air, if you come out early then I have to leave you up on the screen while the seconds tick away. The reverse is also true. If you talk past the time of 09.36.20 then I'll have to cut you off in your prime so I can get into network. Either way, you look a dick. The only way you can look good is to talk to time. Can you do that?'

'Yes, George, I think I can.'

'Well if you can do that, you and me are going to get on just fine,' he said.

Boy this was pressure like no other, definitely *not* the easiest job on the planet. Reading out a list of events is no problem but when someone says you have to do it to an exact time, it really does take some skill to perfect. You had to read the script, not look like a nodding dog, watch the clock and finish bang on the button, while all the time trying to look cool and professional. Remember, this was my very first stint on TV. But there's one thing I know about myself. I love pressure. I absolutely adore it. The bigger the pressure, the better I perform. I don't know why, but give me as much pressure as you can throw at me. I become totally focused.

I later learned Eric Hadwin had the car warming up on his drive just in case I failed badly and he could race in and take me out of the studio. That was never going to happen. The result was excellent. I finished ten seconds early and then filled with an off-the-cuff remark that allowed George to slowly fade into network. Praise was never that forthcoming at Border, but the door opened and George popped his head around the corner. He was a Geordie and had a lovely way with words 'Well,' he said. 'Ya didn't do so badly … for a freelance!'

Apparently, George didn't like freelance presenters but he was good enough not to mention it to me before my broadcast. Eric Hadwin also called in to say well done. I had passed the first test.

*

My contract at Border TV was then extended from three days to three months to cover for Alan Cartner, who was on sick leave. Alan was a lovely man, with a wonderful rich voice. As long as Alan was ill, Eric would continue to give me shifts and very soon I had so much work on my plate that I was struggling to fit it all in. At one stage I was on the early breakfast show on Radio Tees, lunchtime on Red Rose and the late shift on Border TV.

*

At my interview I'd asked about the fee for this job. Eric told me there was a set rate for continuity work and I should see Fred in accounts. After that first weekend, I wandered across the car park to a Porta-cabin to check out how much I would be paid for my three days. I had to sit down. I was earning £25 a show for going all the way to Red Rose. Here, they were paying me £65 a shift plus a clothing allow-ance, and a three-course meal in the staff canteen cost just ninety pence. On top of that, I was on the telly and living at home. Two weeks into the job I got a visit from a union rep asking if I would support a strike. 'You guys don't know you're born,' I said and I meant it. I'd been on crap money for years, I was starting off in a new career, getting my head above water financially for the first time ever and they wanted me to go on strike. There was no chance of me walking out, especially as the union couldn't properly explain what the strike was about, except that it 'would wind up the management'. Some of the practices I saw at Border were mind-blowing and, in my view, nothing short of abuse.

*

The big, yet legal, scam at the time was claiming overtime. Employees could see their hourly pay rocket if they had to return to work at the station again within a certain period of time. If, say they had to go back to work within ten hours of their previous shift, that next shift was paid on 2T, twice their normal hourly rate. However, one of the scams I saw was very wrong. The technical team on the late shift would finish when the station went off air, usually around 1am in the days before twenty-four hour TV. One of the staff who was due on shift the next morning would phone in claiming to be ill. The rest of the team would then make sure they were unavailable to cover, so management would be forced to call in the person who had just finished the previous evening's shift in the early hours of the morning. Because he had not had a ten-hour break between shifts, he was now working on at least double the money and, in some cases, as much as 4T, quadruple his normal hourly rate. If the transmission team shared this working practice around themselves across the year they could all increase their salary substantially. Management knew this, of course, but were often powerless to stop the scam due to union power. This created tension and at times it was a difficult place to work. Thankfully, the strike never happened but my card was marked with a few in the union.

*

I was once caught out by one of their scams and it was my own fault for being dumb. Just before closedown, there was always around two minutes of 'continuity' at the end of night. I turned this tiny bit of late-night airtime into a little sideshow of my own with a few jokes and light-hearted banter. I had a trademark wink to all those who lived alone and reminded viewers to turn off their electricity at the socket. I have no idea why we had to make that announcement as people always kept on their other appliances, like the fridge. What was different with the television? My usual end of night monologue was something on the lines of, 'Goodnight, sleep tight, kick that cat out, gag the budgie and come back to join us tomorrow morning at 9.25 for a new day on Border.'

Then, we'd go to the clock to take us up to the final minute. I got a right telling off one day for shouting 'BOO!' after about twenty seconds of dead air. I imagined all the old folk getting up as one to switch their TV sets off at the socket.

'You'll bloody kill some old dear with nonsense like that, Myers,' Eric warned.

On this occasion, as the evening was drawing to a close, one of the technical team came in and asked if I wanted to have an extra-long goodnight closedown. They were happy to play out some promos for the next day if I wanted. This was an unusual gesture as they were usually as keen as mustard to get home. So, instead of a two-minute close down we had a four-minute bonanza of the programmes that were coming up the next day. As I didn't get to bed before 2am after a late shift, I usually slept until ten o'clock. However, next morning Eric Hadwin was on the phone extremely early. 'John, what the fuck happened last night?' he demanded.

Half asleep, I said, 'What are you talking about, Eric? Nothing happened.'

'Well I've just looked at the closedown log and it would appear we finished the night at 1.02 am.'

'You were scheduled to finish at 12.59 and not one moment later. What happened?'

'Well, the lads from VTR (the video play out department) came in and offered to play a few promos to end the night. We had a great closedown, Eric. You'll love it when you watch it back.'

'Love it! I fucking hate it you dumb arse,' he responded. 'You've been conned. It now means that the whole of the next shift starts within a closed period by just two minutes. It means we have to pay them 2T for the whole of that shift. They'll be pissing themselves laughing at that. You've just cost me about *five grand!*'

He was not best pleased.

'Look, It's not your fault, he said recovering his composure, 'but in future do the standard closedown unless I personally give you permission to extend it. Do you understand?'

Later, I walked into the department to a round of applause, so I gave them my view of life.

You live and learn.

*

In continuity you usually had about twenty seconds on screen to make your mark and there was not much chance of success unless you were different. I was different and being the youngest announcer allowed me to get away with murder. All the transmission controllers liked my new approach and were willing to help me try new things. It was fun too. When a cowboy movie came on, I wore a Stetson. When snooker was on, I came into vision carrying a snooker cue. One night a Dracula horror movie was scheduled, so I went into the make-up room and dressed up in a cape, put in false fangs and smeared my face in fake blood. I came on the TV in dark lighting and introduced the film. Viewers complained I was more frightening than the movie but it got me noticed and was my way of introducing personality into the output. One day, Eric called me upstairs to answer a complaint.

'It's from the Cats Protection League,' said Eric. 'They're not happy about you saying 'Kick the cat out' at closedown.

'Tell them to sod off,' I replied. 'No one takes that term seriously; it's just a phrase of fun.'

'Don't say it again. Think of something else,' he warned.

So, at close-down that night, I looked straight at the camera and said, 'Don't forget to gag the budgie and kick the cat in.'

Job done!

*

I still managed to have loads of fun at closedown. One night I announced a brand-new experiment on Border. I said, 'I shouldn't be telling you this but after about fifteen minutes when you've all gone to bed we will be testing out a range of films. The first one is 'Alone Through The Night' with Charlton Heston. Enjoy. Meanwhile, good-night from all of us …'

Blank screen.

The following afternoon, as I arrived for my next shift Eric was waiting.

He ushered me into the privacy of the announcers' room and said, 'Now John, we really like what you do and you do it well but sometimes you push the bar too far. I'm not that keen about getting a bollocking from my own boss for not keeping you under control. You have to help me out.'

I was at a total loss as to what he was talking about.

'Sorry, what's the problem?'

'Last night our security guard took more than a hundred and forty complaints from viewers who stayed up to see a movie you said we were screening that never came on. He was so busy answering the phone he could not perform his duties of checking the building. What the hell came over you?'

I could not believe anyone would have been taken in when I called the movie 'Alone Through The Night'.

'In any case, it serves the poor sods right if they can't work that out surely,' I said.

'Listen to me, John,' Eric said, rather testily. 'The big man is not best pleased. He's had to spend his day answering complaints and that means more trouble for me, which means a shed load of trouble for you!'

I really liked Eric. He was my mentor as well as being my boss and he taught me a lot. I often used to go upstairs and sit with him for an hour and just chat. There was no way I was going to make life difficult for him so I made sure to be on my best behaviour for a short while.

*

20 second break...

You don't look a day older

Border TV was on the look out for some freelance continuity cover and in the post they received a wonderful CV that showed a lady with bags of experience alongside a stunning photograph. The boss was smitten. This lady would bring some much needed glamour to the screen he thought. Trouble was she lived in Devon so they decided against bringing her up to Carlisle for an interview and just awarded her a contract after a conversation on the telephone.

When she arrived for her first day, she came to reception where the manager was called to come down and meet her. When he appeared, he said to her, 'Jeezus, you don't look anything like your bloody picture'. He was later heard asking 'makeup' to get some more supplies in. He had a way with words. Not that she wasn't fabulous, she was just twenty years older than the picture she provided.

With money rolling in, I could at last afford to take my family on a proper summer holiday. Browsing in the shops in Majorca, my daughter, Kerry, picked up a small puppet monkey that wrapped around its arm around your neck, and you put your arm inside to operate its mouth, like a ventriloquist's dummy.

After we got home, it sat on the chair inside the front door and one morning as I went out to work, I grabbed it on the spur of the moment and took it with me.

Part of my shift entailed reading out birthday cards sent in by families. It was really dull for the kids watching, even those with a birthday, until I came on screen with the puppet who, as a tribute to my boss, I named 'Eric the Monkey'. The viewers' feedback was terrific.

Eric invited me upstairs for a chat. 'What's the thing with this bloody monkey, Eric?'

'It's just a bit of fun and the kids love it.'

'Yes, keep it going. I like it,' he said. 'It's not named after me is it?'

'Absolutely not, Eric, it's named after Eric Wallace, a fellow presenter and a hero of mine.'

'It's amazing, John, that I have to find out what you are up to only by watching the bloody television myself. Please let me know beforehand what you are going to do.'

Coming from radio where you just thought things up on the hoof, I was not used to telling people in advance what to expect but in TV it was clearly a must.

The number of birthday cards coming into the station shot up, so I had a much bigger puppet designed and we launched the official 'Eric the Monkey' birthday slot most afternoons at 4.50pm. The team in scheduling were brilliant and used to move things around to give me more time. Very often the slot was five minutes long. That kind of live TV, just you unscripted without a safety net, would never happen today.

Browsing in Hamley's toyshop in London one afternoon, I noticed a toy fireman that climbed up and down a big ladder. I'd been looking for a prop that would move on the screen and this was perfect. I had to come up with a name for him that would be a long tongue twister that the kids would love to try and say. The following week I announced Eric the Monkey had a new friend, *Fearless Fireman Fred from the Fife Fire Fusiliers who's a fierce fire-fighter and he can't 'arf fight fire, coz he's a flipping good fireman is the fearless fireman Fred from Fife.* The moment I said that, and you have to say it very fast, the team burst out laughing. This was brilliant. To get the cynical old buggers at Border laughing was an achievement in itself. The kids absolutely loved it, too, and once again we managed to refresh a part of the output that had gone stale. Eric saw this and came down for a chat. He often popped into the studio for five minutes. He made me laugh when he said, 'That tongue twister has a lot of 'Fs' in it for kids' TV. Now, if you ever slip up, you know that I can't save you. You'll be doomed, son.'

'Don't worry Eric,' I said, 'that's part of the reason kids like it, too. It comes with an element of danger.'

But the warning was clear and noted.

*

One Friday I received a call from the schedules department. They had a bigger than normal slot on Sunday afternoon and had noticed I was on shift. Would I like to do something special for the birthday slot or did I want them to put in a filler programme?

'How long is the potential slot?' I asked.

'Nine minutes.'

Wow, nine minutes. How could I refuse?

'Look, if you could find me a couple of cartoons to use, we can announce it's Eric The Monkey's birthday and I'll work on something special,' I said.

So, I arrived on Sunday to find the slot had now been extended to thirteen minutes. I went to the canteen and asked if the staff could make a cake for me to use on air.

Then, I went live and announced that later we'd have a special edition of Border Birthdays.

That afternoon, I put the cake on the front of the desk in the Continuity Studio, lit two small party candles and launched into the slot. I went through all of Eric's friends on the desk with me and, as it was his birthday, we were wearing paper hats. All was going well until the paper hat on the monkey's head fell off right on top of the candle and it erupted into a giant flame. In my ear, I could hear the Transmission Controller saying, 'Oh fuck'n'ell, John, go to a cartoon so we can sort this out. The place will catch fire.' I was patting the burnt-out paper on the desk, telling kids to make sure this sort of thing didn't happen at home while hoping that the sprinklers didn't come on. I hit the cartoon and all hell broke loose in the studio. The TC came in and cleared up the debris, we changed the front of the desk and when we returned to air, we had discarded the paper hats but the team were concerned we'd soon be soaked by the automatic sprinklers. At the end of the programme, I was dripping with sweat.

The door flew open and the TC said, 'Well, that was a first, bloody hell.'

Just then I noticed the studio direct line was ringing. It was either my wife or Eric.

'Are you taking that?' I said to the TC.

'Not on your life,' he replied. 'It'll be for you.'

And it was. It was Eric. 'John,' he said. 'Words fail me. I can't believe what I've just seen. Thank God you got out of that but it was close. Let's discuss how we can do things a little better next time.'

Eric was a good man and a keen supporter of Myers. It's a good job. A lesser boss would have thrown me out well before now.

*

We even recorded a special Christmas Eve programme with Eric the Monkey. Santa Call featured cartoons and the real Father Christmas coming in to the studio to talk live on the telephone to excited children. Santa was usually my good mate Clive Champney, who was excellent, but one year he was unavailable so we asked Neville Wanless, a fellow continuity announcer from Newcastle to stand in. Neville was an experienced broadcaster, he had the perfect voice for Father Christmas and could carry the Santa suit off in style. As the show got under way, we knew there were two advert breaks to take before the end and thank goodness for that. As the show started, we plugged for calls from children who wanted to talk to Santa and went to a cartoon. The studio phones went into meltdown. It seemed every household across Cumbria and the Borders was dialling in. Technically, it was an easy show to do and one I'd done for years on radio. There was no reason this should be more difficult just because it was TV. I was working with the flamboyant director Harry King, who was as insane as me. It looked as though we were talking through a phone in the studio but all the sound actually came through an earpiece in the presenter's ear. The show was in full flow and we went to the callers. It was chaos. Santa couldn't hear the kids asking for their gifts. Instead, he constantly shouted 'Hello! Hello!'

And the kids were all shouting, 'Hello, Santa I'm here. Can you hear me, Santa?'

It was terrible TV but gripping at the same time. You could not have planned the disaster that was unfolding before us if you'd had a month to put it together. Harry screamed for us to hit the ad break early and try and sort the problem out. During the break, Neville casually announced the reason he couldn't hear was because he had his earpiece in his deaf ear.

'You what? Why the hell didn't you put the earpiece in your other ear?' I asked.

As he tried to re-insert his earpiece, his beard fell off and the horror-struck children in the studio were suddenly aware this was not the real Santa. The floor manager counted us out of the ad break and I shouted, 'Boys and girls, we've sorted out our special Santa phone, isn't that correct Neville err … I mean Santa?'

So, we hit the phones again and what I heard next nearly gave me a heart attack. Normal practice for a Santa call was to always say to children phoning in that you would do your best to get them what they wanted but there were no promises. That was fine. However, our Santa was not fully briefed because this fool had not prepared him properly. It was my fault, certainly not his. I still have the tape of the show. I just dare not watch it. Santa was on the phone to a delightful boy. Asked what he wanted for Christmas, the young lad suddenly began reading a long list of toys, including that year's most sought-after toy, Tracy Island, a plastic replica of the secret base of Thunderbirds, complete with a swimming pool that moved aside to allow a rocket to be launched. This was a toy so rare nobody could get their hands on one, which made kids want them even more. Blue Peter even resorted to showing viewers how to make one out of toilet roll holders and sticky-back plastic. If you were lucky enough to have a Tracy Island you were the king of your street. This lad was going hard at it and I expected Santa to give out our usual disclaimer line. Not this Santa. All I heard was, 'Well, we'll make sure you get everything you ask for.'

'Everything?' asked the boy.

'Yes,' said Santa. '*Everything*. You have a wonderful Christmas now. Bye, bye.'

The camera panned back to reveal me looking as if I'd been smacked by a golf ball. 'Err, thanks Santa. Time for a break.' Off air

I turned to Neville. I wanted to shout, 'Are you fucking mad?' but we were surrounded by a gaggle of seven year-olds, keen to get their hands on Santa's autograph. I was keen to get my hands on Santa, too.

'There's no-way that kid is going to get all that stuff but you've just told him he *is*,' I hissed.

The final part of the show was a blur. Eric the Monkey read out some Christmas cards, the kids had some sort of a dance and then we opted into network. I was exhausted. As I came out of the studio I learned the mother of the young lad was on the phone demanding to know what the hell we were going to do. We had guaranteed, no promised even, that he would get every single present he was asking for. She was going off her rocker and I couldn't blame her. It was pointless raising this with Neville. It was my own fault for not briefing him properly. At the same time, staff were walking past me in the corridor saying, 'John that was brilliant. That kid was a set up right? I mean you haven't really told him he could have stuff you don't have.'

It was now seven o'clock on Christmas Eve and the boy's father was also on the warpath. He wanted a direct line to the station's chairman. We had ruined his son's Christmas as they had only managed to buy about a fifth of all those toys he wanted.

I told the production team, 'Look, we don't have to get all the toys the kid wanted we just need to get the main one, Tracy Island. If we can get that, we're out of jail. The lad won't care about the rest.' Where the hell were we going to get the most sought after toy on planet earth at seven o'clock on Christmas Eve? I knew the name of a man who owned a toyshop in Carlisle. I'd no idea of his home phone number and three of us went through the phone book and found three possible candidates. We were successful on the second and, of course, he knew who I was. I explained the position and asked for help.

'Let me repeat this. You want me to find the most sought after toy in the UK right now, at this hour on Christmas Eve due to a cock up at your station?'

'Yes, you have it in one. Look,' I pleaded. 'I'm sure Paddy our sales director will look after you magnificently for an advert if you could do this for us, but we need a miracle.'

Fifteen minutes later he called to say he had found one and we dispatched a car to the boy's home for delivery. Tracy Island saved the day but it aged me by ten years. The boy was delighted, the parents pacified and I escaped a near-heart attack. That was one turkey of a show.

*

Border TV's professionalism was never in doubt, though. On 21 December 1988, a Pan Am jet was blown out of the sky over the town of Lockerbie, just north of Carlisle. Almost everyone from Border was arriving at the studios for our Christmas party but it turned out to be far from a celebration. In 1988 television coverage was technically very different to today, with no such thing as 24 hour news. Yet, somehow, this tiny TV station managed to provide pictures and reports to every corner of the world, as the team rose to the occasion with great skill. I watched a colleague constantly on the telephone to news organisations around the world, agreeing a price for all the footage we had before it was handed over to foreign channels to be shown in other countries. It was weird but that is how it works. It is also at times like this when the real professionals earn their money. People ask why presenters earn the sums they do. Of course it looks easy when things are going well but it's when they are faced with these type of challenges that they earn their corn. While I was desperately upset for all those affected by this disaster, I have never been more proud of the people I worked with at that time.

*

My problem is boredom. I have to keep learning new skills or taking on new challenges. While at Border I set up by own door-to-door soft drink business called Mr Pop and a good business that made cassette tapes for the motor industry. In the late Eighties, nearly every car in Britain had an instruction cassette in their glove box with (mostly) me or Mike Smith, Mel Smith and Griff Rhys Jones, for example, who would be on the tape saying ... '*thank you for buying your new car from*

Ford UK' followed by some instructions on how to use the dealership's services. It was all part of my efforts to keep busy and while it did not make huge profits, it did allow for a certain lifestyle. On one occasion, I heard that a rival was going around car showrooms telling fibs about the way I ran the business. I was a little grumpy about this so I hired a private detective from West Cumbria who arranged a meeting in London with this idiot after placing a camera in the eye of a wooden file on his desk, recording everything. The man came, lied, and we recorded. I sent his boss a cease and desist letter the next day alongside some stills of the colleague in action. Rather than have any hassle, the boss just closed this part of the business down and I was left to get along with life once again.

The moment I become bored I become dangerous and that's never good, either for those I work with or myself. I do things to cheer myself up and many a time I've landed in trouble for no other reason than this. As I was leaving Border TV's studios at the end of a late shift, it dawned on me that it was now April Fools' Day. It was one o'clock in the morning and I was travelling home past BBC Radio Cumbria's studios on top of the city's old gallows hill. I had a crazy idea. In the boot of my car was an old chain and padlock. I drove right up to the front door of the station, fed the chain through the door handles, padlocked it tightly and put a notice on the window.

FOR SALE due to lack of listeners or entertainment. Any reasonable offer considered. Might swap for an old banger. Contact Conrad Ritblat Agents, London.

I drove home and went to bed until I was woken at eleven o'clock the next morning by a call from Border.

'John, can you confirm to me - and I very much hope you can do this - that you had nothing whatsoever to do with the padlocking of Radio Cumbria this morning. Your name is being bandied about as someone who might have found this sort of childish humour amusing.'

I told a lie. 'Nothing to do with me, why what's happened?'

Apparently, when David Lamb and the news team turned up for work at Radio Cumbria at four thirty in the morning they couldn't get in. Only the intervention of a night watchman from the nearby hotel, who cut off the padlock with a giant pair of cutters, enabled the presenters to eventually get into the building moments before they were due on air.

'Oh really,' I said. 'That's very sad news and quite right, very disappointing of the idiot who did it.'

'Umm, if you're sure it wasn't you then fine but the writing on the cardboard beside it looked suspiciously like yours,' Eric said. 'Rubbish, I was nowhere near the place,' I bluffed.

Sadly, I now confess. At the time it was close to it being the last straw, despite my popularity as a broadcaster.

I was now reasonably popular with the public and in demand for personal appearances. I made it my business never to refuse one so that I became as well known as possible. A garage gave me a free car with the words 'John Myers and Eric the Monkey' plastered all over it. It was a great car but if I had a pound every time someone asked my wife if she was the monkey I could have retired years ago. I've always said that no matter how funny you think you are, the funniest people are those you meet every day on the streets.

I was asked to do two personal appearances in one day. The first was in West Cumbria to officially open a new Spar shop. Although it was not in the best of areas, as you might say, there was certainly a great turn out. The store manager had booked some PR but completely forgot about security. It was a hot day in the middle of summer yet everyone I met wore a big coat. I made a speech, cut the ribbon and stayed around for an hour signing photographs. As I went to say goodbye, I noticed the shelves were pretty empty.

'Wow!' I said to the shop manager. 'You must have had a great opening.' He thought so, too, and hit a button on his till to reveal the day's total. Turns out he'd taken just £98. It suddenly dawned on me why so many people had big coats in the middle of summer.

My next stop was to open a fish and chip shop in nearby Workington. A big queue was waiting when I got there. After about ten minutes, I noticed a boy aged about seven waiting for a photograph.

Suddenly he was right beside me. 'Hiya,' I said, smiling. 'Do you want a picture, son?'

'No, I don't,' he replied. 'I fucking hate you and that monkey. My dad fucking hates you, too. Now sod off and don't come back.' Charming, I thought. That brought me down to size. I hear he's in the Government now.

*

This was an amazing time for Border TV. We had a brilliant new programming boss, Paul Corley, who together with Managing Director Jim Graham put this tiny TV station in the furthest corner of England well and truly on the broadcasting map. We started getting network commissions like Get Fresh with Gaz Top, The Krankies, Highway with Sir Harry Secombe, and Stu Francis's kids' show, Crush A Grape. A large number of these were directed by Harry King. One minute he was working with me and a deaf Santa, the next he was working with the stars of the day. Perhaps the weirdest moment of all was when the production team had a crazy idea to make Kylie Minogue, who'd arrived in knee-length white boots, sing on top of a car in local dealer Ron Morton's scrap yard. The producer of this show was the one and only Janet Street-Porter.

Meanwhile, the station's best-known product, Mr And Mrs with Derek Batey, was still going out. The show was a nice, warm affair featuring couples of a certain age trying to win a carriage clock and a few quid by answering innocuous questions about their marriage. Who would have thought a couple of pensioners would walk off with the star prize of four thousand pounds with a simple con that managed to beat the show's producers. It was so easy but, amazingly, no one had done it before. All the crafty couple did was answer every question in alphabetical order. Simples. They didn't have to tell the truth, they just had to know the alphabet. When they were asked a question about which side of the bed the got out of, left or right? They just chose the earliest letter in alphabetical order and – bingo – they won. When the programme was shown in the Border area no one guessed a thing. Not a single call. However, when it was later shown across the London area as a network show the balloon went up and it made front-page news in The Sun. I had to laugh. Well done them. The old buggers could still show us a thing or two, I thought, and we had to devise a way of making sure this didn't happen again. The couple insisted they'd given out true answers and so they kept the cash. On one episode of Mr And Mrs, a British Airways steward and his wife failed by just one question to win the star prize. The week following his appearance on the show he was working in the first-class cabin on a flight between New York and London when he was serving a woman who asked 'Do I know you?'

'I don't think so,' he replied and carried on. Over the next couple of hours the woman insisted she knew him and he kept insisting she didn't. Then she revealed she had seen the Mr And Mrs show the week before and that he had failed to win the star prize by just one question. She told him that she'd have got the question right and would have won the prize. That lady was former Prime Minister Margaret Thatcher. Everyone seemed to love that show.

*

Border was such great fun and the local stardom that came with being on regional television was like a drug. The first year I absolutely loved it. In the next year it was much less exciting and by the third anniversary of my first appearance, I was pretty much over it. I had done TV and now wanted to return to my radio roots. I missed the medium so much. I'd done a few shows for Red Rose again and realised I missed the buzz and excitement of live radio. This of course was madness in that most people's career path went from Press, to radio and then TV. I had gone from radio to TV and was now returning to radio. Some would say it was a giant step backwards! Being recognised on the street was good for a time but it had lost its magic and I was clear that, while I was good at this level, I was nowhere near good enough to become a national presenter. You have to know what you are best at and this was just a good interlude before going back to my real love.

The day before I handed in my notice, I had to announce the afternoon matinee. Films on television are always cut down to fit the time slot available. They are edited but you would never notice. If the film needed to be shortened by twenty minutes a skilled editor would take out lots of little bits that did not affect the viewer's enjoyment, such as ten seconds walking from the car to the door. The editor could spend a whole day taking out a few seconds here and a few there to get to the right duration. On this day, the Equity union had an issue with the chosen movie and we were going to have to find a replacement. I would make an announcement that there was a change to the advertised programme. We always had a stock of movies for times like this. The replacement movie was called Submarine X-1, which tells the story of how a brave sub crew used midget submarines to penetrate Nazi defences and blow up a German ship by placing explosives under the hull. Nine minutes needed to be lost from the film but the only person available to make the cut was a trainee. This was an easy job, even considering the time restraints. Submarine X-1 is a great film and as I love war movies I introduced it with gusto. Everything was going fine but gradually the transmission controller became a little worried about running out of time. We'd just got to the part where the crew had placed their explosives. Suddenly, the credits started to come up. The whole point of the movie was the blowing up of the German warship, yet we had stopped before the climax! Would they succeed or wouldn't they? Now we were into the credits and the phone started ringing off the hook in reception. Viewers had been cheated out of the big finale. There was no explosion, just me announcing… 'and now it's the Australian soap, The Young Doctors.' The boss was on holiday but we all wanted to know what had happened. We pulled the apprentice editor in for a grilling. He explained that as he'd been short of time and it was obvious the British were going to be successful and had won the war in any case, the final scene was exactly nine minutes long so he just cut that bit out.

'Job done,' he said. 'Who would notice?'

Who would notice? Just the thousand of viewers who were on the phone wanting to know why the hell they had just spent ninety minutes watching a movie that had no end!

Then stupidity moved up a notch when I was ordered to apologise for the error and tell the viewers that we would play out the missing nine minutes the following afternoon at 3.30 pm.

'What!' I screamed. 'You must be joking. We're going to show the missing nine minutes tomorrow when most people would have forgotten about it. Those watching tomorrow who missed the movie today will now see nine minutes of a ship blowing up with no explanation whatsoever. It will look ridiculous.'

I was overruled and at the end of The Young Doctors I had to go on with this bizarre announcement. I insisted on reading it out of vision over a slide. If I'd been in vision I was sure the viewer would know I was blatantly lying.

'*Some viewers have called in after our afternoon matinee, Submarine X-1, ended prematurely, just before its conclusion. This was due to a technical error and was beyond our control. We apologise for this disruption but for those who want to know how it ended, we will be playing out the final part of the movie again tomorrow afternoon at 3.30 pm. Once again we apologise for any inconvenience this may have caused you.*'

Mind you that's not the best apology ever given out on Border. This one still makes me chuckle to this day:

'*We apologise for the loss of sound and vision in that programme. We hope it didn't affect your enjoyment too much. Coming next, Coronation Street!*'

Chapter Seven

I'M NOT QUITE READY

I got into the crazy world of broadcasting partly as a result of looking for an easy way to make a living. My first job on leaving school was as a plasterer's mate. I've never worked so hard in my life and never been so thin. There had to be an easier way to make a living. I tried washing cars at County Garage and working at a butcher's shop in the Carlisle Market Hall but both were boring. The final straw came when I joined the city council on a youth training programme and they asked me to join a team that was measuring the size of every sewage pipe in the city. It was the only time I thanked God for being overweight as I was much too big to go through the manholes. Instead, I stood at the top of the hole, writing down all the measurements, as my poor colleagues descended into the crap with a tape measure. Why we had to do this, I have no idea. In those days you didn't ask, you simply did as you were told for a miserable salary of £14 a week.

Next door to the Pink Panther record shop in Globe Lane was the Kings Hall, where they held teenage roller discos. I dropped in one day and watched a guy I knew from school days play a few records on a Roger Squires Disco deck. I was amazed when he said he was paid £4 a night for doing it. What? £4 a night, that'll do for me!

I convinced him to give me a go and the first time I spoke on the mic my voice boomed. What I said was utter rubbish but that didn't matter, we all spoke rubbish in the Seventies. Over the next few weeks I got to know how to work the equipment and eventually I told my dad that this was something I wanted to do. He went with me to RSC Audio in the city centre and shelled out for a twin deck, with its own built-in 100watt amp, mic, speakers and a few lights. A complete package for two hundred pounds and Dad had given me all the money he had to get me started. He had no idea if I was any good at this lark but knew it was better than having me walking the streets, getting myself into trouble mucking about with women.

The Myers family were pretty well known in Carlisle as my dad used to own one of the city's bookies. I was one of nine kids. Yes, nine! My mum was just 5ft 2in tall and I was the fourth youngest and the lightest at birth of all the children she had. It appears I was trouble from the start. Mine was the most difficult of births with mum having to have two full blood transfusions to survive. In 1959 that was more dangerous than it is today. The nine of us were born separately in just thirteen years. I used to joke that Mum was practically a resident at Carlisle Maternity hospital and was the only mother who was invited back to their staff Christmas parties. Whatever my dad was good at, he was good at making babies. He was always there at the conception but never at the birth. No father was in those days but he knew how to celebrate afterwards.

The reason my parents had so many kids was that we were big Christians and churchgoers. As Catholics, my parents didn't believe in birth control but after the ninth was born, even the priest turned up to the house to tell my mum and dad that enough was enough! In those days we lived in a three-bedroom council house. All the boys slept in one room, the girls in another and my parents in the third. Thank God for bunk beds. We had lino instead of carpets, a TV from Radio Rentals where you had to put money in to watch it and a pay-as-you-go electric meter that took fifty pence pieces. My dad used to throw his giant coat on our bed for warmth and before getting up I breathed out in an effort to gauge how cold it was. If you saw your breath, it was freezing. We had a Ford Zephyr outside and loved it. It was life back then and a good one, too.

At the age of seven, I was expelled from my Catholic school by a nun called Sister Basil. The nuns always seemed to be a lot stricter than other teachers I came across. She used to come into the class and ask if everyone had gone to church that weekend. Those that hadn't were told to stand on their chair. I went to the toilets, which were outside, and it was a time when having a pee was always a competition between us lads to see who could write their name on the wall. On the way back I noticed that the break bell was standing on a cupboard. I picked it up and rang it loudly. The kids started rushing out of their classes and I was caught red-handed. At seven years of age, I was caned on the stage in front of the school for that offence. When I look back now, it was nothing short of barbaric.

We lived in Lingmoor Way, Harraby, and the school bus stopped at either end of this long road. Our house, number 35, was right in the middle and every time one of my brothers asked if the Myers lot could be dropped off near our home and save us a long walk the driver always refused. One day council workmen were repairing the road and, as the bus slowed down to a crawl outside our house, I opened the emergency door and jumped out. As this incident came just days after my caning for ringing the bell, my mum was informed that I would be leaving the school. I was sent to another school, St. Cuthbert's. I am ashamed of this even today.

When I joined the Newman senior school there was a Myers in every single year and I sailed through untouched by bullies or idiots. I used to think it was because I was a big lad but the truth, that I only discovered later, was that my eldest brother, Eddie, was not to be messed with. Anyone who bothered a Myers had to contend with Eddie, who rarely started a fight but always ended it. I was just thirteen when a lad came up to me, as I walked home through a shortcut, and said, 'Hey, tell your brother, Eddie, he's a poof.'

'Okay,' I said, 'I will.'

I had no idea what a poof was but when I told Eddie, he just smiled and said, 'Thanks, message received'.

Three days later, as I walked through the shortcut again, there was this same guy, only this time he had a black eye and was on crutches.

'I told Eddie,' I said.

He replied, 'Yeh, so I see, now sod off.'

It turned out that this guy worked shifts at Carr's biscuit factory. Eddie knew he started his shift at 6 am, so he got up the next morning at five, waited for him outside his front door and when the guy stepped out Eddie managed to convince him that he was no poof, as he described it.

Dad's decision to buy me the disco equipment changed my life forever and it's my deepest regret that neither my mum nor my dad lived long enough for me to shower them with the rewards this brought me in later life. Dad died in 1985 after a fight with cancer. It was not long after I'd started at Border and just a few months after Linda and I were married. Enduring enormous pain, he came to the church and heard the speeches, but he soon had to return home to rest. He was just sixty-three. How and why it happened remains a mystery, to the family at least. At the time I was selling a red Ford Granada 3.0GL and the man who bought it worked at the local hospital. My dad had trouble going to the toilet and was in pain trying to pee. By then he was a long distance lorry driver for a local sweet maker and over time his job became ridiculous as he would practically have to stop at every second service station. He plucked up the courage to go to the doctors and they sent him to hospital. I went along with him to hospital where he discovered he'd have to undergo an operation. Surgery appeared to go well and he was expected to stay in for at least a fortnight but within a few days I received a call from the surgeon who turned out to be the man who'd bought my car. He asked me to go in and see him where he told me that my Dad had cancer. It was such a shock. Those who have lost their parents in this way will know the deep gut wrenching feeling that hits when you are suddenly faced with news like this. The surgeon said they would give Dad the news in a couple of days but he wondered if I could tell the family first. He also thought it might be wise if we told Dad ourselves too. Today, that would never happen and in 1985 it should not have happened, either. It was the worst thing I've ever had to do. With members of my family, I went to see Mum. It was one of the few times I've cried openly. You feel so helpless. You want to take away the pain but you can't. Both Mum and I went to see my dad and I couldn't bring myself to tell him. At the end Mum said, 'John has got something to tell you'. Through tears and a broken voice, I told him as best I could. He just sat there and started to well up, although trying desperately to hold in his emotions. I couldn't and neither could Mum. To tell someone you love so much that they have cancer is something that, even now, plays in my mind like a colour recording on constant replay.

I came out and told the ward sister that we had given Dad the news. She went nuts and told us there was a procedure for delivering this kind of information to a patient. I explained to her that we'd been specifically asked to do so by his surgeon. She was aghast at that and, as I understand it, blew her top to all concerned. She went to comfort my dad and, even today, that moment still brings me great sadness. Could this news have been delivered by someone else in a much more caring way? I will never know.

Soon afterwards, Dad was admitted to the Freeman Hospital in Newcastle. His condition had become more serious as the cancer spread and surgeons were going to undertake an operation called a penectomy, the complete removal of his penis. He would be fitted with a bag for the rest of his life. For any man, this would be difficult to accept, let alone someone who was a man's man. Nevertheless, in one of my rare moments of a deep father and son discussion, he told me, 'There's nothing for it, son, but to get this done and to get it done quickly'.

He was pragmatic even then and certainly was not going to give up. We hugged each other; it was not something we did a lot to be honest, it was just how it was back then. The operation went ahead and all seemed well. Once fully recovered, he would be released to get on with his life. Dad was sixty miles away in Newcastle and we went over every single day but the last time I went to see him, Mum said she would stay at home and get things ready for his return. Everyone was delighted with his progress as we thought the worst was over. When I arrived at the hospital, Dad was sitting up in a chair in the TV lounge watching the racing. It was such a wonderful sight and he was upbeat because for the first time in weeks he'd been allowed solid food. This was the last hurdle before he'd be allowed home for the weekend. As I left him, I walked out of the room but for some reason, I vividly recall stopping and turning around to wave goodbye. That picture is frozen in my memory, it was the last time we ever spoke.

We will never know for sure what happened but, from what I understand, the move to solid foods killed him. Something had not connected properly internally and the food began to leak from his stomach. Dad was in desperate pain and the surgeons were forced to place him into a deep sleep to deal with the crisis. The phone rang at home and we were told it was best if we came to the hospital as soon as possible. We arrived to be told the surgeons had to operate again but soon afterwards we were told there was nothing more they could do. It was only a matter of time as by then Dad's body just couldn't take it anymore. He passed away without ever regaining conscious-ness, as we sat around his bedside with Mum holding his hand. My mum never forgave herself for not going with me to the hospital that previous afternoon. After all that suffering, all that bravery, the opera-tions, the amputation and the belief he had got through the worst, life was suddenly taken from him. We don't blame the hospital or the staff. They tried their best but we always wonder what if? It was particularly difficult for my mum. A heavy smoker, a few years later she contracted Chronic Obstructive Pulmonary Disease, COPD for short. The whole family watched helplessly as she found it increasingly hard to breathe. It was agony watching someone you love die a slow death. The doctors told my mum there was no point in giving up smoking. It was too late. I used to visit her while she sat there with an oxygen bottle by her side with a mask on her face. She wouldn't go out in case she couldn't catch her breath or that urgent help would not be available. The whole family played their part in nursing her through it and for a time, she went to stay at the home of my eldest sister, Jennifer. As her illness became more serious, she moved into a twenty-four hour nursing home. In the end, she was admitted to hospital where we were advised to say our goodbyes as it was thought she wouldn't last for long. She lasted much longer than anyone thought, eventually passing away on Dad's birthday. As I write, tears are flooding down my face as I recall holding her hand while telling her what a fantastic mother she had been. How proud I was to be able to call her my mum and to thank her for always being there. She had dedicated herself to her family. As a result, all nine of her children are alive today, in good health, a close-knit group with a zest for life and a love of people. I miss her so very much. For some time afterwards I caught myself picking up the phone to call her before realising it was no longer possible. It's a natural reaction I guess.

I tell every male friend I know of the importance of checking for prostate cancer. I go for yearly check ups myself and any male should do the same if they get up to the toilet more than once a night. It is so important.

As you would expect, pictures of my mum and dad sit proudly in my home. They are a constant reminder of where I came from and the standards expected of me. I try my best not to let them down. I often touch their faces for luck and thank my lucky stars to have been born through their love of each other. My dad once told me that we didn't have a lot of money but he was richer than anyone alive because of the family he had. I have that lovely man on my shoulder guiding me through the curvature and difficulties of life today, giving me advice and telling me what to do. I've been lucky enough to be nudged in the right direction when common sense was saying the complete opposite. I talk to him every day, if only for a second.

*

In death there is always humour and thank goodness for that. Both my parents are buried in Stanwix cemetery in the city. It's a small church and plots were becoming very difficult to find. My brother, Eddie, became nervous that they were going to run out of room before long so he suggested we buy our plot now to be sure we had somewhere to be buried in the future. Why we would care I have no idea but it seemed a sensible idea at the time and three of us, Eddie, Jen and myself purchased a plot each. People would find this ridiculous but it was taken to another level when I received a call from Eddie who was at the council offices filling in all the paperwork. He was stuck on a question that only I could provide the answer to. It was personal, he said, but it was important he got it right. He asked me the question and it turned a dull day into one filled with laughter. In fact, my sides were aching so much we both started laughing and it took us ten minutes to calm down. He was calling because on the form we were asked to stipulate, when the time came for our burial, if we wanted to face the hedge or the church. There was no room for error. We had to be precise and furthermore this specific question could not be left blank.

Eddie said, 'I'm going to face the church because the sun comes up that way in the morning and I like that.'

I loved the simplicity of that and agreed to do the same. If you go to Stanwix church right now and wander around the graves, you will come across my brother's plot. You can't miss it. A big sign on top of the grave reads:

Here lies the plot of Steady Eddie.

I'm on my way, but I'm not quite ready.

Chapter Eight

DINKY DOO

I arrived back at Red Rose as part of the management and I also took over as host of the mid-morning show from a great jock, Dicky Duncan. Believe me, starting at ten o'clock in the morning was a luxury but I knew it wouldn't last because the station bosses had decided to split frequencies. Red Rose on FM, soon to be called Rock FM, would be a much more modern pop music service, while on AM we'd carry on playing a mix of music across the years with lots of personalities in between. We had some great jocks, including Derek Webster, Dave Lincoln, John Gillmore, Dave Shearer and a guy from Scotland I brought in to start his new radio career.

I'd first met Colin Lamont at Border TV. He was a freelance continuity announcer, part-time actor and all round good laugh. Colin was also a frustrated radio broadcaster. He was considering returning to a life as a schoolmaster but I thought he'd be great on air, if I could get him trained up. I really wanted to do something different at night. Red Rose Gold was on the AM band and when it gets dark it's not the easiest service to tune in to, so you had to have something different to make people put up with the night-time crackle of the waveband. I decided to launch Colin as a late-night phone-in host, although I had two immediate problems. First, his name was not catchy enough. There's no showbiz in Colin! Second, he had absolutely no idea what he was doing. The third possible issue was that by now I was on the breakfast show as well as being the station's Programme Director. That meant the most inexperienced jock would on the air at a time when I was either in bed or half asleep. Never a good combination. I told Colin that for his first week on air, I'd sleep during the day and come back into the studio in the evenings to ensure he got into the swing of the late-night phone-in format. If he made the grade then I could happily leave him on. If not, then I'd get someone more experienced.

'What the hell can we call you? I pondered.

Colin came up with a few boring possibilities and then I remembered someone from my childhood. When I was a kid in Carlisle, we used to go to the ABC Minors' Club, where for sixpence you could go to the cinema, play games on stage, win a few prizes and watch films, usually made by The British Film Foundation. Those of a certain age will remember how BFF films always started with a picture of pigeons taking to the air in Trafalgar Square. When the film got really exciting the kids would stamp their feet and clap their hands. The host of all this Saturday morning mayhem was a Scottish bloke called Scottie Buccleugh, known as Uncle Scottie.

'We need something mad like this, Colin, so people will remember your name the first time they hear it,' I said. We eventually came up with Scottie McClue.

'It sounds totally different and crazy enough for you to use the name as your launch pad to become a larger-than-life character,' I told Colin.

I spent a few hours practising with Colin in the studio and put callers through from the office next door to see how he would do. I knew there was wonderful potential here. Colin is hugely intelligent and if he wanted to, could have a serious debate about any subject under the sun. To generate talkability on the streets he had to have a view of life that was slightly eccentric, even bordering on the mad.

'Colin, the absolute golden rule of this phone-in is fun, fun, fun,'

I explained. 'You need to take the listeners on a journey. This is *not* Radio 4, it's Red Rose and we're a station that doesn't take life too seriously. There are tons of other stations that do that, we don't. I want the listeners to understand that you are nearly always just pulling their leg but they must never be a hundred per cent sure. That said, you must believe in the core point you are making. Presenters who just make stuff up don't last that long, in my experience. You have to believe what you're saying and ensure the listener believes it, or wants to believe, so they can play along, too. Any argument you put forward must have a strong line of defence, even though some of what you say may be absolutely bonkers. Only those who have views get callers. Only those who have opposing views to listeners get callers. A caller who agrees with you is a boring caller. But, remember, what we really want is fun. Think of this as theatre,' I said. 'We're in the entertainment business so enjoy yourself and the listeners will enjoy you. Finally, I'd ask you to understand that this is "your" show. This means you set the rules. Don't worry about the callers' feelings, worry about the entertainment value. Sermon over!'

Those first few nights I was deeply worried. Colin was trying to be too nice and he was constantly thanking people for ringing in, my pet hate. The problem was he'd had a lifetime in TV and theatre where everything is so nice and lovely but in radio he was failing to hit the spot. He was failing because he was predictable. The cancer of all great shows. I kept going over the show the following day, caller by caller. I reviewed how he got into a call, the way he took the conversation forward, how to phrase certain words and why some comments are more helpful than others.

'Thanking people for ringing in was a definite no-no,' I said. 'This is *not* the BBC. Stop it. You only thank guests or those who need thanking. Sometimes you might believe the caller has offered up such wonderful content that you want to stop and say thanks. On those occasions of course it is right that you do so. However, ninety-nine per cent of the time you have to take the view that when a listener rings you it's a great privilege for them to even be on the show. Take that stance. Once the callers come to realise it's an honour they'll perform because they also want to be famous. When you thank a caller, they have the power. Reverse this by getting them to thank you for taking their call before they tell you what they want to talk about.'

Another bug of mine was that I felt each caller was a separate silo where I wanted the callers to mix into each other, as a bunch of people in a pub might get involved. I said to him, for example, even though the next caller might be wanting to talk about something quite different to the person currently on the air, when they come on ask them what they thought of the previous caller's point. This may throw them for a moment but what usually happens is that you get some radio gold from an unprepared, off-the-cuff remark.

*

It took ages for Colin to get his head around these thoughts and I was starting to think it would never work. Then, one night I heard him move from A to Z in one giant step. He skipped through five callers in less than a minute trying to find someone interesting and used a range of one liners that made me laugh out loud. He was beginning to learn the phrases that worked and the things you say to gain more callers. To a phone-in presenter, there is nothing worse than no one calling. In your brain it means you are failing and you start to panic. In fact, what often happens is that the listeners are actually listening intently. When that occurs you need to give the audience a reason to call. Make them want to pick up the phone and speak to you. Scottie opened one show by saying he did not want to talk to anyone called Brian. Straight away every listener named Brian was on the phone wanting to take him on.

'That was perfect.' I said. 'You're the leader of the gang, so take them with you. Your view is the only one that matters, Scottie. Adopt that stance and the audience will follow.' This was a very different type of commercial radio phone-in programme and you would not do the same for every station but on AM, late at night, you needed to be edgy.

Sure enough, by the fourth week the show was in full swing. He'd got it and he even invented a new catchphrase: 'Dinky Doo, it's Scottie

McClue'. I loved that. It became very clear that this show would be about scale, with huge numbers of listeners wanting to ring in. Scottie was able to entertain an audience with brilliant put-downs. Mind you, some nights he took it to extremes. The Isle of Man should be the place we put all single mothers was one topic I'll never forget. I didn't even have to wait for the audience figures. We always knew we were onto a winner when people called me to complain about a show. I used to pull the presenters together and tell them that minor complaints were good. It meant even the people who didn't like you were talking about you. I've never understood managers who tell their presenters about the complaints they receive. What's the point unless the boss agrees with the complaint? Sometimes that can happen and an effective manager will raise this at the right time with the presenter. However, far too often I have seen good presenters lose their confidence because the manager didn't do their job. Keeping letters penned by nutters away from presenters is important. One boss would share his troubles with everyone all the time and that is not the best way to operate at all. I once asked a manager if he agreed with the complaint he was telling me about that day. 'Not at all,' he said.

I blew my top. 'If that's the case, then why are you bringing it to my attention?' I barked.

He replied that I should be aware of what people are writing in about. What a fool. It was his job to deal with crap like this. It was simply weak management and all it did was make great people lose their nerve on the air. It was moments like this that made me want to move over into management and show them how to motivate people more effectively. I liked to think many of the stations I ran operated a bit like a pirate radio station.

'Just have fun.' I would say. 'We'll sort any trouble out along the way.'

We were in no way irresponsible but we were in the world of entertainment and few things made me more angry than those who had been promoted above their competence or were simply unable to manage effectively. In the end, the only way I was going to do what I wanted to do on the air was to run the whole station myself.

*

The Scottie McClue show got tremendous ratings and ensured Red Rose Gold continued to be the best-performing AM radio station in Britain by some distance. At his peak, he would be on my list as one of my top 20 hires of all time. Of course personalities like Scottie are a phenomenon for a time but not for ever. The act has to change to work effectively or move stations. In my view we had a two to three year shelf life at best but while we had it, we had some fun although I doubt it would work as well today given the political nature of the digital world we live in. Having said that, Scottie's still on the air via the internet from his own website.

*

Red Rose was the home of personalities, sport, phone-ins and great music not to mention an on-air spirit that sounded as if we were all just having a ball.

'Life's not serious,' I kept saying. 'It's only radio.'

I did end up in serious trouble with Scottie on one occasion, though. A few years after his spell at Red Rose, he was working for Scot FM in Edinburgh. Bored one night, I called him up on the air. I can mimic an old man very well and invented a character called Mr Martin, who was seventy-eight years old, had fought in the war, was a miserable old git and his prized possession was a Birmingham Roller, a breed of pigeon! For years I'd used this character as a wind-up call on my breakfast show but I also brought him out at night when for a laugh I'd call up lots of phone-ins. I rang up Scottie and straight away he knew who I was and played along. In an old man's voice I told him I was disgusted by what he was saying.

'I fought in the war for people like you,' I said and demanded an apology or I would write to the Queen immediately asking her to take action against the station. It was good kick-about stuff but how could I end the call? I decided, rather unwisely looking back, to have a heart attack on the air. It sounded realistic, brilliant radio. The next day, I received a call from Tom Hunter, the station's MD.

'John, did you had anything to do with a mad call to Scottie last night?' he enquired. 'We've had more than a hundred complaints from people suggesting Scottie killed off an old bloke who was a former soldier. The phone calls and faxes are building up, The Daily Record have been on, we need to sort it out.'

'Okay, Tom, don't worry,' I reassured him. 'I'll go back on tonight and tell the world I'm fine.'

'Please do, you daft sod,' he said. 'It was fantastic call, by the way. I heard it on the way home and was falling over myself with laughter.'

That night, Scottie apologised and I went on air pretending to be Mr Martin and told him I would still be writing to the Queen but wouldn't demand his severed head on a stick. That would have been the end of the matter if only a number of callers had not complained to the regulator. When investigators from the Radio Authority questioned the station about what had happened, Tom told them I was to blame. By then I was the MD of my own station, Century North East, and the regulator thought I had completely lost it. I got a call from them and was told not to do it again. The Radio Authority's next bulletin contained the complaints from Scot FM listeners about Mr Martin. The regulator's comment was that the incident had been resolved and the station was reminded of their duty not to 'dupe' the listeners again in this manner. Some stations really do need better call screening!

*

———— 90 Second Break ————

It's all for Charrrrrriiiiitty.

To raise money for Red Rose Radio's charity appeal, I staged a sportsmen's dinner with a well-known comedian and a famous ex-football manager as guest speakers. The comedian wanted £900 in cash. I told him we would obviously require something in writing.

'Send me a fax,' he said. 'And write on it "See you at 9 pm". That's it, nothing else just "See you at 9 pm".

'How's that a contract I asked?' I asked.

'I'll draw a circle around 9 pm and return the fax to you and that's our agreement to £900. There's no point in making it complicated.'

'Christ, is that it?'

'Yes,' he said, 'that's our contract'.

A couple of days before the event, Michael Connelly, Red Rose's group MD, asked to see the contract for the star turns I'd booked. I showed him the fax, which said 'See you at 9 pm' and then another fax from him with the 'see you at 9pm' circled.

'What the hell is this?' Michael asked.

'Err, it's our contract with the comedian,' I said, although not convincingly.

'This is no bloody good' he shouted. 'We'll need more than that to satisfy the accountants. We need a proper invoice and proper paperwork, not a bloody fax that simply has a circle around, "See you at 9 pm"!'

'Don't panic, we can sort it with a raffle, which always produces at least a couple of grand of floating cash. That would cover both him and the football manager,' I explained.

'Where's the paperwork for the football manager?' he asked.

'There is none,' I said. 'Just a telephone call and a verbal handshake.'

'What's a bloody verbal handshake?' Michael asked, exasperated.

'It's where I agreed to shake hands on the deal over the telephone.'

'John, I'm going to have a walk and when I come back this will either be the result of a bad dream or I've started to go mad.'

'Please, Michael, trust me.' I said. 'This is just the way sportsmen's dinners go. It's how we get these people to appear for a discounted rate otherwise they charge 50% per cent more to cover tax and VAT.'

'I don't want anything to do with it. We have not had this conversation,' he warned.

The night was sold out. We were on course to make at least a couple of grand for the station appeal, big money in those days. The dinner had started but the ex-football manager had not arrived yet. That's nothing unusual, as sometimes these people will do two events in one night if they can. This famous man was due on at 9.30 and the comedian would end the night an hour later.

When the manager arrived, he walked around the room saying 'hello' to a few people. The buzz of his impending speech was apparent. Then he asked to see me outside, where he promptly announced that there were too many people in the room and he wanted another £200 on top of his agreed fee of £500. I told him straight. We had a deal. We'd verbally shaken hands and a deal was a deal as far as I was concerned.

'Of course we've sold out, we're a radio station,' I shouted. 'Getting people to buy things is what we do, you idiot.'

Would he have given anything back if it was half full and we were losing money?

'That's it,' he said. 'I'm not saying a word unless you agree to a further two hundred quid.' By now it was now nine o'clock, just thirty minutes before he was due on.

'How do you expect me to pay you another two hundred pounds?' I demanded.

'I have a ball in my car signed by the players,' he revealed. 'Get your girls to go around with another raffle prize and that'll earn you at least another three hundred quid and you can have the difference. Plus, I want my fee and the extra two hundred in cash in my hand before I stand up.'

I was livid. I could have strangled the sod right there and then. I went to see Keith Macklin, who was in the room. He agreed we were in a tight spot.

'Look, here's what I think we should do,' I said. 'I'll jump on the mic and inform the audience we have a brilliant football manager here to speak to them this evening. I'll thank them for paying their hard-earned cash for their tickets to help kids in need across Lancashire. Then I'll tell them how this sporting "hero" is holding us to ransom by demanding another two hundred quid on top of his agreed fee because too many of them have turned up. I'll ask them what they want me to do? The audience will throw him out so fast we'll save on his original fee, make more money for the charity, get great Press and he will look bad. I wouldn't give in to him at all.'

'Hmm, that's one plan,' said Keith. 'The other is to do the deal and make another hundred on the night with the extra raffle. Then, never hire him again.' It was probably the more sensible solution as it would have spoilt the night for the people who were there, but if I'd have had my way I'd have kicked the money-grabbing sod all the way down the M6.

He was a brilliant speaker, by the way. I never laughed once.

Scottie McClue was doing great business for us at Red Rose but I was always on the lookout for new ideas. After watching a medium perform at the end of the pier in Blackpool, I thought this would be wonderful for the radio. Someone recommended James Byrne. I rang him up. He had a warm Lancashire accent. As soon as he answered, I chastised him. 'Look, I'm after a medium to come on the air once a month with Scottie McClue and now I'm wondering why the hell I've called you. If you were any good you'd surely have rung me before I found the time to ring you.'

Silence.

'Well, I'm not always switched on all the time, you know,' he replied.

'Well are you interested? And if so, how do I know you're any good at this lark?' I said. 'There are so many fakes around. I also have to tell you we actually broadcast from a church, would that bother you?'

'Look, John,' he replied. 'I'm not going to justify myself to you or anyone else and this is definitely not 'a lark' as you call it.'

I liked him instantly. He came right back to me and I thought, 'I can work with this guy. '

He then said, 'There's only one way I can demonstrate to you that I'm as good as people say I am and that's to read for you right now down the telephone. As you'll be the one hiring then you're the one who needs convincing.'

'Okay, go ahead. I'm telling you nowt, by the way,' I said.

'You don't have to tell me anything,' he replied. Believe it or not, for the next twenty minutes he told me things about me and my family, covering a range of personal information that only someone with a gift for this sort of thing would know. I was hooked.

'Brilliant,' I said. 'Come in and see me pronto.'

The next month we trailed James Byrne, the world's best medium on the show. Now, while I agree that might have been a little over the top, I've always been told that if you have to blow your own trumpet then make sure you it's a bloody big one. That night James was magnificent. I have absolutely no idea how he does it. I don't even know if it's a trick, real or whatever. I don't care. What I did know for sure was that this was fantastic radio and I continued to use James for more than five years. One of the funniest lines he used to use on the show was:

'Do you have a red car outside your house?' he'd ask a caller.

'A red car, James?'

'Yes, love, a red car.'

'There's one about four doors down, James.'

'That'll do, give me that, love. Give me that. Close enough.'

That line had me in hysterics every time and he used it at least twice a night.

*

The worst decision I ever made while at Red Rose was to appear in pantomime. While good at many things, I am no actor. I received a call from an agent who wanted to know if I'd be interested in a six-week run at St George's Hall in Blackburn. I was just about to say no, when I wondered what the pay was for this? When he told me the amount I'd earn, there was no way I could turn it down. I'd be paid the equivalent of six months money for just six weeks work. So here I was, PD of Red Rose Gold, host of the station's breakfast show and now also performing afternoons and evenings as Alderman Fitzwarren in Dick Whittington. What the hell had I done? I was forced to put a bed into my dressing room so I could get some kip between shows. I was performing with a great friend, Donald Scott. We knew each other well from Border TV but the difference was he really was a proper actor and the best pantomime dame I have ever seen. He was also my other half in The John and Gladys show, which ran for three years on Red Rose and was enormously enjoyable. I was Ernie to his Eric, feeding the lines so Donald, as Gladys, could hit 'em for six every weekend. Great radio.

I love panto but hated performing in the theatre. From the first rehearsal, I knew I was out of my depth and so did my fellow actors but the agent told us ticket sales were at an all time high. Blackburn is not the easiest place to get to but because of our connection, Red Rose plugged the show like mad and the box office numbers were great. I was terrible, tired and wanted my bed. I kept telling myself to think of the money but then the first review appeared in the Black-burn Evening Telegraph, which still haunts me: *I fail to see why John Myers is the star of this show. He spits out his words in the same way as a bulldog chewing a wasp and he's more wooden than Woody the Woodpecker.*

Sometimes you just have to take failure on the chin. I read out the review on my breakfast show the next day. We turned it into comedy but like all comedic lines, I was really hurt. Mainly because it was the truth.

Chapter Nine

HITLER AND THE SECRET PIE FACTORY RENDEZVOUS

I loved working for Red Rose, it was a great station with great people and life could not have been better. We launched the AM service on 1 June 1990 and Red Rose Gold was enormously popular right from the start. When the first audience figures came in, we had better results than our sister station, Rock FM. That was unheard of at the time and showed how good the AM output was. Later, I took control of the programming on both Red Rose Gold and Rock FM, while still presenting the breakfast show Monday to Friday and another programme at the weekends. To me it wasn't hard work, just a way of life. Rock FM was given that name because it was going to be based in Blackpool but the agreement for the premises faltered at the last minute. The name stayed, even though we ran the station from Preston. It's slightly confusing because many people believe it exclusively plays rock music when in fact it's just another great pop station.

*

By now I was twenty-nine years old and approaching the upper end of Rock FM's audience, which was eighteen to twenty-nine. But I was desperate to drive Rock FM forward. To be fair to the station's previous

PD, Mark Matthews, he'd done a great job with the imaging. Rock FM's 'Breakthrough' jingle package from the world's greatest jingle factory, JAM in Dallas, was the best I've ever heard and is still used around the world today. On AM, we had a good music head in Dave Shearer. He knew his stuff and was able to mix the right songs at the right time. On FM, I made an error giving the same job to Dave Sanders. He just didn't have the flair of a Dave Lincoln and would often schedule songs that didn't sound right. The other jocks complained about the music, added to this our in-house audience tracking showed listeners were leaving us in droves. We had a music image problem and it was something I had to tackle. It was my own fault for picking the wrong guy as Head of Music. It was certainly not his fault and as a talented presenter he later joined us some years later at Real Radio in Yorkshire. The art of scheduling music is so important on any radio station but within a competitive market it can mean the difference between winning and losing. I've always been very clear that what I know about music could be written on the back of a postage stamp. As a manager, it's vital you know your strengths and weaknesses and music was certainly not one of my strengths. Therefore, I always tried to hire people who could do the things I couldn't. In fact, whenever I hired people, I always wanted to employ someone who was better than me. It was one of the reasons for my success. Sadly, in this instance I got it wrong and was about to solve the problem when I received a call from a man claiming to be my Uncle Jim. Considering I didn't have an Uncle Jim, I was intrigued.

Uncle Jim turned out to be James Graham, boss of Border Television, one of the loveliest people on the planet. He was also a winner and a sharp operator with years of success in broadcasting. It turned out Border Television, in partnership with Scottish Radio Holdings and West Sound Radio, had won the franchise to launch a new commercial radio station in Cumbria, to be based in state-of-the art studios in Border TV's car park. The potential audience was just 150,000.

Jim wondered if I would be willing to come up to Carlisle and have a chat with the board about this new radio station. At that time I was running the programming of two stations broadcasting to over a million people across Lancashire. There was no way I was interested in dropping down to a station that was so tiny in comparison. Also, I'd spent most of my professional years trying to get into a bigger station, so going back to Cumbria would be impossible. I told Jim that it would be difficult for me to come back, despite my love of the city, because the role was too small. I did, however, offer to help him find the right person for the job. I said I'd be happy to come and chat to the board if that would help but I was certainly not interested in returning to my home town. There was another problem. After years on the TV, I had become very well known in Cumbria and if I was to be spotted at Border's studios word would get back to Red Rose within minutes. The local Press, and indeed my own bosses, would think I was being headhunted for the Carlisle job. I didn't need that hassle so we'd have to meet somewhere else. Jim understood the position and came up with a plan that was so hilarious even today it makes me laugh. One of Cumbria's biggest employers is Cavaghan and Gray, who make meat products sold in shop chains throughout the United Kingdom. Their factory was directly across the road from Border's studios.

Jim suggested, 'How about meeting in the boardroom at Cavvy's factory?'

'Isn't that just as bad?' I protested. 'You can see Cavvy's front door from Border.'

'Don't worry,' he said, 'it's all sorted. Just turn up, park your car right outside the door and come straight in.'

'Okay,' I conceded, 'but it's fraught with danger.'

*

I told Linda I was heading up to Cumbria to meet with the management of the new Carlisle station, to give them some advice. My wife instantly knew this was dangerous. I make decisions more on gut feel than common sense and she warned me that under no circumstances was I to take this job. We had a great home in Garstang, lots of friends, a wonderful life and our children were happy in school. So why would we want to move, especially to a station where the audience was so tiny? The whole idea was idiotic. I kept telling myself that I was just going to help a friend.

I arrived at the pie factory car park and headed straight to the front door, to be greeted with shouts of, 'Hey, there's Uncle John!'

Wonderful, I thought, some secret this will be. Jim Graham greeted me in the pie factory boardroom and, for the first time, I met Richard Findlay, Chief Executive of Scottish Radio Holdings, a giant in radio terms. Also there was Joe Campbell, the head of West Sound Radio, and Peter Brownlow, Border's Finance Director. We chatted about the new radio station. How I would launch it, who they should hire, the style of music and even the personality of potential listeners in Carlisle. It was a great meeting and we all got on well. Jim asked if I could wait in the pie factory boardroom while they went back across the road to Border TV for a chat. I really liked the idea of this station, it was in a building complex I knew from my years at the TV centre, plus I was a Carlisle lad and launching a new station would be fun and something I had never done before. The job was not for me but I hoped I might at least get a show when the station was launched. I would have loved that.

Jim phoned and asked if I'd pop over to Border TV's studio. This was madness but he begged, 'Just drive into the car park and come up through the back stairs into the boardroom. It will be fine.'

When I got there the discussion changed dramatically. The board loved me, Jim said, and wanted me to launch the station for them. Even though it was crazy I was tempted, yet I could hear Linda's words in my ear.

'Look, I'd love to,' I said. 'Nothing would give me greater personal pleasure than this but I'm at a radio station nearly ten times the size of this. I have a senior management role and I'm on the air as much as I want. On top of that, I don't think you can afford me.'

I had already seen the budget and had gone through all the numbers. If this went further I had a plan. They convinced me that I was the person they wanted and were open to ideas. I was on £32,000 a year at Red Rose, which was a good wage in 1992, though it wouldn't exactly fund a rock 'n roll lifestyle. I might be interested if I could get my salary up to £50,000 a year. Richard and Jim said the budget could not afford that much for an MD.

I replied with the classic sales line, 'If I can show you a way to pay me that salary within the current budget, would you be willing to consider it?'

This put them in a dilemma. They kept saying the budget did not have that amount of cash and I kept reiterating that if I could show them a way, would they consider it? In the end they all nodded.

'It's simple,' I said. 'You have £30,000 in the budget for the MD and you have £20,000 in there for the breakfast show. I'll do both. You get a brilliant MD, a wonderful breakfast host and furthermore a guaranteed superb launch of this radio station. The only stipulation is that I also get a great car and it's to be a maximum two-year deal. I'd like to launch the station in my hometown but exit again after a couple of years.'

I waited in Jim Graham's office while they discussed it. Jim came back and said they were up for it if they could negotiate a little. They needed a little win to feel good about it. The problem was that many of Richard Findlay's own MDs at SRH were not on salaries anywhere near that and they were running much bigger operations. That was not my concern but I could sense they needed to at least feel they had got me down a little. In the end we agreed a deal slightly short of my objective but I was now panicking. What the hell had I done? I was the PD of a station I loved and now here I was coming back to Carlisle. Linda was going to go nuts.

I sat in my car outside Border TV, wondering how to tell my wife. She knew me better than anyone. As soon as she picked up the phone she said, 'You've signed haven't you?' I kept silent. 'Oh God, when do we move?'

'Well, yes, I have signed and I want to take the job but it's only for two years,' I explained. In any case, even though I had signed and said yes, I was still not one hundred per cent sure. Linda was great about it but it was clear this move was going to cost me.

I never believe in going to your boss and saying you want more money or you're leaving. That is **never** the way to negotiate. Instead, I went to see Michael Connelly, who was running Red Rose at the time, and asked him for a tiny £2,000 pay rise. There is a business lesson here. When you consider that after tax and deductions this was not a big amount, any sensible boss would know that the person asking for this usually just wants a bit of loving. They want to know they're appreciated and highly thought of. It was not so much the money but if he had paid it, I would have stayed at Red Rose. I just needed an excuse. Michael didn't get this and gave me a flat 'no'.

'Sorry, John, not a penny more can be found from our budget,' he said. That made my mind up. If a radio station cannot find two thousand pounds for someone who was PD in charge of two stations and doing six shows a week then they didn't deserve me, I thought.

*

On top of the drama of leaving a huge station for a smaller one, Linda said she wanted her old house back in Carlisle. I'd sold the detached house on the outskirts of the city to a motor dealer from West Cumbria, so I knew him well enough to put a call in. As luck would have it, he'd been trying to sell it for the past year.

Luckily for me, I sold the house at the top end of the housing market but by the time I arrived at his door property values had dropped. He was pleased to see me until I told him I was offering forty thousand less than he'd paid me for it. He was so upset he chased me down the drive with a face like thunder. Linda asked how my meeting had gone.

'Great,' I lied. 'He likes the idea and is thinking it over.' I had to do this deal but there was no way I was going to pay more than the house was now worth. That's just the way life goes. If the market had gone up, I would have had to pay more.

In the past, I'd worked with a character called Michael Eubank, who ran the Talk of the Border nightclub in Carlisle and Cinderella Rockefellers in Leeds, and was a wonderful businessman. When I told him my problem he instantly had the solution. The next day, I rang up the owner and told him that my offer still stood. He told me to sod off. In spite of this, I informed him that I was going to deposit the money I had offered into his solicitor's client account that day. If he wanted to sell, all he had to do was accept the money and sign the papers before five o'clock on Friday. On Thursday afternoon he called and asked me see him. When I arrived he was smiling. As a businessman he was used to doing deals and this was just another. We laughed, shook hands and the deal was done. I actually liked the guy, who was a self-made man and appeared to live life to the full.

∗

I arrived at the new station, now named CFM instead of Border Radio. There is no doubt I had some moments of regret. What had I done coming back to Carlisle when I was making great inroads into radio elsewhere? Presenters I'd hired in the past did not want to join me in my latest venture. They were much more sensible and were never going to come to such a small station when they were broadcasting to much bigger audiences. I had to scout around for new talent and found some in jocks like Dave Croft and Derek Flood and a new guy called Chris Moyles.

∗

We launched the new station on 14 April, 1993. Looking back, this is one of the best moments of my career. I absolutely loved my time at CFM and I'm so delighted I didn't pass up the opportunity. Not only was the station enormously successful, with a reach of over fifty per cent, but it was the gateway to a career that would allow me to make my name across the UK. It's amazing how life turns for you. I had gone from radio to television, back to radio and then to a station nearly ten times smaller because I wanted to launch something in my home town. It was emotional, it didn't make sense but it just felt right to do. It proves the point that you should always go with your gut. The plan was to launch the station by helicopter. When the pilot arrived the day before, he landed in the car park and immediately started asking who the hell put that big X on the tarmac?

'Err, well it's been there for ages since we did Krankies TV,' I said. 'Well, it's not bloody legal and I certainly can't take off from here with passengers and definitely not with someone of your size in the cockpit, John,' he said.

We had to come up with plan B, which was to leave from Newby Grange Hotel and arrive the next morning. We could land together but we couldn't leave together it seemed.

'It's not a Chinook,' the cheeky git kept saying. We launched the station with Tina Turner's, *Simply the Best*. We raised cash for charity by having a fun fair right outside the studios, complete with dodgems and a big wheel.

*

Running CFM was brilliant fun and it was here I learned the art of management and motivating a small team. In fact, looking back it was the best time, although I was doing huge amounts of work. As well as being MD, I was the breakfast host, presented the now infamous Friday night phone-in, plus a weekend show. The night time phone-in was hilarious and I loved it because in those days you could get away with a lot more than you can today. So much fun has been taken out of radio over time by regulatory creep and a fear of complaints that the output we hear now is much more vanilla in sound and, for that reason, it can be less entertaining. A remark from a presenter that most people would regard as offensive should quite rightly be dealt with properly but listeners do not have the right NOT to be offended. There is more than one radio station on the dial. I copied a lot of my style on the phones from the great Allan Beswick, but threw in my own humour. I also knew the people, locations, history and the culture of the place and was always two steps ahead, especially if they were coming on the air to take me on. I fell out badly one year with the local mayor, a delightful soul but also a gobby lass who angered more than a few by telling people what to do and how to think. I was giving her some grief over the air one night when she called in. Now, this can go two ways. She mistakenly thought she'd take me down a peg or two, while forgetting another golden rule of radio - whoever has the microphone wins. That's always the result. She came on and started to give me a lot of stick. I never said a word. When she'd finished, I gave her it in spades. So much so, she threw the phone down. That's the best compliment for a radio host. It means you've won and they've lost the argument. Carlisle loved this and boy did she get some stick for weeks to come after that. It served her right, too.

The Friday night phone-in was always guaranteed to be interesting. One night a group of streakers came in to say hello, ten men stood totally naked in the studio for a dare. Linda, who was answering the phones, got a right eyeful. Very often the show was the talk of the town until the following week but all this changed when I started a new Sunday lunchtime show, Fun On The Phones.

It was a simple idea but you needed the right callers to make it funny. People who are fairly intelligent are not funny. What you need are people who have no clue whatsoever about general knowledge. They're not thick, they are just funny and the humour comes from these people trying to guess the answers to simple questions. We had a great way of getting the right callers on the air. When they rang in we asked them a pass question, something like 'What's the capital of France?' If they didn't know, they were on! We took the questions for the game from a quiz book for eight to ten year olds. The fun came when I always insisted they asked for a clue if they didn't know the answer. Sometimes, a caller would be on the air for over half an hour trying to guess one question. Other times, I'd fly through loads of them. It all depended on who you had on air. It's never an exact science and the ones we called 'golden callers' were often the people you thought were not that great in pre-production. I used a roulette wheel for this game. As I spun the wheel, the ball landed on different numbers and I would use that to ask them a range of questions. However, if the caller was boring or they were getting the questions correct, I would say they'd landed on black. That meant they were dumped. The star prize on this show was three yellow plastic ducks. Radio lesson here. If you give callers the potential to win something big, they take it too seriously so you can't fool around too much. If you invent a prize that is idiotic and worthless while creating 'kudos', you can really have some fun with it all.

Some of the callers who came on Fun On The Phones were hilarious. Often, I would be laughing so much that I struggled to get through the show. One day, Mary from Maryport came on:

'Hi Mary, are you ready for your question?'

'I am, John, yes.'

'Okay, here goes. Who was born on Christmas Day?'

'Oh my God,' she said. 'That could be anyone. How the hell would I know that, John? Giz a clue.'

I told her to go next door and talk to her neighbour. When she came back she said, 'I've got it, John. I've got it.'

'Go on Mary, who is it?'

'Santa!' she shouted.

On another occasion Paul, from Currock, came on. He was a great caller and lots of fun.

'Right Paul, are you ready?' I asked.

'I'm ready, John.'

'Anyone to help you at all?'

'Yes, I've my whole family with me.'

'Brilliant.' I spun the wheel and it stopped on a history question. 'Okay,' I said. 'Who built Hadrian's Wall?'

'For God's sake, John. That was hundreds of years ago, how the hell would I know that?'

'It's a general knowledge question, Paul. A lot of people would know this ...'

'Well, I don't John. Giz a clue.'

I was now laughing so much I could hardly talk.

'Listen Paul, the answer is in the question.'

'I don't get that at all. Giz a clue, John, Giz a clue.'

'You must know this, Paul. Ask your family. They're with you.

Little me. The year I was
expelled from school.

▲ Happy days at
Tiffany's in Carlisle
– Management
accused me of
making people dance
too much.

◄ Tiffany's once
more, although I was
sporting a perm in
those days

My wonderful Dad,
Jimmy. Do you think I
look like him today?

I've always said I was an athlete

Main PR pic for Border TV

My wonderful Mum, Helen

The colour press pic from Border TV with Eric the Monkey - perhaps the biggest star the station ever had

Eric always had fans coming in to see him.

Me and local business guru Michael Eubank. He was also best man at my wedding.

The worst decision of my life - appearing in Panto

A smiling David Lamb... before he got locked
out of the radio station

Working with the boss at Red Rose,
Mike Henfield

Photo courtesy of Cumberland News

Two legends. Keith Macklin, left, and Hugh Mullins, right.

John and Glady's at Red Rose.
What a show that was.

The Red Rose crew with myself, Dave Shearer, Simon Tate, Geoff Webster, Ian Calvert, Derek Webster and John Gillmore.

I never turned down a public appearance...

Getting ready for another night of phone mayhem on CFM

John Myers' Century Radio seems to be beating the BBC in the north-east at its own game – speech. Now order Radio Holdings' boss plans to export the format

Radio station strikes gold with DJ Simon

Speech maker

By JON FLINN

FORMER Radio One DJ Simon Bates is to resurrect his popular *Golden Hour* show in an exclusive deal with listeners.

The show, which has an audience of 25 million around Europe, will be the region's newest station Radio when it starts in...

Century managing director Myers said yesterday the deal would draw a da...

> "I'm delighted *Golden Hour* is coming back and can't wait for the first show."

and Middlesbrough studios from 9am each weekday when Century goes on air on September 1.

Simon Bates said: "I've a lot of friends in the North-East of England...

By Sid Smith

Big Hairy Monster axed for scaring off listeners

He was infamous for his firebrand left-wing politics during the eighties. Now Derek Hatton's turbulent career has taken a whole new twist and shout at the age of 50

'We've never had so many complain'

by ANDREW RUSSELL

FORMER Radio 1 DJ Dave Travis has been dumped by another radio station after one week.

DLT – who calls himself the Big Hairy Monster – was voted an old-fashioned turn-off by listeners.

He launched the morning show – based on his old Radio 1 format – on 17 independent stations after quitting the Beeb.

Carlisle-based station CFM broadcast it for the first time on Sunday – and received a string of angry calls.

IT'S DJ DEGSY!

BOUNDING into the offices of Century Radio's plush new HQ, Derek Hatton strides over to the window to survey the view across Salford Quays. Above the row of penthouse flats and glass-fronted office blocks, he spots the jutting outline of Old Trafford.

"It's not a bad place here, is it? Shame about the view, though. Mind you, at least it's not Anfield. I'm an Everton man. I'm fanatical. I've got blue blood running through my veins..."

With that, he's off. Once in full flow, there's no stopping him. His cheeky-chappy banter hurtles along in top gear, occasionally only broken by...

MarketingWeek   Page 14   Date Thursday 30th October 2008   media_en

TV man Myers in monkey business

YOUNG Border TV viewers have found a new puppet hero in Eric the Monkey.

Cuddly Eric hangs around presenter John Myers' neck whenever he reads out the birthday greetings.

You've probably seen, Eric can be quite a handful and John has had to start weightlifting sessions to build himself up so that he can control the naughty ape.

Analysis

GMG Radio left vulnerable as Myers stands down

John Myers, the outgoing chief executive...

GMG chief executive plans to keep it real

WHEN the fourth-quarter Rajar results were announced this week, GMG Radio chief executive John Myers had several reasons to be cheerful.

Following the latest Rajar Results, John Myers has a lot to smile about. He talks all that jazz with **Allison Brodie** about the future of his radio brands and his plans for expansion

A RADIO SHEPHERD TENDS TO BUSINESS

ONCE THE PRESENTER OF A FARMING PROGRAMME, JOHN MYERS IS NOW RUNNING ONE OF THE COUNTRY'S BIGGEST RADIO COMPANIES. HE TALKS TO RAYMOND SNODDY

THE RADIO career of John Myers could so easily have ended the...

Myers believes that GMG's radio business is worth £150 million – and he wants to expand it

THE MONTEGO 2.0 DL
Turbo Diesel
75 MILES PER GALLON
in stock now
COUNTY MOTORS
ROSEHILL, CARLISLE
☎ 24387

Myers is out to prove doubters wrong

John Myers, chief executive of GMG Radio, has come a long way since his days as a country-music DJ. He tells **Sarah Crawley-Boevey** of his mission to open up the airwaves to the middle-aged

John Myers is a busy man. Not unusual for the chief executive of an ever-growing media business, perhaps, but then, this particular CEO does make life hard for himself.

In an average working week, the 47-year-old GMG Radio chief travels to the road and, with the help of his brother Steady Eddie, who doubles as his driver, covers 1,000 miles of the nation's fine motorways to "wander the shop floors" of the company's 32 radio stations.

When we meet on Wednesday, he has already visited Scotland, Manchester, various parts of the Midlands and now London. But that's all part of the fun, according to Myers, who has recently brought seven new stations into the fold by snapping up GCap's two remaining Century stations for £60m (which he reportedly persuaded the GMG board to buy) and then Saga Radio's...

you would have to ask your agency for a good reason why not."

Heading into uncharted territories like it, must, surely, be hugely beneficial to be a private company? "I'm happy that we don't have to report to the City and make short-term decisions when it isn't for the long-term gain of the station or group," says Myers.

"We're able to make decisions based on what's best for the division going forward."

For the time being, that is integration. Smooth Radio will launch on 26 March and while Myers will not be drawn on whether Century will rebrand as Real, the stations will still be worked properly into the mix over the next 12 months.

But what does the future hold for the industry as a whole? A supporter of the digital world, Myers is keen to spread his optimism far and wide,...

Evening LATE FINAL
NEWS and STAR
Thursday, June 8, 1989   Price 20p

Switch by TV ace!

By ALAN AIR

POPULAR Border TV presenter John Myers is quitting the Cumbrian station in a surprise move to radio.

John, 36, has been snapped up by Piccadilly-based Saga Radio to host its prestigious morning show.

Border's programme controller, Paul Corbett, said: "We are very sad to lose John but he is one of the most popular-ever...

John Myers quits Border for radio

...action on Border TV and his viewers will be sorry to see him go.

"His vacancy always comes over. We wish him well in his new venture and would be delighted to welcome him back in the future. He's going to help us out with the Christmas Toy Appeal so we're not losing him completely."

being, I could be on screen at Border for a few weeks yet until a replacement is...

John's de-...

Myers, married with a young son, has already started his new job and bought a house in Preston.

But, he is keeping on his heavy bungalow near the Metal Bridge, Carlisle.

He explained: "I'll be commuting for the time being, I still have my other...

...action on Border TV and his viewers will be sorry to see him go.

"His vacancy always comes over. We wish him well in his new venture and would be delighted to welcome him back to work as a newsreader and continuity announcer. When Jim Graham, who was chairman of Border, decided that the company should expand into...

Wednesday, October 13, 1993   Forecast: Sunny Intervals

SACKED... veteran DJ Dave Lee Travis

CFM axes Dave Lee Travis

FORMER Radio One disc-jockey Dave Lee Travis has been 'SACKED' by Cumbrian station CFM.

It comes just over a month after the star DJ was labelled out-of-date by the BBC.

By JONATHAN WILLOUGHBY

The shock split came after DLT's first programme, broadcast on the Carlisle-based commercial station on Sunday, produced an avalanche of complaints from listeners.

DLT's album based music was said to be out of tune with local listeners who preferred pop chart sounds.

DLT said today: "I can't really comment at the mo-

ment because I have absolutely no idea what is going on."

But CFM managing director, John Myers, said: "We have never had this volume

Turn to page 2

The daytime line up of presenters for CFM 1993. Derek Flood, Dave Croft and Paul Evans (seated)

Marketing material and the famous bus at Century North East with our last minute slogan.

Consult with them. Who built Hadrian's Wall?' I said. 'It's easy.'

'I've got it. Yes. Got it.'

'Go on then, Paul. Who built Hadrian's Wall?'

'Was it Laing Builders?'

*

Across the UK there were many quizzes like this taking place. Billy and Wally in Liverpool had, in my view, the best quiz show on the planet. It has never been beaten for humour. Scousers are just very funny people but these two presenters were masters of their craft and I was a real fan. I loved the way they got the callers to be happy to have the mickey taken out of them and I learned from their style and greatness. They had one caller on who was perhaps the best I'd heard in a long time. A few weeks later, I replicated the question on CFM. Even today, no matter how many after dinner speeches I do, whenever I am in Carlisle people always remind me of this caller. My brother, Eddie, was in his car in the town and when the call had finished he looked around him and saw that just about every driver was laughing. That's a wonderful compliment.

Two women came on the phone, Brenda and Susan, from the Raffles area of the city. They were great fun and so far had answered two questions correctly. They were well on the way to getting the show's star prize, three yellow plastic ducks.

The main caller was the mum, Brenda, with Susan shouting in the background, trying to be helpful.

'Okay, Brenda, it's time for another question. Let's spin the wheel.' As the ball landed, I threw in the question I'd heard on the show in Liverpool.

'What was Hitler's first name?' I asked.

'Oh, my God, John, that's a tough one. Please give us a clue for that.'

'C'mon Brenda, the whole world knows the answer to this and it's in your head somewhere. You know the answer to this!'

'We don't, John, we need a clue?'

'Do you know anyone next door or across the road?' I enquired.

'We do, John,' said Brenda. 'We know Mavis next door. She might know and she's seventy-eight.'

What that had to do with it I didn't know. 'Go on then,' I urged. 'Put the phone on the table and go next door to ask.'

After they disappeared, I turned up the gain on the fader as loud as possible so we could hear their footsteps coming back. Very soon, Brenda walked through her door. We heard her come closer to the phone and pick up the receiver.

'We've got it, John. We've got it,' she said.

'Go on then, Brenda. Shout out aloud. What is Hitler's first name?'

'Heil.'

I dropped to the floor in tears. I just couldn't speak. My sides were aching and I struggled to talk. 'Brenda, are you saying Heil?'

Then in the background, the daughter, Susan, realised her mum had made a terrible mistake and picked up the phone herself.

'Hi, John, sorry that's wrong. It's not Heil. It's Hail, as in hay.'

That was it. There was nothing more I could do but give up.

I told them, 'Look that's close enough. You win. The ducks are yours. You're a winner!' I hit the winners' jingle with the pair of them shouting down the phone, 'I'm a winner on CFM!'

When people say radio doesn't connect with an audience, then they didn't hear that show. It was the talk of the city for months to come. For me, that was perhaps one of the funniest moments I've experienced on the air and it was all down to listening to Billy and Wally. They did it first.

*

For a quarter of a century Dave Lee Travis had been one of the main-stays of BBC Radio 1 but during his Sunday morning show on August 8, 1993, he resigned live on air.

He told his stunned audience how he did not agree with changes that were being made at Britain's most popular station.

'I really want to put the record straight at this point and I thought you ought to know,' he said. 'Changes are being made here which go against my principles and I just cannot agree with them.'

As if anyone in the BBC would care what he thought about it all.

After storming out of Radio 1, it wasn't long before he was offering himself up to the commercial radio network. Despite thinking he was daft to resign, I was interested in hiring him. He was still big news and having his show on at the weekends would give CFM some PR and a bit of stardust. His first show was a shocker, self-indulgent prattle with music that was totally out of place on CFM. Although at that time he was known at the time for playing songs that were off the play list, I was so concerned about his choice of music that I called up the producers of the show and asked them to play more hit songs. This did not go down well. He was a big name, we were lucky to have him, he had years of experience and he was certainly not going to be told by a tiny station in Carlisle to change the running order of his programme.

'Quite right,' I said. 'He doesn't have to listen to me at all and I certainly don't have to listen to him.'

I immediately cancelled the show and sacked DLT after just one week.

Considering the row he caused when he left Radio One, the Press thought this was hilarious. One of the smallest radio stations in Britain had just fired one of the nation's biggest jocks and pricked his ego with a loud bang.

I didn't care a jot. The problem with a number – not all – who have been on national radio is that they start to believe they are bigger than the station they are on. They forget they are only powerful when they have the mic. If the microphone is taken away from them, they quite quickly become yesterday's news and find it very difficult to adjust to real life. It is a privilege to broadcast, not a right.

The following week, I attended a function in London and as I walked through the door who should be standing there? The one and only DLT.

I said 'hello' and shook his hand.

He had no idea who I was.

I was not for telling him either.

'Quack, Quack. Oops…'

All was going well but now there was another job in the offing.

Chapter Ten

NEWCASTLE OR BUST!

I'd only been at CFM for eight months when Border TV won the franchise for North East Radio. Peter Brownlow, who had been promoted to MD at Border, came over for a chat. I hadn't known him that well but over the months at CFM we became great friends and often used to spend an hour or so just chatting about the station. He loved radio and he also found the medium exciting.

Border was the smallest TV station on the mainland and to survive it had to build another media arm so the board had decided, while I was busy launching CFM, to apply for the North East regional radio licence, part of a new tier of commercial stations. These regional operations would cover the larger local TV network areas and offer radio listeners a different type of output to their existing local stations. In giving a large coverage area with a less-popular format, the regulator hoped these regional radio stations would still be financially viable. The Myers Report into Local Radio, published in 2009 by the Department of Culture Media and Sport, highlighted the failure of this strategy. There were two key components to an application for a regional radio licence. First, you had to offer a genuinely different kind of output and you also needed quite deep pockets to keep the station going in the early years of operation. The winner would be carefully chosen by the regulator in what became known across the industry as 'the beauty parade'.

Border had been slightly caught out. Their application had very much been a dummy run for the soon-to-be advertised regional service in Scotland's central belt, which was the licence they really wanted. So, winning the North East licence came as an added bonus. When I saw the programme format the board had promised to put on air, I told them they stood as much chance of getting an audience as I had of losing ten stone and there was absolutely no chance of that. Peter and Jim Graham, Border's CEO, came to see me. By now CFM was enormously successful, following a textbook launch and they wanted me to replicate this in the North East. I explained their proposed output needed a radical overhaul to stand any chance of success. The format was set out in a legal document that came when you were awarded a broadcasting licence. It outlined in detail what you had to do on air every hour of the day. If you strayed away from that format the regulator could revoke your licence. So I'd have to negotiate some changes with the regulators before I could agree to take over as MD in the North East. I called up the Radio Authority and their response was interesting to say the least. I knew the people there well and they revealed how they'd had many a laugh reading some of the suggestions put forward from the wide range of applicants for the North East licence but apparently ours was the 'most wonderful'. They agreed I could do whatever I wanted in speech terms but I had to maintain both the maximum music and the minimum news commitments set out in the original agreement. The rest, I could play around with. Thank God for that, I thought. This at least gave us half a chance of succeeding. I was dreading putting on the show that showcased championship leeks! The format also had a twenty per cent commitment to bloody Country music. Would I never escape this part of my life? I told Jim that on this basis we could move ahead. We struck a deal for me to become MD in the North East and waited for the board to make the formal announcement. There was a period of deathly silence before Jim came to see me.

'We have a small problem,' he admitted. 'The radio station's board of directors want me to formally advertise the position of MD and furthermore, they want to play a part in the selection process.'

'Well, that is a problem, Jim,' I replied, 'because you've already given me the job and I have a letter of confirmation from you to that effect.'

'Yes, John, that's correct,' he said, 'but you need to help me out. You're clearly the best man for the job and will walk the interview process but we have to keep the board on side, so can you formally apply and come along to the interview?'

'What, you want me to apply for a job I already have?'

'Yes, I'm afraid so, we've jumped the gun and I could do with you helping us through it. They won't feel happy with an MD they hadn't interviewed.'

It was utter madness but I understood the position Jim had found himself in. These things happen from time to time so, of course, I agreed to go along with this charade provided it was a done deal and there was no chance I could lose the position.

'Of course, John, absolutely,' he insisted. There are very few people on planet Earth who would not do something for Jim so I agreed to play along. This did not mean I wasn't more than a little miffed. In fact I was quietly working myself up about the absurdity of it all. I submitted my application and the day of the interview came along. It was held at the world-famous Barbour jacket factory in South Shields. The owner Margaret Barbour was a member of the new radio station's board. I turned up early and waited outside the gates before casually walking in with just five minutes to the appointed hour. A security man told me I was at the wrong factory. Oh God, this was not good. I jumped back in the car and quickly drove to the other factory. Now late and sweating, I drove through the gates so fast I skidded to a stop on the tarmac outside the main offices with a loud screeching of the tyres.

We got under way some fifteen minutes later, although I soon got into my stride, despite one of the board members being Kath Worrall. To be blunt, I didn't like her despite the fact that she was one of the people who put the application together. Kath and I had some history, as she'd been my boss for a time at BBC Radio Cumbria. She wound me up even then and the best thing I can say about her is absolutely nothing. However, I batted back all of the board's questions and by the end had them in the right place. I was getting warm comforting nods from Peter Brownlow. Job done, I thought. Time to get out of here and go home. Then Kath had to ask one more question, just one more, but I'd had enough by then.

'John, what do you think about women presenters?' she asked.

I responded unkindly and incorrectly aiming to imply that women tended not to score that well with commercial audiences.

I pointed to research by one of my previous stations that suggested women did not appeal to an audience as much as male presenters.

There was silence. You would have thought I'd just let one go in front of the Queen. Considering Margaret Barbour was present and as close to Her Majesty the Queen as you could get, this was not good. I glanced around the table. Oh, God, I had just given the wrong answer. Even my mate Peter Brownlow, who moments before had been giving warm and comforting signs, was now transfixed by something on the floor.

*

Over the years, the facts have become much clearer on the issue of female presenters and indeed many are heading up some of the biggest radio shows in the UK right now. That said, this was 1993 and in the North East especially my comment would have been widely regarded as fair and correct, despite the fact it wasn't true. Stood in front of a board of at least four women I could see I had probably snatched defeat from the jaws of success. My answer should have been much more politically correct and indeed it was a good question from Kath but the whole episode had me wound up. Here I was, being interviewed for a job I already had, I'd been late for the meeting and skidded into the car park and now they were looking at me as if I was Darth Vader himself. The meeting closed and I went home. That will be an interesting debate I thought but I was angry at myself for rising to the bait.

Next morning Jim Graham rang after my breakfast show and told me that the job was confirmed as mine but he then outlined how difficult it had been for Peter to make this happen.

'It took some doing, John,' he said, 'especially after that reply about women presenters.'

He warned that even though I'd got the nod it was certainly not universal and I'd have my work cut out to get everyone on board Team Myers. In fact, I believe Peter had pulled Jim Gardner, the local chairman aside to have a word in his ear. Still, I had the job now and I'd learned a little along the way. That's the only way you can look at these things.

---

20 second break...

Eye popping candy!

I've seen some sights in thirty years of radio but few are as good as when sales people hit target. At one station I worked at, the sales manager was a woman with enormous boobs and she knew how to use them, too. When target was reached she performed a ritual that only those lucky enough to be there at that precise second would experience.

Sales numbers are always displayed to constantly remind the team how much they need to deliver to reach target. There is a formula for hitting sales targets that many stations follow for success and always works, it's called the Giff Gifford system, after the world sales guru Dave Gifford. At the beginning of every month you have to be eighty per cent booked for the current month, fifty per cent booked for the following month and twenty per cent booked for the third month. As long as you were there or there abouts, you pretty much achieved your goals. These numbers worked both for individual sales members and for the team as a whole.

At this particular station, which was mostly staffed by men at the time, they would receive a 'Brucy bonus' from the sales manager for hitting target. As the target sales figure got closer to being achieved word got around the station that it would be tomorrow ... then some time today, moving to ... any time now. At 'any time now' every male in the building would find himself loitering around the sales floor. We would find any excuse to be there.

When someone secured an order that took the team to target, a Klaxon would sound, followed by the sight of the sales manager leaping onto her chair and lifting her jumper to reveal those massive bazookas as she shouted, 'TITS FOR TARGET!!!!'

This was usually followed by a large cheer and rapturous applause. The guys in the sales team would break their necks to hit the target each month.

This lady no longer works as a sales manager but she is still in radio.

*

In February, 1994, I moved to Newcastle to set the station up and hired my first three employees – John Simons, the man who had employed me at Radio Tees some years before. Joanne Riordan, the receptionist at CFM, who became my PA; and Clive Douthwaite, the Sales Director of Red Rose Radio in Preston. In one swoop, we had programming, sales and leadership. From this we could build a team I said, but I had also secretly hired one other, local radio presenter, Mike Parr.

At the time, Mike was a presenter at BBC Radio Newcastle and we'd also worked together at Radio Cumbria. I really liked his style and I needed someone who could mix music and speech together and Mike was that man. Sadly, three months before we launched, he pulled out and remained at the BBC. It was a blow but then we jumped for local TV presenter and journalist, Paul Frost. What Paul lacked in radio skills he compensated greatly by being a nice guy with a good nose for a story and, of course, everyone knew him.

I studied the station 'promise of performance' more closely. What a dog's dinner this application was but it had impressed the regulator. All the new regional radio stations were barred from launching before September that year because the existing radio stations, like Metro FM in our area, had convinced the Radio Authority that this extra tier of commercial competition would seriously affect them and they needed time to prepare. Instead, what really happened was that the existing stations went to all their key advertising clients and signed them up on long-term, often exclusive, deals. When we arrived, most of our potential clients had no money left to advertise, which seriously affected our commercial performance. It was a brilliant move by our competitors but luckily we were owned by a TV station with deep pockets. Any local consortium would have gone bust within the first few months. This was not going to be easy. The top man at Metro was John Joseph, who at the start I liked and disliked in equal measure. Initially, we were often at loggerheads. On the flip side, he was a wonderful businessman who would watch the pennies while not being restrictive. He was impressive and I marvelled at the way he ran his business.

*

As we started the launch process, the board's opinion of me had improved and we operated with an air of comfortable confidence. At least that's how it was going until I cocked up again when I revealed my first marketing campaign. We'd hired a great advertising agency, Smarts from Edinburgh, who produced a number of proposals. I was used to working in commercial radio and knew for certain the competition was not going to allow you to walk into their area and just take their audience, and definitely not in the North East! Therefore we had to make a statement, a big splash; we needed to get talkability. The brief to Smarts was to deliver something totally different. Believe it or not, the budget for launching this massive radio station was just sixty thousand pounds, a miniscule figure in 1994, and today it would buy you nothing whatsoever. Nowadays you need at least a million to launch a station of this size. There is no point having a great station if it's a secret.

Smarts presented me and my management team with their ideas for the launch. We all loved them, especially me. Looking back, I can't for the life of me think why the hell I did. The posters were something to behold. This was not a great campaign but that's not what I thought at the time.

'This is brilliant!' I proclaimed.

The first poster they presented had a stunning Page 3 beauty with huge knockers in a tight swimsuit, holding two brightly coloured CDs across her nipples. The strap-line was: WE'VE GOT THE BIGGEST HITS.

The next giant poster showed a workman digging a hole in the road with his jeans halfway down his bum showing the gaping gap in his backside. The headline read: AND WE'VE GOT GREAT CRACK TOO.

Yes, I know what you're thinking and, yes, even now I'm appalled they got through the first presentation but at the time I was genuinely delighted with the concept. Remember, this was 1994 and that sort of stuff was ultra new and looked great. Before presenting it to the board, I decided to show the campaign to Jim Graham and Peter Brownlow to gauge their reaction. They say life is a constant learning experience. Well, I learned the art of chairmanship right there. Jim did a brilliant job of saying next to nothing but the few words he did say didn't register with me at all. I just didn't spot the signs and the reason was simple. I wasn't listening for them.

At the end of the campaign presentation, his face broke into a big smile. 'John,' he beamed, 'this is a very different and interesting poster campaign and I'm sure they'll get a reaction from the board. Do you by any chance have a plan B if the board doesn't like it?'

'No, this is the campaign,' I said, forcefully, 'if we show them something else they'll want to have a debate and all that will happen is that we won't make a decision and time is getting on.' 'In that case, Peter and I very much look forward to the board meeting later this week,' he said.

I left the meeting thinking they liked the campaign. I should have listened more closely.

*

The board meeting got underway with a full turnout of directors, which included many of the great and the good from the North East. Local businessman and well-known local government Chief Executive, Jim Gardner CBE was in the chair, Jim Graham and Peter from Border sat alongside him. At the other end of the table sat the highly redoubtable Margaret Barbour. She was wonderful, engaging and kind but she was also rich and powerful and a giant step out of my league. We skipped through the agenda with ease until the moment came to reveal my proposed marketing campaign. I not only had the two posters I'd showed Peter and Jim a few days before but now I had ten more under the table, all similar ideas. Jim was looking at the floor and smiling but I took no notice.

I stood up and explained our ambition – to gain traction and to get people talking.

'We need something big and bold,' I announced. 'We need to get the people of the region talking. We want chatter on the streets that there's a new radio station on the dial. I believe our poster campaign will deliver that for us.'

I held aloft my first poster, the big-chested woman and the head-line 'We've Got The Biggest Hits'. Suddenly, Margaret Barbour was having a coughing fit. As I asked if she was all right, I noticed Peter laughing into his handkerchief.

Margaret looked at the chairman and exclaimed, 'Oh my word. That's not the positioning I'd hoped we'd be using, Jim. I joined this board because we were presenting a mixture of informative speech and lovely music.'

Jim Graham jumped in, 'Please show us the next one.'

I stood up and held out the board featuring the workman with his jeans down his bum and the headline, 'And We've Got The Best Crack Too!' It was then that I really started to fear for Margaret Barbour's health.

'Please no,' she spluttered. 'I have to tell you that if we go ahead with this campaign I don't believe I could continue to be a member of this board. I just could not be associated with this style of radio station. We can't go with this surely?'

I now looked at Jim Graham and Peter Brownlow. They were desperately trying to keep a straight face but it was absolutely clear this campaign was never going to fly. Peter, being the mischievous sod he was at times, asked 'John, do you have any more to show us?'

At this point Margaret Barbour said, 'I don't think I could take any more.'

Peter knew I had others beneath the desk to bring out but there was no way I was going to risk putting up any more and in particular the one I had featuring the sprinter Linford Christie in Lycra which had a play on words about 'moving the big radio knob up the dial'.

I looked at him and said, 'Sorry, those were the only two examples I have.'

Margaret Barbour was downing water like it was going out of fashion and waving a handkerchief in defeat. There was a silence around the table.

James Gardner pulled the meeting together, 'John,' he said, 'I think you've received the flavour of the feeling around the board and I wonder if you could come to the next meeting with a revised advertising campaign for us to consider.'

'Yes of course, no problem. I'd be very happy to do just that.' When the board meeting ended, the two Jims and Peter went to my office and laughed their socks off.

'John, that's the funniest hour I've had in a long time,' Jim Graham said, wiping his eyes, 'but we do need to consider another creative.'

'Don't worry, guys, I get the message. I'm just worried that Margaret might not come back at all,' I said. But Jim Gardner assured me he would sort that problem.

I called Smarts but there was no problem as far as they were concerned. Clients often don't get approval for some of the creative ideas they suggest. In they came with another campaign, 'The Best Thing In 'Ears'. I could have presented absolutely anything whatsoever the next time around and it would have been accepted but the board all loved this new idea. In truth it was a much better concept altogether. Our posters featured famous faces wearing large pink ears. It did the same job. Margaret Barbour wondered aloud if I had presented the first campaign just to startle them when this was the real creative all along. If only I'd been that clever.

Interestingly, Atlantic 252 went with the same busty woman creative a year later. So Smarts must have managed to sell on the idea.

Chapter Eleven

A STAR IS BORN

Our new station, Century Radio, launched at eight o'clock on the 1 September, 1994, with the song *A Star is Born*. I always used this song when launching a new station for Century and Real because you could guarantee the local press would take the lazy option and print the headline 'A Star is Born' and that's always great to have on the files. The programme schedule on day one looked like this:

6am:	Morgan in the Morning (That was me)
9am:	Simon Bates
10am:	Tony Fisher
12 noon:	Paul Frost's phone-in
2pm:	John Simons
5pm:	Century 21 News
7pm:	Steve Philips
10pm:	Phil Mathews

As Century was a new station, I decided to treat myself to a new name. I'd recently heard some audio from Robert W Morgan in California and I loved the way he would give a time-check, 'It's five past eight

in the Morgan'. He also had a catchphrase, 'you've been Morganized'.
I could have some fun here, I thought and from that moment on I
broadcast on the air as John Morgan, or Morgan in the Morning.

Because of our licence agreement, we had to keep a very close
eye on the music we played, especially during the daytime. We could
play pretty much what we wanted but were only allowed to broadcast
so much music across the core thirteen-hour peak-time period, from
6am to 7pm. This way of programming was ridiculous and meant we
had to manually calculate the amount of music we played each hour of
the day. At 2pm we'd count up all the total duration of music aired to
that point in the day, which then told John Simons how many records
he could play in his afternoon show. If I'd talked a lot during my breakfast show, he could play more tunes in the afternoon. On the flip side,
if I'd played a lot of songs, he had to talk more to compensate. It was a
crazy way to run a radio station but we had accepted the challenge we'd
been set, so there was no point in complaining. The format was clear.
Forty-five percent of our output between 6 am to 7 pm could be music,
but that percentage was a rolling number. So it had to be no more than
45% music from 7 to 11 am, 8 to 12 noon, 9 to 1 pm and so on. When I
tell people today about that rule they find it hard to believe.

All of this gelled us as a team but it was long hours and hugely
stressful at times. In fact, most days we arrived very early and were
still there some twelve hours later and at weekends. The restrictions
were hard but it actually forced us to come up with programming
ideas and promotions that allowed for plenty of speech. The big creative thought that ran across the day was a simple one; we would do
anything provided it was entertaining. Nothing was out of bounds.
If it worked, it was usually on. If it worked and contained plenty of
speech it was definitely on. Any idea that didn't work was quickly
replaced with something else that did. This was radio like no other.
We were trailblazing a radio station format and we had to find our
DNA quickly, or die trying. The ability to be light-footed and adapt-
able delivered some wonderful and engaging radio programmes that
brought in big audiences.

Programme Director, John Simons, and I didn't have a plan as such, instead we just came up with loads of ideas. What we wanted to do we did. We were both good and bad for each other in that we were as mad as each other. We inspired each other to try things and we certainly pushed the line more than once. That was the huge fun of it all. This unique system was going well. The audience figures were going better than expected and the revenue was starting to build. People were tuning in, but even better, they were tuning in for long periods. Those who listened to us loved us. A loyal fan base becomes your marketing team, delivering up their friends and family along the way. They become as proud and vocal of the station as you are. In fact, current listeners are the best marketing campaign any station will ever have.

*

These were great times. The more our competitors fought against us, the more we rallied together as a team. It was working and people were starting to take notice. On a personal note, the more speech I had to do at breakfast time only enhanced my own skill on the air. I became a much sharper broadcaster, learning how to get the very best out of callers and enhancing the listeners' overall experience. We launched The Breakfast Gamble, a game that at times could last an hour. It was gripping radio and had the added bonus of giving us loads of music to play afterwards.

For a reason that absolutely escapes me, we decided to launch the station using brand-new technology. Yet, here we were going hell for leather with equipment that had been untried in the UK. The system crashed so often it was a real drain on our momentum and at times nearly broke our spirit. There was no greater upset for us than when the whole system crashed on day one in the middle of our two-hour news programme that we'd named Century 21. We had a large news-room compared to other commercial stations. Our commitment to news was five minutes an hour in the daytime and fifteen minutes at 1pm. We also promised an extended news programme. We'd worked out that we could deliver a great news programme of around twenty minutes and, then as the audience rotated in and out of drive-time, we would simply rotate the content every 21 minutes creating a rolling news programme. To emphasise this point we stole the strapline from 1010 WINS in New York and adapted it for our market to say *Give us 21 Minutes and we'll give you the World*. Not exactly original but it had never been heard before in the North East. When the computer crashed, the whole day's news cuts and audio went with it. We had an hour left to fill and not a single bit of audio to play. I was in the studio that day and looked over at the news team who were all staring at blank screens. They needed leadership, so I opened the mic and started singing ... 'Always look on the bright side of life' ... durra durra ...'

They joined in and suddenly the rest of the staff started singing, too. A bad moment was turned into something quite unique and after about ten minutes of news with no audio, I told them to play music and would explain the problem to the regulator. To be fair to the Radio Authority, they understood but, in a letter to us the following week, they stressed this could not be allowed to happen again.

*

One day a month, John Simons had the job of going down to London to record all of the links from Simon Bates for The Golden Hour. The programme was a real hassle to do. We would put the show together in paper form and then Bates would record the links for each song separately. Then back in the studio, we'd fit it all together and mix in the music. Each one-hour show often took four hours to put together but having former Radio One DJ Simon Bates on our station was something special and gave us some much-needed showbiz that got great Press. One day, John explained he would be away on holiday the day he was due to record Simon in London. Could I do the session? No problem, what could possibly go wrong?

John reminded me that Simon Bates was not, at the time, the easiest of people to work with and that he had forged a really good relationship with him over the months. He didn't want me to do anything that would ruin that. Clearly, John knew me better than anyone. Indeed, it's fair to say that I had a reputation for not caring about reputations and insisted that people do a great job no matter who they were. However, I was a big fan of Bates and I really wanted to do the session, so I promised I'd be nice. At that time we used to record him at Capital Radio, just off Euston Road, in London. I did my own breakfast show in Newcastle, jumped on a train to the capital and arrived at the studio all ready to record the Golden Hour links. We were getting on brilliantly, until Bates came to the Fleetwood Mac record, *Albatross*. For some reason, Simon back-announced the record by saying, 'that was a great song by Fleetwood Mac …'

I stepped in on his talkback, 'Can we record that link again please, Simon? That's not a song. It's a tune. *Albatross* is an instrumental. It has no words, so we need to do it again.'

I was producing the session and doing what producers did but it was clear through the studio glass that Simon was not Mr Happy. In fact he was not happy at all.

'John, love,' he said. 'I've been doing this for more decades than I can remember. Believe me, I'm correct. It's a great song it is *not* a tune and I will *not* be re-recording that link.'

I spoke into his ear again, 'Simon, you're a great jock and it's indeed true that you have years of experience but that doesn't mean you are correct. On this occasion I'm right and you're wrong. When did you last sing along to an instrumental? *Albatross* is a tune, *not* a song and, as such, we can't back-announce it as being one. Please can you re-record the link?'

He was now standing up at the microphone. 'Look, John. I'm not recording it again. That's it. Now do you want me to do the rest of the session for you or should I leave right now? It's been a long day, love, and I can't do that link again. I simply can't.'

Shit, the session was only half way through and if he walked he might never do anything for us again.

'Okay, you win.' I conceded. 'How about you carry on and we'll go with your version.'

He came back with a brilliant answer – 'That's the right decision young man!'

We never spoke again during the session. I travelled back with the tape and handed it over to production. Personally, I thought the shows were marvellous and Simon Bates to this day remains on of the finest broadcasters on the planet. His word economy is a masterclass every time you tune in. He's not just a jock, he's a communicator and there's no finer compliment than that. We remain great friends to this day.

When John Simons came back from his break he asked how the session with Bates had gone.

'Brilliant, I said. 'No problem whatsoever, he loves me.'

But when John arrived in London to record the next month's links he had to spend an hour listening to Bates calling me a 'bloody northern idiot' and explaining at full volume that there was no way he was going to record again if I ever went down to do it.

John arrived back at the studio, wandered upstairs to my office and said, 'Hey, just remind me how your session with Bates went? You may recall telling me "brilliant", he loves ya' and there's no problem. Well, you're barred from any more sessions,' he shouted. 'He doesn't think you're brilliant, yes, there was a problem and, no, he very much does *not* love ya' whatsoever!' Simon Bates and I often recall those crazy days at Century with fondness.

*

Part of our weekend output was a two-hour programme, The Crazy Gardening Show. When Simo came upstairs to tell me about his idea for the show, I asked. 'What's crazy about a gardening show?' 'Easy, we don't take any gardening questions. We just lark about. That's why it's craaaaaazy.'

It was totally nuts and that's why I loved it.

'Right go on then, have some fun,' I said. 'Let's see how it works.' Boy did it work. At one stage, it was the highest-rated show on the station, simply because we dared to be different. It was a wonderfully entertaining show, totally different and unique compared to anything else on the dial. Simo, who was already doing six shows a week on top of his job as PD, was the ringmaster, accompanied by Gardening Gary and the lovely Adam Eden. They were actually very good gardening experts who sometimes would actually take a few callers and answer their questions correctly just to confuse the audience before going back to being totally stupid. Perhaps the reason it became one of the best shows was that it allowed people to let off steam and just chat about rubbish. There's a message here for all radio programmers. Music is important but content is king every single time. Bold programming decisions can work wonders and this was a winner. Over time, we split the show into two parts. Fun On The Phones for half the year and The Gardening Show for the other half. It allowed John and me to get some weekends off.

*

We often had complaints about the station and sometimes I'd read them out on air and ask the listeners how I should respond. In turn, this stopped people complaining. If I don't mind saying so myself, it was a brilliant move. However, some complaints could not be batted away so easily. Century Radio had exclusive commentary rights with Middlesbrough Football Club who were, in my view, the most challenging set of managers running a business I'd ever experienced in that their logic was often confusing. Some of their discussions with me over the years were maddening and totally illogical. Once, I was called in to see Middlesbrough's Chief Executive, Keith Lamb, who now works for the FA. I always found Keith quite dull but he was always professional and, while I tried to keep things balanced, he was frustrating to say the least. When we were negotiating exclusive rights to cover the Boro, he told me the club wanted more cash because our commentary was affecting the number of people coming through the gates. He had failed to notice that the reason people were no longer coming to the games was that the team, at that time, were crap. I was one of their biggest fans and really did have the T-shirt. Here he was trying to blame us for low crowds. I couldn't believe it. A typical football club, I thought, wanting to blame everyone for their mistakes.

*

Usually, when you point a finger at someone there are three of your own, pointing right back at you. One day the sports show producer called to say there was a problem with our co-commentator, the brilliant and very likeable former Middlesbrough manager, Malcolm Allison, who had just sworn live on air. Simo and I called Malcolm in to the station and underlined to him the importance of not using profanity. We did a great job keeping the regulator at bay by promising it wouldn't happen again but this was a problem we had to address. We came up with the idea of giving him a button that he was to press only when he wanted to talk. This would resolve it all. Alistair Brownlee was perhaps the best football commentator in the business and we loved him. He was bang on our style, emotive, fluent, passionate and absolutely biased towards the Boro. We liked that. Middlesbrough were our team and we wanted a sound that said bollocks to being fair to each side. We wanted open bias towards our team and the fans loved us for that, too. Century Radio was one of them and it's why we managed to attract such enormous sponsorship alongside our commentary. Everyone wanted to be part of our output.

Thinking we'd sorted the issue, life went along as normal until the day of the big local derby, Middlesbrough versus Newcastle from The Riverside Stadium. I was shopping in The Metro Centre in Newcastle when I received an urgent call from Rod Hardisty, who was producing the sports show that afternoon.

'We have a problem,' he stammered. 'Malcolm Alison has just sworn again!'

'How bad is it?' I asked.

'It's pretty bad, John. It's a swear word on the regulator's A-list.' Oh, oh, this meant a big fine was coming. This may be hard to believe but the regulator had actually listed all the swear words they knew and then categorised them into different levels of offence. A Top Twenty of expletives. Bloody was a slap on the wrist, while fuck was near the top of the list – and a guaranteed big fine. The list is unofficial nowadays but it's still there.

Uttering a swear word on air at a time when children might be listening upped the fine. As thousands of kids without tickets to the game would be listening to our exclusive commentary we were in a bit of a fix. I asked Rod to play the audio down the phone. What I heard drained the blood from my face:

Newcastle's newest player, Asprilla, had just been given the ball and was racing on goal. Alistair Brownlee's commentary was going full tilt when Malcolm hit his button and came in loud and clear.

'Asprilla has got the ball,' said Big Mal. 'He's going to score … He's through … he's … he's fucking scored. I fucking knew it!'

Oh my God. This was not just bad it was very, very bad. I sat down on a chair outside Marks & Spencer's and ordered Rod to tell Ali Brownlee just to cut Malcolm off the mic for the rest of the game. Simo played a blinder by calling the regulator first thing on Monday morning before our competitors did. They always put a call in to inform them we had been naughty and it's always good to tell the regulator first before anyone else can. They listened to the clip and then we told them we would fire Malcolm as a damage limitation exercise. That sort of got us through while we dealt with loads of complaints but we did manage to get away without a fine. We were walking the line so often that we were bound to be fined at some stage, so we accounted for it in our annual budget. If the money was still there at the end of the year we had a good night out in celebration.

We summoned Malcolm. He was such a lovely man that it was hard to fall out with him. However, he was no fool and knew he was coming in to be fired. He was full of apologies for the hassle he'd caused. I wondered how the hell this had happened as we had put in a device to stop him swearing on air.

'I just got confused,' Malcolm explained. 'I was so excited I thought that by pressing the button I was off the air, not on.'

Sadly, this great man is no longer with us but he was a gentleman and will never be forgotten.

*

My new role as Group MD of Border Radio Holdings was increasing as we ran our stations and applied for more and more radio licences. At the same time I presented a live Friday evening debate on Border TV called The Forum, on top of my six radio shows a week. Something had to give and the big decision was to come off breakfast. So, I told Simo to find someone to replace me but it was not that easy to find the right person who could jump into a live breakfast show which contained over fifty per cent speech and had so few resources. You had to be able to talk in an entertaining way for more than half the show. I was used to it by then and my style is very much off-the-cuff but other presenters did it in different ways. After a while Simo came back and suggested we hire former Metro FM breakfast presenter, Steve Coleman. Steve was currently on the air in Yorkshire but was still relatively well known in the North East. Simo did the deal and Steve came back to Newcastle. I'd met with him a couple of times through all the negotiations but I tried to keep out of it as he was replacing me and it's always difficult to hire someone for your slot. While I loved being on the air, I also relished the management role, although I did keep a weekend show. I left the breakfast show on Friday and Steve started on Monday. We'd had a bunch of new jingles and imaging produced for the show and Steve and Simo had gone through the content of the programme. All new shows can take time to bed-in, so I was careful not to get too involved. I stayed away and upstairs. Clients started phoning the sales team complaining about Steve's style. My view was that we should just keep going. I'd been there for some years and it was only reasonable that it would take some time for a new show to settle down. In any case, I certainly didn't want to get up again at 6 am for a while.

*

Any PD faces problems when a personality leaves a show. Changes mean complaints. Look at when Terry Wogan went from his Radio 2 breakfast show, perhaps the biggest radio presenter ever in terms of success. Chris Evans comes in and, bang, the audience goes up despite hundreds, if not thousands, of complaints. You have to keep your nerve.

That said, even I couldn't escape the fact that the new breakfast show on Century was not as successful as we had hoped for. The number of complaints was getting higher each day, not because Steve Coleman was bad but just because he was not Morgan. I know when I talk about myself in the third person it can come over as arrogant but it's certainly not the intention. I'm just being honest about the issue. Simo wanted action to sort it out. It was still early days, I said, and we should continue with the plan while reviewing more forcefully each segment of the show.

'I'm already doing that,' he insisted. 'I'm talking to him every day and in my view he isn't listening or changing the way he performs. He's come back to Newcastle and thinks that all he has to do is turn up. The world has moved on and he hasn't kept up.' I asked John to do some research with our own Listeners' Club. Century had its own club made up of thousands of listeners who were devoted to the station. In those pre-Facebook days, we used them as a research tool and a way of connecting with our audience. We pulled all the team in one day and rang five hundred club members in one go. We didn't quiz them about the breakfast show as such but asked about the station in general. Unprompted, the feedback was that we had a big problem with breakfast and it was not going away. While this was potentially bad news for me, I asked Simo to keep going for a while longer.

'Work with him more, insist on features being executed in a certain ways if you like,' I insisted because I was not keen to go back on the air. I was keen to keep Coleman in place.

The following Wednesday morning Simo stomped up the stairs, sat on the big red couch in my office and said, 'Right, This is **not** for debate. Steve Coleman is history. He's not working out and I'm making the decision to take him off. You are back on the air on Monday morning at breakfast until we find another replacement.' With that,

Simo left the office. Ten minutes later he was back. 'Err, we have a small problem,' Simo said. 'He hasn't actually signed his contract yet.'

I pondered for a moment. 'So, are we saying we want to fire a jock but we can't fire him because we haven't actually hired him?'

'No,' Simo replied. 'We can't fire him under the terms of the contract because he's not actually signed saying he agrees to the terms of that contract.'

'So, what's the plan?'

'As soon as he signs the contract, I'm firing him.'

And that's exactly what happened. Steve Coleman came in on the Friday morning, and signed his contract in front of Simo, who immediately handed him a letter saying that was his last show and we paid him off under the terms of the contract he'd only just agreed.

The Press loved this but it wasn't our finest hour in management. We'd made such a big splash about Steve coming back that this was too good a story to miss. We'd agreed to hold the line and not discuss it with the Press but I received a call from The Sunday Sun in the North East who told me that Steve was saying negative things about the station. Looking back I don't think he did but at the time I felt giving our point of view was the right decision. I regret that now. Steve is a very good broadcaster and only recently I tuned into him on Magic AM in the North East where he continues to be an excellent performer. He was just the wrong fit for our station. The fault was all ours and not his.

Monday morning I was back on air ...

Chapter Twelve

BLIND LEADING THE BLIND

There's a great advantage to being on the air under an alias. As the leader of the station, I was John Myers, Group Managing Director of Border Radio Holdings and MD of Century radio. However, on the air I was John Morgan, genial host of a slightly crazy and off-the-wall breakfast show. Thankfully, my programme was popular but not with everyone. Jocks who want to be liked by everyone nearly always fail to reach the top. People who can't stand your show are just as important as those who love it. Take Terry Wogan, for example. In my view he is the greatest radio communicator I've ever heard. His unique style, the majestic verbal dance with the English language mixed with a gift for delivering observational humour was a daily pleasure for millions. But despite his brilliance not everyone liked him and that's good. It means you are having an impact. The very act of positioning yourself as a personality means you are asking listeners to form a view about what you do and the way you do it. The greater the personality the greater the divide and the really smart broadcasters know this. However, no matter how popular you become, the hurt of being disliked by just one person is always there. You just have to get over it. In fact, I've never come across any successful personality presenter who is not disliked by large numbers of people and with that will always come complaints. At Century, listeners would start to ring me as Managing Director to complain about me as Morgan in the Morning! This happened so often I lost count.

With my managing director's hat on, I would listen to moans about something I'd said on the breakfast show and then say, 'I'm sorry. I've not heard the show this morning, but I'll have a stern word with John Morgan later on.'

That usually placated them. God knows what the latest regulator, OFCOM, would think about that today?

The problem of having two identities at the station got me into trouble on more than one occasion. We tried to acquire the football commentary rights from Newcastle United, the mighty Toon. They had an agreement with BBC Radio Newcastle and Metro Radio and didn't want to give it to us, too. Premiership football is big money and the amount we could pay them, even though it was more than the competitors were offering, was peanuts in reality. Relationships are always more important and Newcastle weren't going to change for a few thousand. Newcastle United's Chief Executive and head of commercial operations was Freddie Fletcher, a fiery Scotsman affectionately known as The Rottweiler with a reputation for having a bit of a temper. He was also the man responsible for bringing Kevin Keegan to Newcastle and was someone who demanded your respect. Having survived the days of Owen Oyston and David Maker at Red Rose, I was used to working with people of a certain bubbly nature, but Freddie was in a different class in that respect. However, he was a genius at getting the money in and absolutely knew the value of his product. There is no doubt in my mind that Newcastle United would never have been half as successful without this man at the helm. Nevertheless, I always made sure that I always offered more money for the commentary rights each year, because I knew he'd not waste the opportunity to go back to the BBC and Metro to get more money out of them. If we weren't going to get a deal, then we'd make damn sure the competition were paying top dollar. This would reduce their marketing spend against us across the year so, for me, it was also just good business. Whenever the receptionist announced Freddie was on the phone for me, it was like a laxative. A roasting down the phone from Freddie was something you didn't forget. It was so hot you could get a tan from it. He was known to ring up the Newcastle Chronicle if he didn't like a headline and ban the paper's reporters from the following week's team Press conference.

*

As we had no relationship whatsoever with the Toon, the football club were fair game as far I was concerned and perfect for my particular style of on-air mickey taking. I took it out of the club's mercurial manager, Kevin Keegan, at every conceivable opportunity. I even kept calling King Kev's deputy at the time, Terry McDermott, Ronald McDonald. The former Newcastle player was the double of the fast food chain's mascot. One night, disaster happened for the club. They were beaten at home by Sunderland and for a Toon fan, there's absolutely no greater shame than that. So, the next morning, just before the breakfast show went on air, I recorded myself crying hysterically down the phone. Later on, listeners heard the sound of a telephone ringing, with my co-presenter shouting aloud that King Kev was on the phone.

'WOW!' I said. 'This is something special. King Kev is ringing Morgan in the Morning. I answered the phone, asked Kevin how he was after the previous night's defeat and then played in the tape of hysterical crying.

In between sobs, I shouted in the microphone '… it's just a game Kev! Get hold of yourself, man … Sober up …There's always next week.'

*

The telephones lit up. I expected a huge backlash, but instead the callers were loving it, the best laugh they'd had in years. All the callers were great – except one, Freddie Fletcher. He was a little upset.

My daughter, Kerry, was the station receptionist and had been well trained to say that the boss, John Myers, wasn't in yet but he would call them back. I'd then deal with my own complaints. This time, Freddie was apoplectic. I was clearly not making friends but I didn't care. We were having fun and getting talked about. Even the Newcastle players tuned in each morning on the way to the training ground. I lived close to Peter Beardsley, a fantastic player who had previously played for Carlisle United, and get on with him well. He told me that when Kev got to the ground that morning, all the players pulled out white hand-kerchiefs and launched into a chorus of hysterical crying. Thankfully, I had heard Kevin's wife, Jean, was a fan of the show so he took our leg-pulling in great spirits. I did mean to reveal the truth to Freddie about my dual identity to avoid future embarrassment but the opportunity never came. I shouldn't have worried. A fall out was coming anyway.

One day, The Sun ran a full page story about Newcastle's young Irish player, Keith Gillespie, apparently owing the bookies thousands of pounds. Keith was a brilliant player but he was not brilliant at picking horses. Yet again, this was too good to miss, so that morning I ran a competition called Gillespie's Donkey of the Day. It was a simple idea where we told them what Keith was backing and our listeners knew to back something else. I had him live on the show, telling listeners about the horses he was picking and how he was doing it. I was constantly promoting this feature, while Freddie Fletcher was ringing the station demanding to know how this was possible as he had just called Keith and had been assured no such thing was going to take place. Just after 8am, I put Keith Gillespie on air and in the interview he revealed his system was nothing more than throwing a dart at the racing page pinned to the dressing room wall. However, this was not the real Keith Gillespie. Instead, it was a man called Keith Gillespie from Byker who I'd managed to find in the phone book and, as luck would have it, he was also Irish. He played along brilliantly and, of course, I didn't actu-ally *say* he was not the real Keith. He sounded genuine at first and then the audience worked it out and loved it.

The big giveaway came when Keith said that every morning before training he ran his hands through King Kev's permed hair for luck. The Irish never did anything unless they had 'something for luck', he said. It was very funny but one man was not smiling. In fact, he was gloriously fuming.

When I came off air, there were half a dozen notes on my desk demanding I telephone Freddie Fletcher immediately. When I called him up he went ballistic. I had to 'get to grips with that Morgan', he said. He demanded a full apology on air and if he didn't get it he would use the match programme to tell all Newcastle fans to have nothing whatsoever to do with Century Radio. Oh God, this could get out of control, I thought. I tried to tell him it was just satire and that he could not blame me for Keith getting himself in trouble. Freddie was having none of it. I told him I would see what I could do. The dispute with Freddie had gone on far too long and I really needed to come clean about who I was but the right opportunity never seemed to present itself. Anyway, I wondered, why did someone who got so wound up about my show always bloody listen to it?

✳

The following weekend the world blew up in my face. While we didn't have commentary rights with the Toon, we did have exclusive commentary with Middlesbrough FC. Both clubs were in the premiership and the local derby was taking place at The Riverside. Our rights to the game also came with a bunch of free tickets in the executive lounge. As the match kicked off, I could see Freddie in the box alongside me. At half time we were unfortunate to walk out together when Middlesbrough's chairman, Steve Gibson, gave the game away.

'Oh, I see you've met John Morgan' he said. To say Freddie was upset is an understatement. I was banned from the club. Our reporters were also banned from the Press conferences. We were never, under any circumstances, ever to turn up at Newcastle's stadium, St James' Park. Considering I'd never had commentary rights, banning me was not that much of a loss. However, I did feel bad about our journalists being banned.

The following weekend, Newcastle were live from St James' Park on Sky Sports. Two days before, I received a call from Sky's advertising department who wanted to know if I'd be willing to take an advertising billboard at the game. They were usually £10,000 per board per game but Sky were offering me one for just £1,000. I was about to say 'no chance' when the salesman added that the board came with two executive seats for the match, as guests of Sky. It was a mad thing to do but I found myself saying 'yes'.

Very few people climb into the executive seats in the directors' box before kick off but I was there in my place fifteen minutes early and bitterly regretting it. What the hell had I done? Directly opposite the directors' box was my board advertising Century Radio in the very stadium we were banned from. This was going to get interesting. The players were just about to kick off when Freddie arrived and scanned the pitch. His eyes nearly popped out of his head.

'How the hell did that board get there?' he shouted.

I was laughing uncontrollably into my coat but at half-time Freddie pulled a masterstroke. He sent a couple of ball boys onto the pitch and I watched as they unscrewed my board and took it away down the tunnel.

Next morning I complained that some kids had stolen my board, while Sky moaned that I should have told them Myers was the Toon's Public Enemy Number One. Over the years, I'd come to know Freddie a little better. He was a wonderful after dinner speaker and, love him or not, he was the absolute best at what he did, generating millions for NUFC and as important to the club as any player or manager. As I wrote this book I learned about his death and it saddened me a great deal. I respected him a lot.

The following season, things calmed down a little and I met with Freddie to ensure our reporters were allowed back into Newcastle's games. We had an IRN licence, so Freddie had to allow us official access but that cut no ice with him. When I met him at the club, we did eventually sort things out and he took the opportunity to twist my arm to buy a couple of season tickets for our clients. There was a catch, I would have to buy what was known as a 'five year bond' because all the other types of season ticket had gone. It was another genius money making move from Freddie but I did the deal as a gesture of good-will towards a better working relationship. When the season tickets arrived, we were in the worst end of the ground with the most vocal of home fans. I decided to go to the first game myself with a friend however disaster struck. I was a lot bigger in those days than I am now and I became stuck in the turnstiles. I couldn't believe how tight the gates were. I convinced myself that if I sued the club and the judge was a big guy, he would immediately award judgment for the plaintiff. Nevertheless, here I was at five to three absolutely wedged tight with thousands of fans trying to push forward, demanding to know what the hold up was. Before long stewards and the police were called. In scenes of utter chaos, I was pulled back out and given entry through the disabled door. Purple with embarrassment, I headed off for a pork pie and an oxo to the sound of, 'you fat bastard, you fat bastard' ringing in my ears. I told the story on air the following Monday and Paul Frost debated the issue of small turnstiles at football grounds on the midday phone in. It turned out I was not the only big guy in the North East who had to watch the game by entering through the disabled entrance. These days, I have executive seats.

*

I loved complaints although I was always careful not to be offensive. There is a fine line between dealing with people who love to complain and making sure you don't air anything that is rude or in poor taste. In the early days I always dealt with complaints personally whenever I could.

I once ran a competition on air with the now defunct Today newspaper. I went down to London and sold them a promotion called Today's The Day, a simple competition designed to get more people to buy their paper. The hook was the chance to win £10,000. For that, the audience had to buy the paper each morning. To make sure they'd made a purchase, when a caller rang in to try and win the ten grand, I would pick a page at random and ask them to read out the headline.

Therefore, I knew they'd bought the paper and, as sales soared, Today Newspapers loved it.

One morning, I went upstairs to be told there was a complaint on line five. The lady had been hanging on for at least five minutes and absolutely insisted on talking to the Managing Director about 'that man Morgan'.

The conversation went like this:

'Hello, John Myers here. I'm the Managing Director. How can I help you?

'Hello, My name is Mary Watson. I'm sorry to bother you but I wish to make a very serious complaint about John Morgan.'

'I've never heard a complaint that's not serious, love. What's the problem?'

'I feel victimised,' she said.

'Oh dear. That sounds terrible. Why's that?' I enquired

'I'm blind, which means I can't read the paper. Which, in turn, means I can't enter your compeition. Which means I'm victimised. What are you going to do about it?'

This could also mean trouble, I thought. Then quick as a flash I said, 'Look Mary, what about the people who are deaf? They don't even know we're doing a bloody competition.'

Silence.

'There's always someone worse off than you, Mary,' I continued.

After a moment's pause, she said, 'You're absolutely right. I'm really sorry to bother you.'

With that, she put the phone down.

Fun times.

Chapter Thirteen

THE MILLION POUND DROP

My show on Century Radio was going well. Audience levels were building but, more importantly, so was the chatter on the streets. To build a successful show, you have to get people talking and it wasn't just the listeners who were talking about me.

Before long I was getting offers to move elsewhere and three in particular stood out. The first I turned down immediately, the second was not for me, and the third, I very nearly accepted.

The first offer was easy to refuse but why I said no was buried in my past. After being rejected by Radio Luxembourg, I'd continued to hire studios to record demo tapes. One of the stations I really wanted to work for was Metro Radio in Newcastle. I spent so much of my salary on making these demo tapes that it was bordering on the obsessive. I sent many of them to Giles Squire at Metro. He was one of the best Programme Directors in the UK at time and had a knack of hiring great jocks. When a radio station didn't like your demo tape, they just sent it back, landing on your doormat with a loud thud. Judging by the number of times he sent my tapes back, Giles clearly didn't rate me much at all. His letter was always the same along the lines of thanking me for my tape, he will keep my name on file but I was not what he was looking for at that time. The usual rejection letter that was now filling two drawers in my home.

*

One day however, instead, of sending my tape back, Giles sent me a letter asking me to pop over to Newcastle to see him. I was convinced this was it. At last all my hard work and investment in those tapes had paid off, he actually wanted to see me face to face. As I lived sixty miles away and had no car, popping over as he suggested was not so easy. The journey to Metro's studios involved getting on a bus, train, another bus and then a walk. It took me over three hours to get there and I waited in reception for Giles to appear. I was nervous and excited at the same time. What show did he want me to do? Would it be week-ends or perhaps some holiday cover? I was up for anything. Giles walked down the stairs and began a conversation that still haunts me:

'Hi, Are you John Myers?'

'Yes, thanks so much for agreeing to see me.'

'Not at all, I really want to help you. Sadly this won't be a long conversation,' he said, pulling me into his office. 'Look John,' he continued. 'You have to stop sending me those bloody demo tapes. You're never going to make it in radio, believe me. I've listened to all of them and, in my view, you're wasting your time. I'm doing this for your own good. I'm sorry, but I wanted to tell you in person because you're clearly not getting the message.'

And with that he showed me to the door. I was devastated. I don't mind telling you I was in tears as I headed back in the pouring rain. My dad, a big guy, wanted to jump into his wagon, drive to Newcastle and chin Giles. Looking back, perhaps he was trying to be kind, I was spending a fortune on the tapes, but instead of turning me away from radio it did the reverse and spurred me on to prove him and any other doubters wrong.

Many years later Giles Squire was still the PD of Metro and I, of course, had changed my name from Myers to Morgan. Metro was still the number one station in Newcastle but I was hurting them with my breakfast show. One day, Giles called asking to meet me. I readily agreed although I'd no idea what he wanted to talk about. I assumed it was because our respective stations had badly fallen out over a complaint they had made to the regulator about us.

*

Century's format agreement with the Radio Authority stipulated we could only play forty-five per cent music during the daytime. Metro were so worried about us they had someone monitoring our output every single hour of the day and on one occasion we had played more than we were allowed. Over the thirteen-hour peak time period, we had somehow managed to play two minutes more music than permitted. Yes, just two minutes over and Metro complained. As I told the team, this was how much they feared us. In my eyes, war had been declared so I retaliated by complaining about them doing too much speech. In turn, they were also reprimanded.

Very soon we were complaining about each other every week. Paul Brown, deputy chief executive at the Radio Authority, announced he'd had enough and was not going to be spending his valuable time listening to tapes from us complaining about each other. The chairman of our respective stations decided to have a peace meeting where it was agreed that if we wanted to complain about each other, we first had to speak to our rival's chairman in the first instance. Only if we couldn't sort it out amicably would we go to the regulator. I agreed but it was not game over as far as I was concerned. I was just getting started. There is nothing I like better than a good scrap and this was my playground. This is what fired me up and motivated me greatly. Over a few weeks I turned up the pace a little. I had a giant poster installed at Newcastle Central train station, which simply read: *Welcome home to the biggest station in the North East. Century Radio.*

The boss of Metro FM saw this and nearly had a heart attack. He was livid and rang me up complaining that it was untrue. I was misleading the public and I must take it down immediately, he claimed. I told him to calm down. What I was saying was absolutely true. Newcastle **IS** the biggest train station in the North East. That's all my poster said. He did not like that at all and slammed the phone down. I laughed all day. He then paid money to have his own poster put up right beside mine which he called 'the facts'. This just high-lighted my own poster even more.

*

The Great North Run, Britain's biggest half-marathon that attracts more than fifty thousand charity runners, was coming up and Metro devised a brilliant marketing idea. They planned to place a huge ninety-six sheet poster just to the side of the Tyne Bridge. As the TV cameras pulled back to show the runners crossing the iconic bridge, their giant poster would be in full view of millions of television viewers. I admired Metro's concept but I couldn't allow it to happen. Century Radio had a double-decker bus totally covered in our logo and colours. In the trade it's called a full-bus wrap. Ours was brilliant yellow and you couldn't miss it. I hired the bus for the day of the Great North Run and told the driver to be outside my studios at nine o'clock that morning. I asked him if it would be possible to break-down in about thirty minutes time, just before the authorities closed all the roads off, and make it happen right in front of the giant Metro poster. He, of course, said there was no way he could do that but, after a little financial persuasion, quickly agreed. I also told him there was a 'Brucy Bonus' if he could ensure the bus couldn't be re-started for at least three hours.

'No problem,' he said.

Before the roads were closed off, I went home and switched on the TV. The moment came when the huge swell of runners came across the bridge and sure enough the camera panned back to see the wonderful scene. Then as the camera dropped back into the crowd there in full view was my broken-down bus in front of the Metro poster. I skipped across the room in delight.

'What a bloody result!' I shouted. Oh how I loved it even better when my phone started ringing. Metro were going berserk, accusing me of being unprofessional. On the contrary, I felt for them but how was I to know a bus would break down right there? It was a pure coincidence, I said innocently. They threatened to call the police. The very thought of the police receiving a call from Metro complaining about a broken down bus on the North East's busiest day of the year made me chuckle. The next day, I received a call from my chairman asking for my assurance that I had nothing to do with this piece of marketing warfare. Even he couldn't keep a straight face.

*

My friends in the Press have always told me that a headline is more important than the story. That's quite true. No one recalls if Freddie Starr really did eat that hamster but they all remember the headline. In a fight for media coverage, I focused on that objective more than anything else. Late in the Nineties, I heard Metro were going to ditch the name of their respected AM service, GNR Radio. I couldn't get it confirmed but on RAJAR day, when quarterly listening figures are published, the opportunity was too good to miss. Newcastle's paper, the Evening Chronicle, loved stories about the competitive fight between Metro and us but they were always baffled by the audience figures and in any case numbers are boring for readers. Stories are much better to focus on. I would talk about our regional listener numbers as that was the only figure we had, while Metro could only talk about the figure for their smaller Tyneside listenership area. Of course, on a like-for-like basis in Tyneside we were much smaller than Metro but we were making a bigger noise. The Chronicle would usually employ young and inexperienced reporters on a story like this and I loved convincing them that I was right and Metro were wrong.

Audience figures come out every three months. When the latest three-monthly figures were released our listenership had risen again while Metro had dropped, closing the gap even further to our advantage. I knew close analysis of numbers wouldn't cut it. We'd gone up a little and Metro had gone down a little but overall there was little difference. I pondered on how we could get more PR. I rewrote the headline on our press release to accompany the RAJAR listening figures to read: *Century kills off GNR*. I'd spun the story and Metro were livid, advising the Chronicle's reporters to ignore my 'idiotic Press release' and go with the more sober figures they were releasing, but Metro could not deny my scoop. In the end, the Press ran with my headline while putting the boring audience facts into the story. Many letters to the editor for clarification followed but I had won the war of words.

―――――――――― **40 second break...** ――――――――――

Fat Fred

At CFM, a brilliant sales lady popped her head around my door.
'Just letting you know I have an appointment to see Fat Fred.'
'Oh God,' I said. 'Only male sales people are allowed to see Fred, I can't let you go on your own.'
'Do you think I can't deal with him?' she asked. 'I've been selling advertising for two years to double-glazing reps and if I can deal with them I can handle people like Fred.'
I explained that the car dealer could be a little dodgy and was known to be rude and therefore I would much rather Darrell, our sales manager went with her.
'I don't need a man to come with me,' she protested. 'Fred really wants to see me and there's a big chance of an order.'
'You have no idea what you are letting yourself in for here,' I warned. 'If you insist on going, then I must insist that if there's any trouble, you'll just walk out and come straight back, do you understand?'
'Of course, thanks John.'
I called Darrell and told him, 'Get in your car and sit outside Fat Fred's office right now. If there's any trouble, go and sort it out. If she can make the order herself then let her have the glory but I want you close by.'
An hour later, the office door flew open. My first-rate sales girl was sobbing. Darrell followed her in with his hands in the air.
'I tried, John but she wouldn't listen.'
I pulled the rep into my office and got the story.
Fred, who was only 5ft 6in tall and the double for Jabba the Hutt from Star Wars, had told her she could have a thousand pounds of advertising but on one condition.
'Show me your tits,' he'd said, 'and I'll show you my cash'.

She promptly told him to sod off and came straight back as directed but despite her insistence that she could handle it, the whole episode had shocked her.

'That's the reason only men go to see Fred,' I explained. 'He's a dinosaur but you wouldn't listen. Now put this all down to experience and next time, pay heed to me when I give you some advice.'

'But he wants to advertise with the station,' she pleaded. 'I'm just a grand off hitting my target for the quarter.'

'You're barred from seeing Fred. Even if you'd had a signed order I wouldn't have taken it without a cheque. He's known for not paying, so just don't go there again.'

I offered her a deal, 'Look, if you get another £500 towards your monthly target, I'll pay you your quarterly bonus. How can I help you get it? Shall we work through your client list?'

The next day, she bounced into the office with both a signed order and a cheque from Fred, along with the copy for his advert.

'Please tell me you didn't show him your tits,' I pleaded.

'Absolutely not, John, I wouldn't do that.'

'Good. Thank God for that.'

'I refused to take my bra off!'

Nice girl.

*

I accepted Giles Squire's offer to meet for lunch. I like the man a lot as there have been very few programmers as good as him in my lifetime. He was a winner and I admired him from afar as I tried to work out his methods. Near the end of the meal, he brought up the reason for the lunch. It turned out he did not have a complaint. What he actually wanted was to hire me as the breakfast presenter for his station. I was stunned but delighted. I smiled and told him, 'Giles, having lunch with you is an enormous pleasure and I thank you for taking the time to do so. However, my answer to you is no. Absolutely not and always will be. It's clear you have forgotten an occasion that happened many years ago.'

I told him the story of my first meeting with him and his expert view that I would never make it in radio. Now, here he was telling me over lunch that I was a great talent, so brilliant he wanted me to join him in Swalwell and pay me top dollar. He seemed shocked as the memory of that meeting slowly came back.

No amount of money would take me to his stations, I said. But he should take comfort that this was one of the best days of my professional life. He had removed years of hurt that had always been there. Giles, of course, denies my account of this story but, as I was the recipient, it's something I can never forget. That said, he is someone I would have liked to have worked with at some stage because I suspect he could have taught me things I didn't know. Giles now lives in France and will always be a giant of UK radio in my eyes.

*

To be successful on the air, you have to talk about things that connect with people. There were many local celebrities on TV in the North East and the king of them all was Mike Neville. He'd just moved from the BBC to Tyne Tees in a mega-deal after the colourful Bruce Gyngell took charge. Alongside Mike, were two other well-known names. Pam Royle, an excellent presenter and journalist who always seems to wear purple, and local weatherman, Bob Johnson. I used to pull their legs on my show and, kindly suggested that the glass of water next to Pam on the TV set was really neat gin. They also had a sports producer, Roger Tames. He was the double of famous TV ventriloquist, Roger De Courcey and was often the butt of many a joke. I always suspected Roger absolutely hated me for that, which, of course, made me do it even more. People with no humour whatsoever are often more comical than those who can see the funny side.

*

Tyne Tees asked me to join them on the air so often that I became a regular fixture. As I'd already spent three years on TV at Border, it was nothing that I couldn't handle and my humour came over rather well. In a big fanfare, Tyne Tees decided to change the format of their evening show and created a new programme, that they imaginatively called Tonight, headed up by Ingrid Hagemann, a lovely young blonde presenter from Metro Radio. Tonight had been a mess from the start and was failing badly. It was certainly not Ingrid's fault. This was a live show that required someone of much greater experience to host it. On top of this, the format, content, and guests were just not good enough and Tyne Tees needed to change it.

*

In February, 1996, I took a call from Graeme Thompson, the overall programming guru at Tyne Tees. He knew the TV programme was failing and thought I'd be ideal for his plans to save it, especially as my name had scored well in some research they'd carried out. I was flattered, who wouldn't be, but I also knew that TV was not for me. I'd got TV out of my system years ago and had no desire to be back on the box full-time. However, doing this show would be fantastic PR for the station and I wondered if it would possible to do both. I rang my immediate boss, Peter Brownlow at Border and talked him through it.

'John, you're currently the Group MD, you're also MD of Century NE,' he said. 'You present a daily breakfast show, you sit on our main radio board and you are applying for licences across the UK. There is no time for this in your life. It would just be too much and I'm afraid you have to decide, TV or radio. If you choose the former, then of course we would understand. If Tyne Tees would let you do one night a week then maybe it might work but you can't be involved anything more than that.'

I rang Peter back the next day and said that as I'd built up the company with him, I wouldn't be leaving for a TV show that was failing. In any case, I loved what I was doing. He was delighted and told me to choose a car of my choice as a thank you. That was a lovely gesture but I made a huge cock-up in picking the same car as Peter, a Honda Legend. He did say pick any car but it was clear this was a bad move on my part. Although Peter never said anything, I could sense it was a source of irritation. I'd never do that again and would never advise anyone else to do the same, either.

Graeme Thompson at Tyne Tees was very understanding,

although I did do a number of the Friday night shows for them and we remain friends today.

*

My third offer came in December, 1997, but it was much more difficult to refuse. When I'd worked at Red Rose Radio in Preston in the early Eighties, one of the rising stars was Dee Ford, a beautiful and extremely talented woman who was, and still is, magnificent. Over the years she rose within the company to become the boss of the whole radio group. Dee's a wonderful motivator of people and was always my strongest competitor whenever we worked in the same markets.

One day, Dee called and asked me to meet her for lunch at a restaurant near Sheffield. I liked her, so agreed and during the meal she threw me an offer that was hard to refuse. The giant publishing group EMAP owned a number of local radio stations and Dee planned to air the first network commercial radio breakfast show. It would broadcast across the whole of the north of England including the North East, Yorkshire, Humberside, Merseyside, Lancashire and Greater Manchester. The potential audience was millions and she wanted me to do that show. This was amazing. Dee pressed all the right buttons and my ego was flattered. However, we would be broadcasting only on AM but the loss of FM would be compensated by a semi-network show and a large financial sum. She knew it would have to be large enough to matter but I was unaware of just how large it was going to go.

*

In any deal I always negotiate the money last. In fact, I never even raise the issue until everything creatively is sorted first, otherwise the cash will never be enough. I've never had a problem talking money with people but I've always insisted that a money meeting should be a stand-alone meeting with nothing else on the table. It focuses the mind if everything else is agreed. Furthermore, it allows you to aim higher as everyone is excited about the plan and won't lose the deal for just a bit of cash. At the time we were only discussing the idea and I must admit I liked it. AM was still doing big numbers in those days and the thought of being ahead of the game and going out on a large network was interesting. I asked for time to consider the idea, as this would be a huge step forward. In further meetings we agreed a management role within the company but I was not stupid enough to think it would be a meaningful one as they only really wanted me for the breakfast show. I would have to be comfortable about leaving a company I'd started from scratch but I did not dismiss the idea. A few days later I called her back as I wanted to be clear about the network offer. In short, I sought assurances that it was a 'done-deal' not just work in progress. We met the following week where she hit me with a deal that had the potential to be life changing.

First, Dee explained that the network show was eighty per cent done, although she expected it to be a hundred per cent within the year. Just one more station needed to be brought into line, she said, although she was confident it could be delivered. This was not what I was expecting. By any measure, eighty per cent is not a done deal. I wanted to know who was stalling, what was the problem, who needed convincing and how this could be resolved before we did anything else? Lots of questions but not a lot of answers. She wouldn't reveal the station and I didn't press too hard. I knew I could find out by other means. I got back to Newcastle and did some digging. I called a few friends high up in EMAP, as I was sure this would have been discussed internally. Radio is such a small community that it's almost always possible to find something out. It became clear that the AM station holding out just happened to be the biggest in their group, Piccadilly Radio. The man who ran this station was the one and only Dave Lincoln, the brains behind the success of Red Rose and someone I admire greatly. He was now the regional boss of EMAP Radio in the North West and was a brilliant operator. His view was that his own local breakfast show was doing rather well thank you very much and while he thought I was a great jock, he certainly didn't need Morgan in the Morning to come in and save it. While others had come into line Dave had not and, to be fair to him, he was right. I suspected Dee hoped I'd present the show for a while, increase the audience and then use that data to convince Dave to make the change. However, Dee was honest in that there were no guarantees and, in any case, Dave Lincoln was an important figure in the group at the time. He also delivered big profits and that gives you power.

Dee and I met again to discuss how to resolve the problem. The reality was that she couldn't. Dee, Dave and me had all been together at Red Rose in the golden years and we all knew each other well. When I think of all the national talent that has come out of the North West over the years it was an amazing breeding ground for those who would lead the industry for many years. Red Rose, Piccadilly Radio and Radio City were tremendous stations and enormously successful. I told Dee that I was going off the proposal as I really needed Manchester, the biggest AM station in the whole portfolio at the time, to be on board from day one. I fully understood why Dave would not want to to be part of a network.

Then she got to the money. This deal would be worth a staggering one million pounds to me. That's right. A million quid! Plus, I could present the show from Newcastle and didn't have to move. I just sat there.

Wow. This really was a great deal. More money than I'd ever been offered before and much, much greater than I was on at the time. It was a wonderful gesture on her part but she was doing this from a business perspective and she knew that figure would get me to a moment of pause. I was really pissed off with her believe it or not. I had come to say 'no thanks' but now she had hit me with a great reason to say 'yes'. I have often talked to people about the way she operates and I learned a phrase from her at that meeting that I would use myself years later.

She said, 'John, tell me how you are going to handle the counter offer from Border? We know they love you and they have built their business on the back of your talent. We want you to come, which is why we are making this offer but we don't want to be used as a stalking horse to just get you more cash if you really want to stay where you are?'

Always the saleswoman, she was closing me. I told her that if I was coming, I was coming. I would not ask Border to match this but I was concerned that I was leaving a great company, a company I had given birth to and also I was leaving an FM radio station. In turn, she was offering me a much bigger broadcasting platform, even though Manchester was not included. It was also on AM but she was more than making up for that with a wonderful financial deal. I gave her my word that if I said I was coming, I would honour that commitment.

I asked her to put the offer in writing. I still have that letter and many people will wonder why I didn't take the deal. Interestingly, I was closer to accepting it than they thought. I drove back to the North East and rang around a few more friends within EMAP. It was not common news it seemed and it was clear that Dee was being absolutely up-front about everything. I thought about ringing Dave Lincoln personally and chatting about the problem but decided this was something she had to sort out, not me. I talked this deal over with John Simons along with Peter Brownlow, at Border, who was also someone we went out to dinner with a lot. I explained the position to Peter and told him this was not me talking to him as a boss but as a friend. He replied that it was a fantastic offer and that Border would never match that deal. Considering it was nearly three times my current salary I had never expected them to. What was really bugging me was the lack of share options at Border. Other people in radio who were connected to Border through radio stations like Scot FM and Radio 106 in Nottingham had share options in place but they had never been offered to me. If I refused the EMAP offer would they at least try and sort this out in the future, I wondered. I didn't want any promises as such, just a commitment to review it. Peter gave me that commitment, although it wasn't certain that I was going to stay.

*

I loved being on the air but I was also a deal maker. I liked running radio stations and empowering people to achieve their own success. I passionately believe that if you can make other people successful, then that success also rolls over into your own world. The deal was a good one but I was not sure I could remain a jock for long, without inter-fering with the overall station output.

In the end, it was a comment from someone I knew well at Metro Radio that finally made my mind up. Over lunch, he told me that this was a double win for them. Morgan would be moved onto AM and it would also hurt Century at the same time.

'You're a pain in the arse, to put it bluntly,' he stated. He was right and it was just the reason I needed to walk away from the EMAP deal. John Simons thought I was mad to turn it down. However, Dee was magnificent about it all. She's such a pro and takes these things in her stride. As events would prove, it was the right decision for both parties.

Chapter Fourteen

TROUBLE AT THE TOP

I did eventually give up the breakfast show on Century to be replaced by Paul Gough, an exciting jock who would not only build the audience even higher but could talk for England. Goffy, as he was known, had an engaging and infectious personality, was totally shameless and best of all was always up for stunts. When he worked as my assistant on the breakfast show he would do anything. He even dressed up as a pink pig and stood on all the famous bridges across the North East giving out pork pies. We called him the Pink Porker and, every morning during the breakfast show, we'd go to him live to wherever that day's pork pies give-away was going to be. It's hard to imagine today how that promotion would ever get to air but Century was all about doing things differently. Goffy was brilliant at getting people to talk and was also a fine broadcaster in his own right. We gave him his own Saturday morning show and he would often come into the studio carrying a giant bag over his shoulder. When management weren't looking, he'd play songs from his own personal record collection. John Simons and I were happy to let him get away with it because it made the station more appealing, as our musical offering was very different to other stations.

I'd been at Border TV for some years and the business about my
share options had still not been sorted out. Phantom share options, as
they called it, was the new way to be rewarded at the time. It was a tool
management could use to reward success without paying out cash. In
my case I kept asking and they kept declining or at best, saying 'not yet'!

However, the whole game changed when we won the radio licence
for the North West. For some reason, I was not keen on applying and
so we left it very late to put in a credible application. I really thought
it was a fruitless task as the North West was the most hotly contested
licence in the UK. By the time we entered the race the chance of
obtaining any reasonable support or a credible board was low. In came
Kath Worrall and, to be fair to her, she did a great job in turning my
dire early stage application into something respectable. In those days,
part of the process involved being interviewed over the telephone by
David Vick, the Deputy Chief Executive at the Radio Authority. Peter
Brownlow and I had prepared well for the questions the Authority
threw at us about the application, the finance, and who would run the
station. However, we had not a single letter of support and we knew
this would be difficult to defend, although we came up with a stance
that our application was based on experience, merit and track record.
It was impossible to gain support when there were so many applicants
in the process, we said. In this case, we believed the support of our
parent company, Border TV, was the only support worth having. The
interview had gone well, I thought, and I told Peter we were very much
in the running, although I had no reason whatsoever for saying it.

Soon after, I was asked to outline my thoughts to the board on all
the twenty-one runners and riders for the North West licence. I had, of
course, read them all by this time and could usually sort out the good
from the bad. In my view we were about the third worst. Not because
it was unprofessional but because our support and lateness in getting
our act together meant we were simply not in the same league as the
one submitted from Chrysalis, headed by my good friend Phil Riley.

'However,' I stated. 'On paper our application is well down the
list but I believe our chance of winning is actually much higher up the

scale. We have a great track record and the analysis of the questions we fielded from David Vick was quite positive in my view. Also, I have a gut feel. I wouldn't back a horse on that but we're not out of the game.'

*

On award day, 5 February 1998, I was sitting in my office waiting for the arranged 5 pm call from the regulators. At 4.57 pm the phone rang. We'd won! I'll never forget that call because I later wrote every word of it in my diary: *'John, this is David Vick. Congratulations, you have just won the most sought-after radio licence in the UK.'*

I was so emotional everyone stopped what they were doing to join in this moment of elation. I even hugged clients I'd never met before, who were in the boardroom next door. I called Peter Brownlow with the news just as he was coming off a train and he was shouting with delight, too.

*

I don't drink. In fact, I never have. There's no particular reason for this. I just haven't found an alcoholic drink I like. Considering I take life to excess, I've even heard people say, 'Thank God for that!' That evening, I took a call from Jim Graham, the CEO of our parent company, Border. He was coming over to give me a bonus and to thank me personally. Remember, this was the most prized possession in UK radio. The biggest licence in the country, worth at least twenty million pounds right there and then and we had bagged it against amazing competition and with zero letters of support. The Radio Authority spent a lot of time explaining this decision to other parties later on but we didn't care. Amazingly, the radio division of Border was now bigger than the TV company itself. What a masterstroke by Jim and Peter to get into radio. They had transformed their business model and collectively we were on a roll. Jim turned up as promised and we hugged, laughed and celebrated. He showered me with warm and lovely words of praise. Then, he said he wanted to give me something. I thought it must be a large cheque. Far from it. Instead, Jim brought out a bottle of whisky he'd grabbed from the BTV cupboard. We'd won the biggest licence and I got a bottle of whisky – granted it was special stuff – but as I didn't drink it was pretty pointless. However, the gesture was a good one. I never said a word and decided to let it be for a few days.

*

The following month I sent a note to Border's senior management explaining my position and asking for a bonus. After a few debates, we got to a point where I was happy but we were still miles off any share options being offered, although they did promise again to sort it out. That was good enough for me. My PD, John Simons, had taken the opportunity to move to London to start a new job as Programme Director of the national station Talk Radio, now TalkSPORT. I started to prepare for the big move to Manchester but refused to move home. Linda and I loved the North East and were determined to remain there. One morning, I received a call from the BBC. They wanted to come and see me about a TV programme they were airing, called Trouble at the Top. It was a fly-on-the-wall documentary series and they wanted to follow the launch of our new station. The programme would show the problems we encountered launching a radio station in the most competitive market outside of London and how we dealt with the competition. The producer of this programme was Sue Bourne and the executive producer was Mark Thompson, later to become the Director General of the BBC. This was where I first met him and that connection was to help a lot in future years.

The station's format would be similar to our operation in the North East, with around fifty per cent speech in peak time. The Radio Authority's decision to give us the licence had not gone down too well with our competitors. They were fuming. It was all so unfair and, on reflection, I am amazed we won it, too. In the end it was a simple decision by the regulator. As I understand it, the Authority were left with two applications on the table. It was a choice between a radio station that played music all day, Chrysalis, or a radio station that played the same type of music but had a lot more news and speech included in the output. They chose us but it was that close.

*

I pride myself on being able to hire great people. It's one of my key talents and people I've hired have often stayed with me for years. It is the secret to any great business. I decided to replace John Simons with Graham Ledger from TFM radio in Teesside. Not one of my best decisions, I must admit. Graham was a good music PD but it soon became clear we were not meant for each other. He was also a little off the wall and I suspected the worst when he bragged he could eat glass and ride a Harley-Davidson motorbike up the stairs of our studio building. His first full day on the job was to meet me in Dallas, to record the new jingle package at JAM studios. I'm obsessed with jingles but Graham wasn't and to me that was a big sin. As a result, I took a more hands-on approach to programming and made sure Graham was not left to his own devices. This was too big a station to allow him a free hand. Every time you hire the wrong person, it is always your fault. When I hear managers blaming the person they hired when things go wrong, it's a sure sign of weakness. It was not Graham's fault, it was my own and I knew it. He's actually a very nice guy.

One of those big decisions was the appointment of a lunchtime phone-in host. I knew *what* I wanted but I didn't know *who*. Whoever it was, they had to have a bit of spark. Simo called and said he'd recently used a guy called Derek Hatton at Talk Radio and he was good. I called Derek and arranged to meet, although I was aware he came with a lot of baggage from his former life as a controversial left-wing councillor in Liverpool. For over an hour or so we talked radio, his life, his view of certain topics and I became convinced he'd be great. On top of that, I liked him. I have never hired anyone I didn't like. You can have talent, you can have the best education but if I didn't like you there was no chance of a job. I hire people first and talent second. I spent more time with my work colleagues than I did with my family so it was important to at least work with people I could get on with. In this case, I simply didn't care about Derek's past as a politician. All I cared about was the future and, if I knew anything about radio, this guy could get the

phones ringing. He had an opinion about everything and could hold a
reasonable line on any subject going. Perfect!

At that very first meeting, I hired Derek for a one-hour daily
phone-in show. He wanted to do two hours but I wouldn't let him.
That was a step too far and, in any case, we only needed one hour
of speech at lunchtime to meet our format requirements. This was all
going on as the BBC cameras followed our every move. I signed a deal
with them that they could come anywhere at any time, except meetings of a personal nature and, of course, board meetings. Anything else
was open for filming. To be honest, Derek was initially hard work in
the studio. He was skilled at many things but he was miles off being a
broadcaster. His skill was in being a communicator and that was the
key to his success but I needed to get him up to speed fast. The cameras
loved this and they filmed hours of me trying to teach him how the
desk worked. I've very little time for presenters who can't drive their
own desk. It's laziness, although Graham Ledger kept asking me to
provide Derek with a tech-op. I wouldn't hear of it. I was so glad I
persevered as Derek was simply superb on the air and his clumsiness
at times endeared him to the audience even more, although he very
much divided opinion, even on my own board. When I announced
who was presenting the lunchtime show, there were some worried
faces. Six months after launch when the audience figures came out the
decision was proved right. Derek had, what we in programming loved
to call 'the penis on the page effect'. Derek would come on air at noon,
the listener figures would shoot up and, when he left an hour later,
the audience would drop back to normal. When Kelvin MacKenzie
bought Talk Radio, he hired Degsy for mid-mornings. Once again
it underlined to me the importance of content. Radio stations think
music is the only route to success. For brands that may be correct but
for radio to work it has to engage listeners at all levels. The audience
have to want to listen, they have to turn from passive to active and
that was what Century was doing. We were making our mark. Degsy,
as everybody called him, was riding high. Mind you, I did pull the
first advertising campaign for his show when it was presented to me. I

looked at it and told them straight. There was no way I would endorse that poster on the buses of the North West. Furthermore, I was not sure the bus company would even accept the copy. The proposal for the campaign was: *mass-debate with Derek Hatton.*

Even for a maverick like me, that was a step too far.

---

30 second break...

WARNING ... WE APOLOGISE FOR THE FRUITY LANGUAGE IN THIS COMMERCIAL BREAK

Excuses, Excuses

Every quarter the regulator publishes a list of complaints received about radio stations. I always spend twenty minutes going through it because it is a highly amusing read. However, even I had to gasp at one radio station's response to a complaint. To this day, it's one of the best ever.

Brick FM, the community radio station for St Boswells, in the Borders of Scotland, played a song with the word fuck in the lyrics. Clearly, this is one of the regulator's top ten naughty words and it soon received complaints from listeners. First thing the regulator does when this happens is to write to the radio station and ask for their comments. This station's response was majestic. First of all, they claimed, the word 'fuck' was not that offensive because it was a commonly used term in Scotland.

I loved that.

The regulator effectively told them in that case they wouldn't mind being told to fuck off and come up with a better answer, (although they used different words) but they also wanted a reply on a song that contained the following line...

"I like to see the girls in the sexy bikini ni ni // Want to take my chilli and push it between ni ni // "I like pun-na-na-na-ni even if it's a virgin."

Punany or punani is an urban slang word for female genitalia. All the station had to do was apologise for this and give some assurance that they would take steps to ensure tighter control of the songs they played in the future. At best it was a slap on the wrist. The station's management decided not to do that. Instead, they assumed the old sods within the regulator would have no idea what the words in the lyrics really meant and gambled with an all-time classic excuse:

'Punany is a sandwich sold locally, made of Italian bread with cheese and tomato which is heated up. Therefore we do not accept the song "More Punany" has sexual connotations.'

With a wry smile, one wag from Media UK replied: 'I think you'll find that's a panini.'

As lame excuses go, that's genius. In fact, it should win the Best Excuse of the Year.

*

I desperately needed something really big for the launch. My top objective was the commentary rights from Manchester United. However, the main man running the club wouldn't see me. His PA kept giving me messages that they had a deal in place with BBC Manchester and Piccadilly Radio. I kept asking for a meeting to table my own proposal but kept being told no. I was getting really frustrated until one day I heard it was the boss's birthday. I sent over one hundred inflated balloons, which totally filled his office and the club entrance. The private line on my desk rang. It was Peter Kenyon, probably the best Chief Executive of any football club in the country, a real gent but a tough negotiator. 'John, what is it you want?' he asked in exasperation.

'I just want ten minutes with you, Peter. as I have an offer you will find hard to refuse. If you don't like what I propose you won't hear from me again.'

'Done, meet me at eight o'clock tomorrow morning.' he said.

I turned up in his office at Old Trafford and got straight to the point.

'We're a regional radio station launching next month,' I explained. 'We want exclusive commentary rights for your club. We know you have a deal with the BBC and Piccadilly Radio but we're prepared to pay more than you're getting from both parties combined. As a regional station we can offer more in return, your fan base is regional, not just confined to Manchester.'

I thought I'd be honest and added, 'I need this deal and I need it to work for both of us and that means you'll get my undivided attention. Best of all, you'll have a brilliant radio partner. The bones of my proposal are this: I'd like a four-year exclusive radio deal. In return, you tell me what I have to pay and I'll simply say yes or no. I won't even attempt to negotiate. If you make the asking price too high then I assume you just don't want our business but if you pitch it just right I'll simply say yes or no. That's it, that's the proposal.'

In effect, I was now asking Peter Kenyon to give me a figure rather than me propose one. By all accounts he was getting about one hundred thousand pounds a year for radio rights and I was happy to pay perhaps fifty per cent more.

'If I understand you correctly, you want me to tell you how much and then you will say yes or no,' Peter said.

'That's correct. I'm not here to negotiate, I am here to do the deal,' I replied.

That was assuming, of course, he wanted to work with a new radio partner. He'd never heard of us before and it's always a hassle to change but I could see he was pondering.

'Is there anything else you wish me to consider before I make my decision?' he asked.

This man was a class act, I thought. My ace card in this game of poker was high risk and had the potential to kill the deal completely. That said, I knew the people involved at our competitor stations and I thought it was worth planting a seed of doubt in his mind.

'Peter, before you make your decision I would like you to consider this,' I said. 'I want this deal. Everyone in town knows I want this deal. My competitors know I'm in the area and wherever I've launched a station I've done so with commentary rights. They must know that I'll be trying to buy these rights from you. I'm willing to bet they think you'll never switch to us. I'm willing to bet they feel so secure of your business they've not even considered you might see me or change media partners. I'll also bet they haven't even told you how important this partnership is to their own business. When was the last time they called to say thank you or even sent you a simple letter of appreciation? If they have been in touch and done all of those things then you already have a great media partner and this is just a cash proposal. Personally, I like to work with partners with a common interest.'

Then I shut up.

Peter sat there and smiled. 'Okay,' he said. 'For a four-year exclusive commentary deal we will require a fee of £250,000 per season, one million pounds in total'.

I pondered. Inside, I was thinking, 'Oh God, that's a lot of cash. This would blow a big hole in my £750,000 marketing budget for the year. On the flip side, there was no greater marketing deal than this. It would mean the only way fans could hear commentary from Old Trafford was to turn that radio dial to us. This was the holy grail of radio marketing. I told Peter he had a deal. He stood up. I had to sign within twenty-four hours, he said. I was happy to sign right there and then but had to see a contract first. Until then, we agreed to keep it confidential. I certainly didn't want this to come out before it was signed and sealed. I called my boss, Peter Brownlow, who immediately hit the gas and air.

'How much?' he shouted.

'Don't worry this is a superb deal. It's just marketing.' I said and Peter was enormously supportive. About four o'clock in the afternoon Peter Kenyon called on my direct line.

'John, can you come and see me?' he asked. Oh God, what had happened?

When I arrived in his office I said, 'Hey, Peter, I've tried for weeks to get to see you and nothing, now I see you twice in a day.'

'I've had a thought,' he said 'How about if I give you the commentary rights for free?'

Peter had my attention but surely something was coming around the corner that was going to hit me hard?

'Look,' he said. 'I'm launching a new executive suite for the really big brands and the cost of a table is £250,000 a season for eight places. I want you to be the first client of that room. In return I'm going to give you the commentary rights as part of that deal but it will be in effect free of charge.

'That works for me,' I said. Even better from my perspective, I thought. Until then I had no tickets to Old Trafford, now I had commentary rights and the best seats in the house. 'There must be something else?' I ventured.

'There is,' he said. 'We've been thinking internally and we all feel that we can do without Piccadilly Radio if you are involved but we really can't boot out BBC Radio Manchester. They've been really supportive in the past and are much more a news station than a competitor for you. Can you help us out?'

I had to think fast. This was not the deal I had in mind but you cannot say a blank no as it was a request and he had played a brilliant card in offering me more. I made a mental note that some time in the future, I was going to attend the school where Peter Kenyon learned the art of negotiation. He was the best and I knew I was learning from a master.

'Peter, I understand your predicament,' I said, 'but we can only pay this amount of money if we can sell the rights on our station to a big sponsor.'

He understood that. Exclusivity is the key to price and we need the best price in order to pay the fee we have agreed. He knew that, too.

'However, I can see you might be in a little difficulty,' I said, 'and our big win is that we are the commercial radio exclusive content owners.'

I offered a compromise. We would be willing to let BBC Manchester have second-half commentary rights, provided we were exclusive from kick-off. He liked that idea and we shook hands.

I was still a little confused about why he wanted the contract to state commentary rights were FOC?

'You were right,' he conceded. 'We've had no contact with Piccadilly Radio and that's been more than a little disappointing, to be honest. So we're going to enjoy telling them we've given you the deal free of charge.'

'Can I sit in on that call?' I asked with a smile. I left the room and did a little hop, skip and a jump as I departed Old Trafford. We signed the deal and the Press launch was great. Piccadilly were fuming, although the truth was we only got the deal because they'd partly cocked up and we'd paid more money. The golden rule to be learned from this is that you must thank your customers for their business and keep thanking them. Customers go where they are invited and remain where they are loved. Piccadilly had failed to do the simple things and took both the club and us for granted. I wanted to rub salt into the wounds and just couldn't pass up this opportunity. As Group Managing Director, MD of Century North West and host of the station's breakfast show, I should have been much more grown up and mature. No one else in my position would have come up with this madness but sometimes you just have to do stuff for the sheer fun of it.

I called up our advertising agency and told them I wanted an advertising lorry, with a poster on each side, to arrive outside in two days time. I gave them the script. They loved it and promised the van driver would be outside Century at seven o'clock on the morning in question. When the driver arrived, I repeated my old trick and gave him two hundred quid to break down right outside Piccadilly Radio's studios. He had to do it at peak time between 8.30 and 9.30am. I wanted their staff and management to see everything. I got a call from my old Red Rose colleague Dave Shearer, who by then was working as the PD at Piccadilly.

'Team, what the hell are you up to, man?' he asked. 'The bosses here are going absolutely nuts!' He was laughing his head off. 'You've got to get that truck off the road. Look, officially I'm saying it's bloody terrible but, honestly, it's a fantastic stunt.'

The truck, broken down outside Piccadilly Radio had plastered on one side: '*Who's not singing any more?*'

The other side read: '*It's all gone quiet over there*'.

I'd called up my dear friend Mark Dodson at the Manchester Evening News and told him to have a photographer there to get a picture. It was a wonderful stunt. Great days. Fun days.

It was a golden time for us to take over the commentary rights as it was the year Manchester United won the Champions League with two goals near the end of the game. The excitement of that game, with people dancing on the streets of Manchester, was quite special. One funny moment came when our sales director, Julian Carter phoned in from outside the ground. He had taken some of our prestigious clients along to the game and it was all kicking off. So we asked him if he could provide a colour piece, which in broadcasting terms just meant explaining what you see to allow our listeners to visualise the picture in their own minds. It was a stark reminder of the perils of asking a non-broadcaster to do this, as Julian totally forgot he was on the air. Halfway through his live piece someone hit him on the head. Instead of ignoring it, he shouted down the phone and indeed across the North West 'I've just been twatted by a bloody copper on a horse...'

*

The BBC documentary crew caught all of this on camera but they were not getting involved in my PR stupidity. They wanted to concentrate on the business side of things, and the events surrounding the launch itself. One day, the documentary's producer, Sue Bourne, came into my office.

'John, we have a problem,' she said. 'Our documentary is called Trouble at the Top and, so far, we can't find any trouble. This programme is turning out to be a forty-minute advertising feature for the station.'

'What's wrong with that?' I said with a smile. The problem, she stated, was that the programme was supposed to be about watching people solve business issues and problems.

'We need to be watching you sorting out problems and if there's no trouble, the show might not get to air.'

Furthermore, Lesley Douglas at BBC Radio 2 was going nuts internally about this programme. Lesley and I were friends but big competitors. When I told her the BBC were doing this show, she went white.

'What, the BBC are going out of their way to promote our biggest competitor?' she protested.

'Yes', I said, 'isn't that lovely?'

She went off to cause a stink but all I could smell was brilliant PR.

I explained to Sue, the producer of the programme, that this was my fourth launch of a radio station and by this time I knew exactly what to do. We had a critical path to follow and all was going to plan.

'But if you want trouble,' I said, 'you'd better come with me to our sister station in Nottingham. Ron Coles has just departed as MD there and I'm now in charge of the station, which has recently been rebranded from Radio 106 to Century 106. There are going to be some big changes at that station so if you want trouble, you'll have to widen the scope of the programme a little and follow me to Nottingham.'

'Brilliant,' she said, 'we'll follow you down tomorrow.'

As we entered the station in Nottingham with a camera crew filming over my shoulder, I overheard the receptionist saying to Sue on camera, 'Every time Mr Myers comes here, someone gets fired'.

Oh great, I thought. The producer was delighted, a promising start in her eyes. There was a lot going on and I met a number of staff and it was good but not explosive TV. Sue Bourne was happier but not yet delighted. She kept asking what was happening and could she film it. I nipped out to the loo and when I came out the presenter of the religious programme was waiting for me.

'When can we talk about my programme?' she asked.

I replied that 'today was not a good day' to see me. I had a film crew with me and as my news to her was perhaps not what she wanted, it would be best to wait a few days. Her reply took me off guard.

'I'm perfectly capable of accepting bad news, Mr Myers', she said firmly.

'Umm, okay,' I said, 'Give me two minutes and then come into my office.'

I walked back into the room and told the film crew to start filming. What happened next turned out to be on the promo for the whole show and whenever people talk to me about this programme they always remember this part. Not everything was included in the final edit but here is what really happened that day:

Knock on the door.

'John, I wonder if you could tell me what's happening with the religious programme?'

'Yes, I can and thank you for coming to see me. I've had a look at the show and the audience figures. The audience for your programme is not good, in fact, there's an asterisk against it. This means the figures are so low they can't be counted and therefore we can't sell any airtime around that.'

I then said something I regret to this day, 'Even God's not listening'.

There was a shocked look on her face. Clearly this had not gone down too well and we had a discussion as to how the religious programme could survive in a new form but my mind was made up.

'I'm really sorry about this,' I said finally, 'but I've decided to keep God but lose you. Sadly, we just can't make this work.'

As she left the office the phone rang. I picked it up, glanced at the camera and said, 'This is God on the phone right now...'

The producer was delighted. 'That's it John, now we have the making of a great show.' Interestingly, Paul Corley the head of programmes at Border TV was not at all in favour of the BBC documentary idea. He was deeply worried the Beeb would cut it in such a way that it would make us look bad. I thought there was no such thing as bad Press and, in any case, I was sure Sue Bourne was a professional and wouldn't do that. The end result was just that, an honest reflection of life at that time.

—————————— **20 second break...** ——————————

Rolling Stones

The Rolling Stones were coming to Manchester and we wanted to plug their gig but it was always going to be a sell out. The promoter didn't need Century Radio but plugging major artists always sounds great on air. Instead of paying us cash in return for our on-air plug for the band, the promoter promised my management team and a few others a meet and greet with the Rolling Stones. Brilliant, that will do for me!

We turned up at the MEN Arena and were immediately ushered into a room where we were told to stand in a set position and not to move an inch. They then took a picture of us. This would later be super imposed onto the main picture if one of us had blinked.

The Stones were coming and we had to stand perfectly still. The band arrived, two pictures were taken and they left. That was it. That picture is in this book and still has pride of place on my wall.

The whole thing took no longer than twenty seconds. Agreement fulfilled. It was the shortest meeting I've ever had.

*

Trouble at the Top went out to great reviews and Century North West was doing well but I was not happy. I was falling out with Border big time over my share options. I went to a meeting where, over the space of two hours, we discussed the value of the radio assets for ninety per cent of the time and the operational part of our business took up just ten per cent. You didn't need to be gifted to work out that Border were preparing for a possible sale and my share options still hadn't been agreed. There was only one possible buyer for the TV assets, Granada, while the real value of the company was in its radio stations. Border's value was rising.

*

In the end I found out, quite by accident actually, that I was being given incorrect information regarding who in the company had been getting share options and how much. How true this all was became difficult to know but it was an issue that could not be overcome in my eyes. It was time to depart for fresh pastures. My trust in them had gone and I felt they had become exhausted with my constant moaning on this subject. To be fair to the board at Border, they did come back with an offer of share options at the last minute but I found myself getting quite upset about the way it had all been handled. Things got quite emotional and when you're in the thick of it like this, it can often tear friendships apart and that was starting to happen. On reflection I could have handled myself better, too. This was not a good period but exiting a company rarely goes to plan.

I told Border I was off and they had to replace me with three people – a breakfast presenter, an MD and a group MD. In any case, Border was soon sold for £151m. The radio division was worth £101m while the TV operation was valued at just £50 million. If I'd accepted the last-minute deal on the table I would have walked away with about a million pounds in cash but it was pointless thinking about what might have been. I'd already agreed a move to Guardian Media Group. This time, I'd learned from past mistakes. My new deal was right from the start.

Chapter Fifteen

HELLO GMG AND REAL RADIO

Mark Dodson was a skilled former rugby player with a face to match and a body made of steel. He was the Deputy MD of the Manchester Evening News and, in my eyes, the powerhouse behind its success. He was the first person to call me when I arrived in the city to launch Century in the North West. He was obviously keen to find out what we were planning. From that first meeting we clicked and he's been a life-long friend ever since. We share the same sense of humour, love of life and work ethic. During Century's first year, we worked together on a range of projects where we promoted our respective interests. Mark was actually the first person in Guardian Media Group to come up with the idea of getting into local radio and he'd managed to become involved with a number of licence bids around the Greater Manchester area. None of these was successful but that's because he was aiming too low. Directly after Trouble at the Top went out on television, Mark called and asked me to a meeting with his group Finance Director, Nick Castro. Nick was a straight-to-the point guy, with a wicked sense of humour and therefore fun to watch. I remember him in later years explaining to an executive at The Guardian that the paper's circulation was falling so fast, while costs remained high, that they now had a journalist for every two hundred readers. Nick wanted me to join GMG and do for them exactly what I'd done for Border. This was perfect timing as I was ready for another challenge but I had to get the approval of their company's Chief Executive.

*

Bob Phillis was legendary in the world of media, a giant of his generation. A former Deputy DG of the BBC, he was incredibly well connected and greatly admired. The moment I walked into his office, he reminded me of my dad and we seemed to hit it off. I later discovered he'd telephoned Jim Moir, the boss of Radio 2, for a reference and the man was kind enough to give me a glowing report, even though I'd never met him before. In our meeting, Bob asked how many licences I was confident of winning. I thought we could confidently win three and told him so.

'Really?' he said. 'I love your optimism and if you believe that, I assume you have no issue striking an arrangement that reflects that confidence.'

The deal we struck was actually a very high risk, very high rewards arrangement but I like that kind of deal. In addition Nick wanted a 'dead-end' to the deal, meaning if we hadn't won anything in eighteen months that would be it. I would leave with nothing, not even a pay-off.

*

In April, 1999, GMG Radio was created with just three employees, including myloveable PA, Joanne Riordan, and a great character called Jon Hewson, who was our commercial director. We based ourselves at the Manchester Evening News in Deansgate, where I thought I was going to get an office on the top floor with carpets and lovely furniture. Instead I was given a shit-hole in the basement, well out of the way of any trouble. Looking back, it was a good decision.

There were two regional radio licences up for grabs. The first was in South Wales and the other in the West Midlands. In the application, you had to prove your station would widen listener choice and you did that through a combination of research and support. Furthermore, if you could find a suitable location you could get permission to run a short test of your proposed service to a small part of the community, through what they called a twenty-eight-day restricted service licence. In Wales, we were too late to do this but we did find a perfect location in Sutton Coldfield for the West Midlands application. I hired the whole of the top floor of a local hotel, chosen because it was the highest point in the town. The hotel wanted payment up front so I put this along with hiring all of the equipment on my GMG credit card. Mark Dodson used to sign off my expenses but I soon got a call from accounts. It turned out that I now held the record for the most amount of money spent on a GMG company credit card in one month. 'Oh lovely,' I said. 'Thank you.'

'My pleasure,' came the reply. 'By the way, Internal Audit want to see you.'

Warmly nicknamed the 'internal police', Internal Audit sent Stuart Kilby to check us out. My office always has sweets on the table. I shouldn't considering my size but it's part of my nature. This day we had about ten pounds of jelly babies in a giant bag and as Stuart arrived through the door he was hit on the head by a red jelly baby, flying through the air. He looked more than a little shocked by our antics. On top of that, Nick Castro had asked him to ensure we were 'all okay' and be our point of call for the finance part of the licence applications process. He came in thinking we were all mad but we soon had him on-side as he started to spend more time in our office than his own. He was reassured of our sanity when we became serious about the job we were doing but that didn't mean we couldn't have some fun the rest of the day. Word got around GMG about the crazy gang in the basement and very soon we had visitors galore from other departments. We also had the radio on!

We only had eighteen months to make an impact and I was determined we wouldn't fail on a technicality or lose out because we hadn't delivered a well-researched, well-thought-out document. The regulator had now stipulated that applications had to be evidence-led and they would dismiss emotion.

*

While all this was going on, GMG had a shareholding in a company called OneWord, chaired by Tim Blackmore and led by Simon Cole, perhaps the best Managing Director commercial radio never had. Simon was direct, smart, full of energy and was running his own very successful business. OneWord, launched on DAB, was innovative and, even though it was costing a fortune to run, there was a reasonable chance it could succeed. That was until the BBC decided to launch a competitor against it called BBC7 (now BBC Radio 4 Extra) which at a stroke killed any chance for this truly creative commercial digital station to have a life. An independent report led by former Channel 4 executive Tim Gardam blamed the Corporation for its demise and rightly so in my opinion. Investment running into millions was wasted and it underlined the need for an independent oversight of the BBC.

The BBC shot themselves in the foot more than once. I complained bitterly to them about their radio marketing campaigns, which were always directed to the areas where we just so happened to be launching a regional station. This was also followed up by BBC trailers for their programmes. The BBC would tell me they welcomed competition, yet at the same time they went out of their way spending thousands of pounds trying to kill it. Up would pop a promo for Terry Wogan, for instance. I am all for the BBC cross-promoting their services but, in my view, there had to be some reason for it. For instance, if Paul McCartney was on TV the night before and a promo came on at the end that said you could hear Paul McCartney on the Terry Wogan show the next day, that's fine by me, this is a good promotion of their respective services. But blatant TV promos that simply said 'tune in to Terry Wogan tomorrow because he's brilliant' was an abuse of their power. No wonder the CRCA and later on The Radio Centre became so aggressive towards them. This advertising was worth millions in real terms and we were excluded from that promotion. We all felt the BBC at that time were bordering on being out of control. It was one of the big success stories for Andrew Harrison and his team in that they managed to bring a halt to this madness. The BBC are not nearly as destructive in this respect as they once were.

*

GMG were also involved in a company called Radio Investments, which needed some attention. Bob called me in one day and asked if I would jump in and see what I could do for them.

'There are a number of issues to resolve. It'll take you, say, one day a week,' Bob estimated.

How wrong that was.

At the time, valuations of the worth of radio stations were bonkers and this group was wheeling and dealing in radio assets all around the country. They had been enormously successful under Robert Stiby. In any event it was eventually sold for a profit to another organisation but they could have sold out earlier for a lot more if they'd taken my advice. At a dinner one night with the key shareholders, I told them the market was at the top and if they wanted to maximize their profit they should exit now. Not all the shareholders agreed with my view, so instead, some sold out and others wanted to own more stock, resulting in a different group of shareholders. At one time Radio Investments had a stake in twenty-eight local radio stations, from Scotland right down to the south coast. Some of these were tiny. I told Bob that there was no way I could get around these stations on my own and he agreed I could hire my brother, Eddie, as my driver. We travelled seventy thousand miles in that first year, darting between the stations. These UK tours nearly always included Joanne in the car with me working on her laptop via a virtual office. How many PAs would do that for their boss today? There were just too many stations and the group was far too complicated. It was like spinning plates on a stick. Just as you got a few going, some of the others were starting to fall off.

On top of that the shareholder mix was, at times, near impossible to manage and far too many people had a say in the direction we were taking. Looking back, it was the most difficult twelve months of my career in radio. If we were going to continue with this group we needed to adopt a new strategy, giving some control back to the stations them-selves. Running the network from the centre was not the answer.

While the discussions around the board table were sometimes complicated to resolve, there were some wonderful people involved, highly educated and certainly a cut above my own school. I'd rarely mixed with people at this level but I was certainly not in awe of them. However, one member was really top drawer and I rang him up, seeking a breakfast meeting the next day. I loved his answer. 'Of course John,' he said. We could meet at a certain club in the City.

'That sounds very posh,' I said, 'Are you sure we can get in?'

'Oh, I think so, John. I own it!'

He put the phone down and I imagined him punching the air after delivering that line. On another occasion, I was invited to dinner by a very senior figure in the Tory party and, as we chatted, I asked if I could use the lavatory.

He said, 'Of course, just go down the hall and it's left at the Monet.' I had to open every single door laughing as I went along. I'd no idea what a bloody Monet looked like. Even when I saw it on the wall, I was not that impressed. When I came back I told him that I loved his collection but I felt it was missing the picture of the girl on the tennis courts scratching her arse. He had a look of total confusion on his face. I often wondered if he put a call in to his art dealer the next day to enquire about it. You can take the lad out of Carlisle, but you can't take Carlisle out of the lad!

*

We held a board meeting of Radio Investments at GMG plc. One of the members was Ralph Bernard, perhaps the best radioman in the busi-ness at that time. I learned so much from him over the years that he's worth a section all on his own. GMG had been offered The Marcher Group of stations and I'd been negotiating with the owner for a few weeks. I'd agreed a price and the GMG board had approved the deal. However, I also knew that Ralph was also in the hunt and he'd been negotiating with the owner for a far greater period than I had. While this meeting was going on, I got a call from the owner on my mobile so stepped out to take it. He was confirming that we had a deal so we had beaten Ralph, which was slightly embarrassing as he was still sitting opposite me when I came back into the meeting.

A few hours later he discovered he'd been beaten on price and was forced to pay an extra million pounds to take the deal away from us. To say he was not happy was an understatement. In his eyes we were working together on the same board and we had tried to pinch some radio stations from beneath him, while he was locked inside a board meeting at GMG. The reality was that we were also in competition and while we were on the same board on one part of the business, we were also competitors in other areas. There was no way I was just going to let him take these stations without a fight. That didn't wash with Ralph and it took some time before we kissed and made up. Even today he often accuses me of costing him a million.

*

I got on very well with David Vick at the regulator and he was, in fact, the real brains behind a lot of what the Radio Authority did. He loved radio and liked regulating and he'd put some good people together to form a cracking team. In my view, they could do with someone like David right now. The moment we won the Wales licence was an emotional moment indeed.

*

We spent months in Wales, working and living out of St David's Hotel in Cardiff Bay, building up a highly respectable board and meeting the movers and shakers of the area. Once all the applicants had submitted their documents, I read through them all and was positive we stood a great chance of winning, until I noticed something that I thought was a killer blow. I read in all the other applicants a question that was not in our own document. I called Joanne and it seemed we had completely missed it out. Not only that, we had somehow managed to delete the question from the main document itself. It was possible we could be accused of deleting a question so we didn't have to answer it. What the hell were we going to do? We decided the best course of action was to say nothing and if the regulator came back to us on it, we'd blame the printer. Thankfully, no one said a word.

A week before the announcement was due, I hired John Simons, my former Programme Director in the North East. Some would call this bullish to say the least but I just thought if we didn't win this one, we'd win another somewhere else.

The date for the Wales award was 5 pm on 6 April, 2000. I wore my lucky blue shirt and waited for the call at home to let me know if we'd won. If you were a winner, the regulator always called up a minute or so before the time indicated. The clock on the phone was checked, we had teletext on the TV to treble-check the time and Joanne even rang the speaking clock at 4.45 pm to be absolutely sure. At 4.58 pm the phone burst into life and history was made. I rang Bob and Nick immediately and my good friend Mark Dodson, who were all ecstatic. I did a jig on the lawn outside, grabbed a bottle of champagne and jumped into the car with my wife and son Scott, along with Joanne and we headed down to Cardiff. We booked ourselves into the St David's Hotel and held a Press conference the next day. What a moment. Underneath it all, no matter how confident you are on the outside, you always wonder if you'll make it. This was a licence application under my own steam and if I'd failed it would have been because either I was not good enough or the work we did was not acceptable. To win at the very first attempt was special for a number of reasons. First, I had just two chances to win otherwise I was out of a job. Secondly, I now had a real job and so did those who put their trust in me. I was back in the radio game and could get on with doing what I did best. And thirdly, I was now financially secure. The high-risk strategy had paid off and all I had to do was make sure this radio station launched successfully.

A couple of days after the awards we were in London and thought it right and proper to celebrate with a few drinks at trendy Soho bar, Suga Suga. Degsy was in town having a beer with ex-Tottenham and Man United footballer Alan Brazil, who is now a very successful radio presenter, so they came along, too. Bob Phillis was there, although he was a bit nervous about mixing with Derek Hatton. However, Nick Castro was excited as he's a mad Tottenham fan and Alan Brazil was one of his heroes. It was a great night, although this was not a venue I would normally go to. Degsy was always larger than life and announced that we should celebrate the GMG Radio's first win with a bottle of champagne and asked the waiter to bring one. Bob was relaxed but, being a finance man, Nick was a little nervous as one bottle of bubbly cost a staggering £125. We all had a drink, except Bob and Nick. They wanted one but there was nothing left after Degsy and Alan Brazil had supped it. The next morning Nick wanted to be assured that we wouldn't be picking up the tab for that bottle considering he hadn't had any! Mind you, he was always a bit wary of how radio folk could celebrate. One night we took our internal dealmaker, Andrew Zelouf, out for a drink at a Smooth Radio event, even though I always drank coke, we managed to put six cocktails, known as Slippery Nipples, on his company credit card. The next week, when his card bill came through, he had to explain to Bob why he had six Slippery Nipples on his expense account. Andrew wanted me to take the blame but I was having none of it.

---

20 second break

White Goods Man

When you work in radio you tend to mix with people who are famous for one reason or another. It's just part of the media circus and while most are reasonable, a few others have lost their sense of reality and I usually just end up laughing at their ridiculous demands.

One famous household name never wanted a fee for personal appearances, or for voicing over a client's adverts. No cash and no cheques. He would always agree to do it for 'nothing more than a little gift' and he had a lovely way of asking, too. He'd say something like, *'That's wonderful, John, thank you. Yes, of course, I could help you out on this. By the way, do you know where I might get one of those big American freezers?'*

Or, 'Yes of course, very happy to oblige. Have you seen those new fifty-inch TVs, John? They're wonderful and would look great on my wall.'

His real love was white goods. Over time, he must have had a fridge, washing machine, deep freezer and even a giant jukebox from clients as 'a little thank you'. Whenever I see him on the television today or hear him on the radio I always smile at his passion for gifts.

*

These really were the crazy days when ridiculous prices were being paid for radio stations and that first licence, in Wales, was immediately valued at twenty million pounds. Indeed, GMG received offers to sell it there and then but that was never contemplated. We launched Real Radio in October, 2000, with the voice of Tom Jones starting off a great breakfast show with Terry Underhill and Sarah Graham. From the first day it became a huge station. Without doubt, the reason for its amazing success was due to the people we hired. I'm just the leader, the person who inspires people to do their best, and we employed great people with amazing talent.

That first year in Wales we demonstrated just how our attitude to life, radio and, indeed, competition hadn't changed despite the fact that this station was owned by one of the largest and most sober media groups in the UK. Make no mistake, we took the business of radio seriously but the business of on-air entertainment was even more important. We certainly were not going to be put off by petty regulation and rules we thought were just plain daft.

Part of our success was down to our commitment to local news, with five minutes an hour every hour and extended bulletins twice a day. We invested in news and local reporters and it paid off. Listeners knew that if something was important to them it was important to us and we covered it. At Century, I came up with the idea of paying reporters a bonus if they managed to get their mic flag – our station logo – on the local TV. We called it 'logo lolly' and if a reporter went to a news conference they not only had to get the audio but they had to get Century's name seen on TV. For every success we paid £25 in cash, which turned a reporter into a rottweiler. They were magnificent and many turned winning logo lolly into a skill. The best used to wait until the very last second, just before the news conference started and then jumped up and moved their big mic into a more prominent position. Our competitors cottoned on to this and after a while logo fights erupted. Today, the size of some of the logos on mics is outrageous, often larger than the microphone itself.

We were also very big on fun.

'It's only radio,' I kept saying.' It's only radio!'

While the music was important, what we did between the songs was the killer ingredient. I encouraged a pirate radio attitude to life right across the board although people like John Simons in programmes and Jon Hewson in sales did not need much persuasion. That suited me just fine because, as the boss, I had to be able to stand back just far enough so I could step in if the fun was seen to be going too far. As a politician might say, I needed deniability. Around the time of our launch, Talk Radio, owned by Kelvin MacKenzie, caused quite a bit of fuss when he announced that the station was going to provide live match commentary even though they had no official rights to games. His team would simply commentate from a hotel bedroom, while watching the game on television. The BBC was outraged, especially as they had paid for exclusive rights and Kelvin hadn't parted with a penny. Despite the right and wrongs, it was genius in its simplicity. What's more, there was no legal precedent so all the parties involved marched off to the High Court to get a judge to decide on the rules. The decision was typically unhelpful. A radio station could do this provided they made it clear to the listeners that the commentary was not actually being broadcast from the ground.

In our first year in Wales, BBC Wales acquired the rights to an important football international in Cardiff. We had no rights of any sort and were effectively barred from covering the game. We had been issued with one Press pass for recording reaction and interviews but that was it. We pondered on Kelvin's idea and hatched a cunning plan. While we had no rights, we did in fact have a TV licence and the BBC were kind enough to broadcast the game for us on BBC1. We swung into action with a full PR campaign alongside non-stop promos on air proudly proclaiming we would have full and comprehensive coverage of the game that week. The BBC went nuts and the more we said it, the crazier they became. The more upset they were the more we played the promo. I learned years ago that winding up your competitors is the best way to get them to take their eye off the ball. Worse still for them, we would often go on air and tell our listeners that the BBC were getting upset with us. The listeners would then complain to the BBC accusing them of bullying our station. A member of the BBC management team rang John Simons, who had to hold the phone far from his ear as the man shouted down the line, 'How the hell can you say you are doing this? We have the rights! You're not allowed in the stadium. You're telling lies!'

Simo thought the man was going to have a minor heart attack, as he demanded to know what we meant by 'comprehensive coverage'. Simo replied that it was 'whatever he wanted it to be.' That did amuse me, I must admit.

Our plan was simple. On the day of the game, we turned up at the head quarters of the Western Mail newspaper, which were right outside the ground. We sat in an office looking directly at the stadium, turned on the TV to watch the game and dangled a mic outside the window for sound effects.

We were talking to fans and bringing the atmosphere of the game to our listeners while match officials and people from the BBC marched around inside the stadium trying to find us. They came across our reporter who only had a simple tape recorder and a mic with him to record after-match interviews. They confiscated his equipment, demanding to know where we were. Little did they know we were outside looking in. We knew the rules. We told our listeners we were bringing coverage of the game from the Real Radio Monitors. The public thought this was just another name for our sports staff. Those that knew we were simply commentating from the television screen didn't care a jot. They just wanted our partisan style of commentary.

It was fun but like all things in life you have to sober up eventually and agree to come to some sort of an arrangement. The BBC called me to ask if I knew what was going on and the local board of our radio station were starting to ask some awkward questions. I told them that what we were doing was perfectly legal, although perhaps not within the spirit of a sensible working relationship with our fellow radio friends in Wales. As it was an international game, it was just a one-off event so we agreed not to do it again. We had, though, won the battle. Best of all it brought our team together under a wonderful spirit that said to the staff, we work hard but at the same time we won't be beaten up by the big boys.

Doing things like this makes radio so much fun. It creates a winning team.

*

Highlight of the year was our first set of audience figures, which confirmed Real Radio was the best regional radio launch, in audience terms, anywhere in the UK to date. I thought it didn't get much better than that. Even today, the station remains at the very top of my emotional register. In the middle of all this I got a call from someone at a council office in Cardiff who told me I had no right to erect a flag pole outside our building without planning permission and they were not minded to give it. We were flying the Real Radio flag but I quickly changed it to the Welsh dragon and told the man that I would go on the air and tell the audience that the 'flag nazi from the council office' was demanding I take down their national flag. He never called back and that flag is still flying today, still without planning permission I believe.

*

GMG loved radio and I loved them, especially Bob Phillis and Nick Castro, who were hugely supportive and inspirational. They loved it partly because they thought we were all slightly mad and radio was certainly much more fun than newspapers. The medium was full of wonderful characters and we always regaled Bob with amusing stories of people in the business. It was while we were running Real Radio, that we learned the regulator had given the West Midlands regional licence to Saga Radio, headed up by long-time radio executive, Ron Coles. His applications were always first rate and there was little doubt that it was aimed at a gap in the market. The problem was there was little chance of it making any money. People learned from each other and ideas were being swapped and copied each time.

*

As we left the team to get on with the business in Cardiff, I moved on to putting another application together, this time for the Yorkshire regional licence. Once again, we put a great local and influential board in place. At one of our earlier meetings, I forgot that I was mixing with a different class of people. Part of the application process was that we had to ensure we had support from the community and so I asked if they could ensure business partners and friends submitted letters of support to the regulator. One of the team said, 'Don't worry, John, I'll ask members of my 50-club to provide you with some letters.'

In an effort to flannel I said, 'I have to say you don't look over fifty.'

She smiled and said, 'I meant people with fifty million pounds or more!'

Joanne and I chuckled for months about that.

Once again, when all the licence applications were submitted I went through them and this time I was more confident than ever. So much so, I went on record that we would win it, which was actually quite a foolish thing to do considering the way the regulator seemed to allocate licences willy-nilly. In my view, we had the best application by far, miles better than anyone else. I have absolutely no idea why that confidence was there. It just was.

*

I had to walk a tight line in my early days at GMG. The company didn't know me as well as others I'd worked for and I had to have my semi-serious business head on when mixing with some of the directors and senior staff. But having a weekly show on Real Radio in Wales allowed me an outlet for my stupidity. The show was Fun On The Phones. My co-host, Sarah Graham, is one of the best female presenters I know. She was perfect and we both knew when to allow each other the space to deliver the punch line to a topic or any running gag. What is more she wasn't a giggly girl. So many presenters in a dual role talk over each other. That was something we never did. The chemistry was just right and Sarah was as much a central plank to the programme as I was. One weekend, she was talking about having had her bikini line 'sorted' for her holidays and like any couple would do, I simply asked her what shape that line was taking, a Brazilian perhaps? It was one of those moments when you had to hear it to understand the humour. It was what wasn't said that allowed the humour to breathe and, after all, we were a radio station aimed at the over thirties. Interestingly, there were never any complaints and the audience for this show was terrific.

Bob Phillis rang me later in the week to say GMG's Chairman, Paul Myners, had been travelling along the M5 the previous Sunday lunchtime and had called him to say 'the idiot on Real Radio at lunch-time should be fired'. He asked if I could look into it, send him a note and deal with the presenter if I felt he needed some direction. Could I let him know who it was, so he could report back to the Chairman? Christ this was me! I managed to stall him long enough for the crisis to go away but it was touch and go. Once again, I thanked God for having a different name. It wasn't long before I had to come clean to Bob and Nick who just loved this and never let me forget it. They told the Chairman I'd sorted it. To be fair, if someone like Paul Myners had enjoyed a show called Fun On The Phones, I would have been much more worried!

*

I have a lot of time for Paul, now Lord Myners, who was hugely supportive for all things radio and, indeed, me personally. He was perhaps the best chairman of a board I have ever seen in action. I used to sit there and watch him skilfully work through the numerous difficulties of running a large plc. Perhaps his greatest strength was his ability to stand back from all the emotion and make a decision. He was certainly not the easiest person to deal with at times and you always felt you had to be on your mettle. Make no mistake, he was a very demanding chairman but a first class operator. I like that in a leader.

*

Around this time I decided that I no longer liked my title of Managing Director of GMG Radio. It seemed rather old fashioned to me so I simply changed it to Chief Executive. That seemed much more credible, I thought, so I ordered some new business cards, changed my email signature and carried on. I forgot to tell Bob Phillis, who one day called and asked if I had been promoted to a new position over the summer. I had completely forgotten about changing my title so I had no idea what he was talking about until he explained that he had just received an email from someone else in the wider GMG group, who was currently Managing Director, asking if they could also change their title to Chief Executive to match mine. It was the first time he'd heard of it and asked who had agreed to this. I was in a tight spot and had to think on my feet a little. I told him that he was such a busy man that I didn't like to bother him with trival matters such as this as I was sure that he would see the value in ensuring those around him were motivated and happy within their work. I also suggested that as I was negotiating contracts with Chief Executives across the industry, it was absolutely essential they believed I was their equal and were happy to negotiate with me directly. I also added that in changing my title to Chief Executive I had not asked for a salary increase which would have been normal practice in any discussion such as this but as this was not about reward instead it was just a title change with no difference in work load or responsibility, I was sure it would have been acceptable.

'Bob, if I have someway jumped the gun and you believe that I am not worthy of this title them of course I will go back to being the Managing Director although I would want to immediately put a date into your diary where I can discuss the move to CEO more formally,' I said.

The phone fell silent for a few moments before Bob replied that there were some things in life that he would risk his time being taken up with and handing out titles to executives was something he would, at the very least, wished to have been consulted about. He was absolutely right on this of course and I should have sought permission beforehand. He was going to consider asking me to move back to Managing Director overnight. I had to think quick. 'Okay, Bob, of course,' I said. 'That is right and I apologise for doing this. It was very silly of me and I am annoyed at myself for not being both courteous and indeed professional. I wonder Bob, if you could consider this request. I really like being called the CEO. There is a ring to it that I like and I know that you always wish to have your team motivated and happy. If you want me to refrain from calling myself CEO could you please allow me to be called President? That is much more showbiz and I think it really does works. This name is very popular in America and it has real showbiz and gravitas. In fact, the more I think about it the more I love it. *John Myers, President GMG Radio.* What do you think, Bob?'

Silence again and then a chuckle. 'John, there is absolutely no possibility whatsoever that I will endorse that suggestion. President of GMG Radio, the Guardian would have a bloody fit. Look, keep the title CEO and I'll sort it out elsewhere. But, please, do *not* do anything like this again without consulting me.

'Absolutely, Bob. Thank you.'

Chapter Sixteen

LEFT WING, SANDAL-WEARING ARSEHOLES

I struck up a friendly relationship with Kelvin MacKenzie, the former editor of The Sun. Kelvin is one of life's rich characters. We first met soon after Kelvin had acquired Talk Radio. He invited me to lunch. I got on with him immediately and liked his forthright style. He competed hard but also loved life. It appeared to me he'd got the measure of the various characters in the radio industry at the time. As you can imagine he was no idiot and was keen to buy up radio licences. In turn, this drove up the price for everyone else. It was a gold rush and, while GMG were always in the hunt for radio licences, we kept with our strategy of only acquiring large regional licences. In any case, we had a shareholding in Radio Investments that housed nearly thirty small local stations, so there was no point in having small stations within GMG itself.

One of the stations Kelvin owned was Scot FM, which broadcast from Edinburgh to Scotland's central belt and was losing money at a burn-rate of about three million pounds a year. The station had been poorly launched in a market already dominated by commercial radio giants, Clyde and Forth. They were also outgunned in PR and made a fatal error in saying they were going after a Radio 4 demographic, while airing the infamous Scottie McClue.

Kelvin had been buying up quite a few radio stations across the UK at a time when he had to pay top prices. His bank was now asking for some of that to be paid back, and quickly. Banks are like that, they give then suddenly panic and want their money back. Kelvin was really angry about this but he was in a tight spot and had to sell something to keep the bankers happy.

Kelvin invited me for coffee at The Savoy and, when I arrived, it turned out he'd hired a private room. He asked if I was interested in buying Scot FM and enquired how much I'd be prepared to pay. He wanted thirty-five million pounds. I told him to sober up and come back with a more realistic price but we would enter any competition or sale process he wanted to conduct. Over the next few days, we got the price down to £25.5m, subject to our board approval.

It was still a huge amount considering the losses Scot FM was making and GMG put me under enormous pressure to justify paying this figure. You can convince yourself on a number of fronts why businesses are worth the money you eventually pay. It depends on your strategy of course. Usually it is a combination of turnover and profit, it could be the market or an attempt to gain more assets. From my perspective, a business was worth what you were going to do with it. We were building a radio group and were fully aware we might have to pay over the odds in order to achieve scale. That said, all I could do was just give the board my view of life and hope they believed in the business case. First, I had to persuade Kelvin to agree to this figure and secure a period of exclusivity to do the deal.

*

I put the plan together with Stuart Kilby, who had now moved from Internal Audit to become our own finance director. We tabled this to Bob Phillis and Nick Castro for first approval and I was then asked along to the main plc board meeting to present my case. This was bum-clenching time. How the hell was I going to convince them that a radio station losing three million a year was worth more than twenty-five million?

The great and good were there in the boardroom. I stood up, gave them a short presentation, supported by Bob and Nick and answered their questions. The board members were all polite but I could see that this was not an easy 'yes', despite the one station I'd just won.

One of the board said, 'John, You've done very well to win one station. We have no idea how successful that may be. You're awaiting the outcome of another licence and now you want us to buy one that, on the face of it, is hard to justify at this price. If only we knew if the Yorkshire licence was going to come our way, it would reduce the overall risk.'

I took a deep breath and replied, 'What you're saying is correct. It's true also that I have no idea if we will win Yorkshire or not. Winning licences is not an exact science. All you hope for is that you're up for debate when the regulator meets to decide on the winner. However, I know the regulator and despite some of their recent awards, the staff do want to make sensible decisions. I know about licence applications and we have submitted a great one, even better than Wales in my view, and furthermore I know how to run radio stations. Wales is going to be enormously successful. I cannot give you a cast iron guarantee of success but we have everything in place and have done everything we can to give us the best possible chance. We take educated business risks every day but if we can acquire Scot FM and we have won Wales and Yorkshire, the next time we meet up we will have built up a radio group valued at sixty million pounds at today's prices for the outlay of just £25.5m.'

I left the room and Bob called to say that he had permission to complete the deal on the best possible terms but we could not extend our offer.

I now had a problem. Kelvin had gone quiet on me, very quiet indeed. This was not a good sign. At the same time, my very good friend Phil Riley at Chrysalis had also gone quiet. You don't need to be a professor to work out what was happening. Phil was trying to scoop this prize out of my grasp and Kelvin was going for a bigger offer. Through other sources, we also found out that Scottish Radio Holdings were also involved. Nick and Bob called me in to talk strategy. How were we going to get this deal done bearing in mind we had general approval from our board but for no more than our original offer? We were not for moving.

Then Kelvin called to say he now wanted twenty nine million pounds in cash, otherwise he was selling the station to someone else. You can't blame anyone for this. It's just part of the normal swing of business and I absolutely love this part. In fact, I quite admired Kelvin for it and I'd be doing the same in his position. This was a prized asset. Could we come up with more cash? Already sceptical about paying the current offer, Nick was against doing that and was a firm 'no'. It was then that Bob demonstrated his experience. Bob and Nick realised that both SRH and Chrysalis would have to get shareholder approval, yet Kelvin was under pressure from his bank right now to reduce his borrowings. Bob called in his PA and dictated a letter to the chairman of Kelvin's bank. In the letter, he outlined that GMG were offering £25.5 million for Scot FM and not a penny more. However, it was a cash deal. It was not negotiable and, furthermore, if we had not bought this radio station by five o'clock the following evening, we would be gone and would not return to the table. It was a great letter and we meant it.

That's the bluff. You have to be ready and willing to walk, no matter what. In other words, Bob was telling the bank's chairman that we had the cash and we could do the deal now. We were a certain buyer. On the other hand, both Chrysalis and SRH who were offering two million more would have to wait to get full shareholder approval and even then that might not be forthcoming.

The next day, we turned up at the offices of Kelvin's lawyers. Chrysalis and SRH were in separate rooms and we were in another. It was not a good atmosphere. As the clock crept towards 5pm, Kelvin had been to see both of them and told them straight. They had to sign today and for their increased offers, or they would be losing out to us. In fact, it was slightly worse than this as Kelvin had told Chrysalis that because GMG had already approved the paperwork that should be good enough for them too. If they wanted the station they would have to hand over their money after being given given just one hour to go through all of the files for due dilligence. We knew they couldn't do that and they eventually just walked out. Suddenly, at 4.58 pm the speakerphone burst into life. It was Kelvin.

'Who's with you?'

'Er, me, Bob Phillis and Nick Castro,' I said.

'Right well let me tell you,' said Kelvin. 'This is the worst fucking day of my bloody life. To have to sell something to you left wing, sandal-wearing arseholes has really pissed me off. Look I've done the deal, I've signed the forms and, John, I really hope you make a success of it. But for now, you can all fuck off.'

The phone went dead.

I was delighted that we'd won and had our second licence. But Bob was stunned at being subjected to such foul-mouthed abuse.

'John,' he said. 'We have just given that man twenty-five and a half million pounds for a radio station that's losing three million pounds a year and he has just told us to fuck off.' I told him that meant he loved us.

'You should hear what he says to people he doesn't like,' I said. 'We have got what we came for so let's move on.'

A couple of days later, Kelvin called Bob to apologise for his language during our purchase of Scot FM.

Thinking this was a lovely gesture, Bob started to relax, 'Well Kelvin, that's really kind of you and it takes a very good man to ring up and apologise and I am delighted to accept.' Then he said, 'Look, Kelvin, why don't you come and have a coffee sometime?'

That's when Kelvin exploded, 'What, come into the Guardian? You have to be fucking mad. I'm not coming in there, you can fuck off ...'

The phone went dead.

*

The fourth of July, 2001, was decision day for the Yorkshire regional licence and the pressure was really on. I had all but told the main board that we would win this and, based on that confidence, we'd just spent over twenty-five million pounds buying Scot FM. Once again, I wore my lucky blue shirt and waited by the phone at home. With me were John Simons, Joanne Riordan and Jon Hewson among others, along with my family. There had been thirteen applicants, all of them strong, but my confidence remained high. Our Commercial Director, Jon Hewson, needed this win more than most. In those days he lived a champagne lifestyle on lemonade money and a win bonus would get him out of his current financial predicament.

We double-checked the clocks but as 5 pm approached, nothing. We just looked at each other. If the regulator was not calling us, they must be ringing someone else. I was gutted. It was now 5.01 and still nothing. We all knew we'd failed. Someone else was getting the call. I was almost in tears as the phone started to ring loudly at 5.02 pm. I answered it and Neil Stock from the new regulator, OFCOM, confirmed we'd won. Jon Hewson jumped up onto the table with delight, while I was punching the air. When I'd calmed down, I asked Neil why the call was late.

He replied, 'We knew you'd be waiting and just wanted to wind you up a little.'

A little? I'd nearly had a bloody heart attack but we'd won and that was all that mattered. We now had Yorkshire, Wales and Scotland. We hit the Chinese restaurant in celebration. We knew how to live!

GMG couldn't believe it either. For years, they'd been trying with no success and here we were winning two out of the first four we applied for. They were both big licences, too. That's a brilliant scoring average but I was more delighted for Bob, Nick and Mark Dodson who had put their faith in radio and me in particular. Once again the high-risk, high-reward strategy had paid off.

20 second break

Barrow boy

Kelvin MacKenzie, the larger-than-life owner of TalkSPORT and a number of local radio stations, decided to take his group public.

He summoned his executive team to a meeting where he offered all his staff share options and proudly issued each one of them with a green wheelbarrow. They would 'need the barrow to take home all the cash they were going to make from their investment', he proudly announced. Kelvin was met by a sea of confused faces, all wondering how they could get the wheelbarrows back home on the tube, trains and planes.

Two years later, he wrote to all the staff asking for the wheelbarrows back. He needed to sell them to raise cash to help pay the bills...

*

With Yorkshire in the bag, I turned my attention to Scotland. We'd paid an awful lot of money for Scot FM, so we had to really focus on getting it right. The station had been poorly launched by any measure; although they had entered a market where the competition had such a big share it was never going to be easy. That said, the previous management had shot themselves in the foot by making the classic mistake of suggesting to the media that the station was a kind of upmarket BBC Radio 4. That was never going to work and, sadly, neither did the first record they tried to play. The music failed to start and the great launch turned out to be anything but. Scot FM's statement about being upmarket was further ridiculed when they later hired Scottie McClue as their late night phone-in host. The Press murdered the station at every opportunity and Clyde and Forth were certainly not helping them either.

Now we'd bought the station, Richard Findlay, who'd been part of the team that hired me at CFM and the boss of Scottish Radio Holdings who owned our rivals Radios Clyde and Forth, was kind enough to tell his team that Scot FM under my leadership was not to be confused with the last regime. We would be much greater competition, he said, warning his team to be on their mettle but even we didn't think the door would open so wide.

Soon after the purchase, I was at the Scot FM building on Leith docks, just outside Edinburgh, thinking, well, if all goes badly at least we can watch the ducks screwing. There was not a good atmosphere and I was absolutely sure we couldn't stay there. It had been a mistake to base the station in Edinburgh. The people of this historic city were used to receiving their media from Glasgow, but there was no way people in Glasgow would ever accept anything from Edinburgh. We had to give the audience in the West permission to listen. You can't change that, it's just the way it was. We'd have to move our studios to Glasgow to stand a chance. This meant that at least ninety per cent of our staff would not be able to move with us, and over time, it proved to be the case.

Time was limited and I needed to be totally focused, so my PA Joanne kept me away from people I didn't want to meet. However, she'd been flannelled by a salesman from a media magazine called The Drum and had arranged a slot in my diary to catch up with their commercial director, Billy Anderson. On the day, I asked Joanne why the hell this appointment was in my diary but she just told me that I had to meet him. A message to sales people everywhere, here. Always make sure you make friends with the PA. They have enormous power over the boss. I was not ready to advertise just yet but Billy convinced me of the value of taking out a double-page spread in his magazine to announce our arrival to Scottish advertising agencies. I never buy anything from anyone I don't like and I liked this guy a lot. He was sharp, to the point, had some humour and best of all, integrity. He also knew how to make a sale.

The magazine came out the following month. I scanned it and laughed out loud. He had used us to sell full pages to every single radio station in Scotland. That edition turned out to be the magazine's biggest revenue earner of the year. Instead of blaming the smooth-talking salesman, I told Jon Hewson to employ him immediately. If he was this sharp for a magazine, he could work wonders for us in radio. Billy Anderson turned out to be one of the best employees I've ever hired and I soon promoted him up the ladder to become one of our key executives.

We decided to re-launch the station as Real Radio and I was sitting at my desk in Leith listening to radios Clyde and Forth, trying to work out where the gap in the market was. Where could I position this station? We had to have a USP and we needed to find the music gap to have maximum effect. What we could not do was take on Clyde and Forth head to head, as we would lose. Why would listeners change for the same thing? Instead, we needed to promote and sell our difference but what was it? Then, like a parting of the waves before us, Clyde and Forth made a huge error. I couldn't believe it, so I made a point of listening to them every day. I kept saying to the team this was terrific. Our biggest competition and the barrier to our success was handing us the gap on a plate and we now had our biggest chance to succeed. When you re-launch a radio station you need two things to happen to achieve the required success. You need to be at the top of the game yourself with a very clear plan and you also need the competition to cock it up a little. In order for the latter to happen you need a bit of luck and a little bit of persuasion. I was going to go for it in PR terms in order to make that happen.

*

The regulator had awarded a second regional licence to Beat 106 who had among their shareholders footballer Ally McCoist, TV presenter Carole Smillie and singer Sharleen Spiteri. This station was losing money, yet it was soon sold to Capital Radio for thirty-seven million pounds, a staggering figure that made its shareholders, including the Scottish celebrity investors, very rich indeed. At the time Beat 106 was playing dance music and it was starting to have an effect on the younger end of Clyde and Forth's audiences. Both were deeply worried about this and panicked. They decided to compete with Beat 106 on the music front and much of their output started to change, from what their current audience liked, to music many of their listeners had never heard before. In short, they were abandoning the very foundation they had built their stations on. I thought if we could go in hard as the station that plays the songs the listeners know, we would have a big impact. We did some quick research and it was clear the loyal Clyde and Forth audience were becoming grumpy. I pumped up the marketing spend, hit the air as the 'classic hits' radio station with larger-than-life personalities such as the wonderful Robin Galloway on breakfast, huge competitions and songs the listeners could sing along to.

Outside Real Radio's new studios in Glasgow, there is a big white horse made out of wire. You can't miss it when you drive along the M8 motorway. The rivalry of Scotland's central belt made me laugh. One client told me it was good to see the arse end of the horse pointing towards Edinburgh. This was why moving to Glasgow was so important.

Our executive team couldn't run this station ourselves, as we had to launch the Yorkshire station, so we launched it and then left it in the hands of people we trusted.

*

In the early days my management style was quite hands-on but I soon learned this was a mistake. It was not getting the best out of people and, if you do everything yourself, then everyone expects you to make all the key decisions. To be a true leader, you have to be out in front allowing the staff to follow and make their own decisions and, of course, their own mistakes. This in turn empowers them to succeed. If you really are a leader of a business then success is all that matters. Making people feel valued, appreciated and loved can work wonders. Radio can be like McDonalds, and a number of brands are emerging that on the surface all look and sound the same but to me radio is personal and there are some differences between the audiences of Wales and Scotland for example. I learned that quickly, and allowed each of my stations to have slightly different styles, even though they were under the same brand.

I hire people first and talent second. We show them the way to do it and then I very much like to get out of the way. I found a great MD in Shaun Bowron, whose big attraction to me at the time was his level headedness and strong ethics. Billy Anderson came in as Sales Director and we hired Jay Crawford as Programme Director. Even though Shaun was a Geordie, he'd spent considerable time in Scotland

and was well accepted by the Scottish media. Shaun called me one day, just a month after he'd started his role. He asked me to take off my CEO hat and replace it with my presenter's hat. I was presenting Fun On The Phones across the network at the time and Shaun had received a complaint about me. I listened carefully and after a few moments said my CEO's hat was back on and told him to forget the idiot who had complained and move on. The sheer joy of radio was right there. Billy and Jay made a great sales and programming team. Jay was a great find. I knew him from my days at CFM and I'd often visited him in Edinburgh. He was kind of handed over to us as an asset when we took control of Scot FM. In my view, the other stations he'd worked for had slightly disregarded him and his success over many years. This guy wanted to prove everyone wrong. All we did with Jay was restore his confidence and allow him to deliver a programming ethos that worked wonders. He's a class act and, together with Simo, they set the stall out for the future and made it happen.

For any business to succeed, you have to allow the staff to succeed themselves. You cannot claim the glory, just the vision. The success was all their own and I wanted them to own every drop of it. The station launched and before long we were rocketing up the league table. The boss of Radio Clyde had made a comment in the Press that they were so far up the mountain they were always looking down on us. Not for long they weren't. Within a few years we became the most successful radio station in Scotland, growing our reach from thirteen to thirty per cent within five years, with listening hours soaring from 2.3 million to 10.3 million.

What a success story. Real Radio Scotland had a buzz like no other. The truth is, and I keep saying it, winning is infectious. Once you start winning it's hard to stop. Shaun Bowron was always the pragmatic leader and the perfect link to Billy and Jay. They were an unstoppable army. The Press also liked us because I always had a quote for them. So many people talk to the Press when they have something to promote but I'm always available, although sometimes I wish I wasn't.

The Scottish Press called me one day for a quote on why Radio Clyde was losing audience. You have to fuel bad news sometimes and I told them that I thought Clyde's strategy was brilliant, well thought out and showed the class of their programming team. They had to stick to their plan of taking on Beat 106. In truth, I felt it was absolutely the reverse but what I didn't want them to do was to start playing more classic hits again before we'd made our mark. Some sales staff had defected to us from Clyde and Forth and they told us about the fear in our rivals' camp about what we were up to. This was good. The more they talked about us, the less they were focused on their own business.

∗

I rarely got a bollocking from GMG but at one of my catch-up meetings with Bob he brought out a story from the Scottish Herald, where I had told BBC Scotland that we would very soon be 'ripping the liver' out of their audience levels too. Bob was not best pleased about that at all and neither were the BBC who had complained directly to him about my overzealous approach. He was absolutely right, of course, and indeed it was immature but it was quotes like this that kept me on the media pages and we were making great headway. The truth was the BBC in Scotland were never a threat. Indeed, they were more of a friend to us. Nevertheless, I was told this was not the GMG way. I was learning from the big man and the lessons kept on coming.

Perhaps my biggest faux pas with the Press came a couple of years later. In May 2005, GCAP was formed from a merger between Capital and GWR. The following month EMAP acquired Scottish Radio Holdings. As well as Radio City in Liverpool, Magic FM and a host of other stations nationwide, EMAP also now had Clyde and Forth in Scotland. However, in January 2008, EMAP was then sold en masse to German media company Bauer. I was in the car with Eddie when I received a call from Broadcast magazine. The reporter asked if I had a quote for them about the recent takeover by Bauer of EMAP Radio. To this day I don't know what came over me. I replied, 'It's good news, I think. The

Marketing posters for Century 105 in the North West

The shirt I bought on the day we signed the Man United commentary deal.

Degsy confirms he's a champagne socialist at the Century launch.

The two posters at Newcastle train station. Metro got a little grumpy about mine.

The exec team and their partners at our annual 'team' week-end away in Marbella

Two of my three brothers. Mike and Eddie (centre)

The famous meet and greet with the Rolling Stones

DEGSY RIDES AGAIN

WEDNESDAY 24th MARCH

9.00pm

BBC2

James Rea, he started life at Century
and now runs LBC.

The BBC publicity card for Trouble at the Top

A collection of all the radio greats in 2006. How times have changed since then!
How many can you name?

Me and Simo having
a lark about in
Marbella

All dressed up - Simo and Isobel, Linda and Scott and Stuart Kilby and my brother Eddie
at The Sony Radio Academy Awards

Life at GMG and the famous boardroom where many a deal was done.

Some of my favourite people - Billy Anderson and Jay Crawford winning yet another award

Our Christmas party and the team had got these lot to wear t-shirts of me for some reason...

Linda and I meeting a member of the 'Royle' family at our Christmas party in Glasgow

The Myers tribe at Carlisle Cathedral the day I received my Fellowship from Cumbria University.

Linda and me with Marcus and Mia. Wonderful grandkids.

Eddie and I at the halfway point on a trip from Chicago to LA on Route 66. We love our bikes.

Germans have not been to the Wirral or the Clyde since 1945, so it's good to have them back in a friendlier manner.'

I also gave him some other quotes that I thought he would use instead but soon the head of PR at GMG was on the phone.

'John,' he said, 'please tell me a senior member of Guardian Media Group and a member of our Plc board has not just told the Press that it was good to have the Germans back as they hadn't been on The Wirral or The Clyde since 1945.'

Silence.

'Oh shit, you have, haven't you?'

'Hey, listen,' I pleaded. 'I gave him some other quotes, too. The comment was just a bit of fun there was no way I said it was my actual quote.'

'Did you tell him that, John?'

'Err, not that I can recall.'

'Shit. Right, leave it with me.'

Over the next couple of hours GMG were forced to make a couple of calls to the right people to ensure that quote didn't go to press. It was the measure of the guy in our Press department that he didn't take it to Bob. If that quote had been published there would have been huge repercussions bearing in mind Guardian Media Group's ethics. He was right again but the tale often came up at future dinners as one of the 'moments of concern' during my employment. It's always interesting how management can pull your leg about something later on but at the time it would have been quite a different matter.

Chapter Seventeen

JUGGLING WITH JELLY

There are times in business when the momentum is going so well for you that it can be hard to see the wood from the trees. It was January 2006 and I was now on the main board at Guardian Media Group and this meant not just being across the radio side of the business but everything else that was going on. You can say what you like about GMG's ethics but they sat well with me. To this day there isn't a company I've worked for which matched them for the way they went about their business, especially under Bob, Nick and Carolyn McCall, CEO of The Guardian.

However, colleagues will tell you that I don't have a lot of time for meaningless meetings and we had loads of them at GMG. The one question I ask about every meeting I ever attend is: what decision or conclusion is expected from this meeting? If there isn't one, then I begin to wonder why I'm there. Of course, update meetings are important in the day-to-day running of any business but I've come to learn that people like meetings and people like to talk. I prefer action and doing things resulting from those meetings, otherwise they are very often just a talking shop. That is not a good use of my time. I learned a trick about how minutes of meetings were often recorded.

If a company circulated minutes of a meeting, say within forty-eight hours, they were usually a fair and correct record. However, if the chair of that meeting wanted to add some confusion about what was said, they were very often delayed and circulated at the last moment. Your memory fades especially when you are busy and a mentor of mine warned me to look out for this sharp practice. It happens more than you might think. If minutes are late, there is usually a good reason for it.

*

Most meetings I attended at group level were about The Guardian. GMG exists purely to fund The Guardian, which is run by the Scott Trust to ensure the future of this left-of-centre newspaper. When the board invests more than a few million pounds in a business you are leading, it's not unreasonable to be called to account now and again. But, to be honest, some of the thinking at these meetings was well above my head and I often used to sit there wondering what the hell they were talking about. There were in a different league to me. I loved and understood radio and indeed I loved business but there was not, on the face of it, a lot of business logic in the way The Guardian operated.

In any case, The Guardian were always hugely supportive of their radio arm and what we were trying to do. The executive management team was top notch and it was good to be in their company. I learned a lot from just listening and they, I hope, learned something from my direct approach. In fact, Mark Dodson, who was now CEO of GMG Regional Media, and myself were widely regarded as the two naughty school kids of the group. As blunt northerners we often just called it as we saw it and that was sometimes off-putting for a few soft southerners around the table. The Guardian's CEO, Carolyn McCall, once ordered Mark and me to sit on our hands while the Head of Social Responsibility gave a presentation. We had little time for this kind of stuff and she knew it, although we did hire people to ensure we were compliant. I was told to hire a health and safety manager for the business. I told my HR Director that anyone who has ambitions to be a health and safety officer should be barred from ever getting that position. If that is the sum of their desire they are not people I want to work with. Instead, we had a great guy in our company who we affectionately called Head of Crap. His name was Jeff Stephenson, one of the loveliest men you could ever wish to meet. He took on the compliance role and did it brilliantly. I was happy to be compliant but at the same time I was determined to work with people I liked. Jeff's best job was to call up anyone who complained about any of our stations. He holds the world record for being able to talk to someone non-stop without taking either a toilet break or a drink. Some of those who complained about a station actually ended up complaining about Jeff ringing them up about their complaint. He could be on the phone for hours and often they were delighted to get rid of him. His best line to complainers was, *'Thanks for bringing this matter to my attention. I'll deal with it for you. Would you like me to call you again later this week to update you on how things have gone?'* Every single one pleaded with him not to do so. I just love that man.

───────── **30 second commercial break** ─────────

Officer Dibble

As Morgan in the Morning, I did a wind up on a young man who had just passed his driving test. His friends told me he would be in his car at a certain time so I called him up as Police Officer Dibble – I nicked the name from Top Cat – and told him I'd just clocked him speeding. He was on speakerphone totally denying it. I asked him to pull over where it was legal and safe to do so and wait there for me to arrive. I advised him not to use the phone until I had arrived, as I may have to ring him back. I called him again after about ten minutes and told him I was still delayed. He would have to wait. After thirty minutes had elapsed I rang him again to say I would not be able to get to him after all. He explained he was desperate to get to an appointment so I said I'd let him off if he promised not to speed again. He could either attend a speeding course or, better still, if he could repeat the Lord's Prayer that would be sufficient. He was startled by this and had no idea what to do or what was the right thing to say. He opted for the latter and started off confidently.

'Our father, who art in heaven, hallowed be thy name...' he lost the thread and I just lost it, bursting into gales of laughter. Then he said he was going to smack me and everyone who had put me up to it. It was a lovely wind up and he kindly gave me permission to put it out on air. A day later, I got a call in the office. The police wanted to see Mr Myers, the MD. When the officer arrived, I thought I was going to hear something really bad about one of my team. Instead, he started to tell me that he could not condone John Morgan, my breakfast show presenter, imitating a police officer. It was a very serious offence and the force always took these instances to court. However, if I promised to have a stern word with the presenter, then they would be prepared to forget it on this occasion.

'Of course,' I said. 'It is indeed very poor judgment on his part and I'll deal with him immediately. Thank you for coming to see me direct.'

The officer left satisfied, while I just wondered if there was not a better use of police time.

＊

Our competitors, and yet close friends, were Chrysalis. I really liked them and, in fact, would champion them internally at every opportunity. My good friend, Phil Riley, ran Chrysalis with support from Don Thompson, a great commercial director. At GMG, Phil and Don were affectionately known as The Everly Brothers. Group CEO of Chrysalis was Richard Huntingford. We all got on well and, indeed, Chrysalis were our national advertising sales house responsible for the national advertising we broadcast on all our stations, so clearly there was a substantial amount of trust and rapport between us all.

The radio market was going through consolidation with stations being bought up right, left and centre. I told the GMG board there were too many commercial radio groups and we would all come together eventually. We either had to buy Chrysalis or Chrysalis had to buy us. The latter was more realistic, as they owned the Heart and Galaxy radio brands and were substantially more successful than us in London. Whoever bought GMG Radio would become very powerful.

This came to a head in 2005 when Chrysalis tabled an offer for our stations. It was a good one, too. We had won some new licences and bought some existing stations with the result that we'd spent about seventy million pounds to date, plus around £10million in running costs, so a total of about eighty million all in. Chrysalis were offering £125million. GMG could have got out of the radio business there and then for a substantial profit but the discussion around the table really threw me.

The GMG board was a wonderful and engaging bunch of people, led by Paul Myners. In reality, they faced a difficult decision. At that time GMG Radio was going well. Through a lot of blood sweat and tears we now had a sizeable radio group but the truth was we were still nowhere big enough to compete and our competitors were just getting stronger. We had to sell out now or commit to buying more stations. Staying still was not an option. However, what GMG was not short of was cash and the discussion around the boardroom table was why they needed another £125m. The company had millions in the bank so how would this sale change their position? It was an interesting debate and not one I'd come across before. Look at it like this, if you'd won the lottery and had ten million pounds in the bank and someone offered you another million it would not change your life whatsoever. This was the situation Guardian Media Group were in. It made their decision to sell or not quite difficult but it also gave them strength in the negotiation.

Bob asked me what I thought. This was not my train set, it belonged to GMG and I was only running it for them, although I was clearly emotionally involved as I'd given birth to it all. The company had invested in me as the leader of that business and, therefore, my view counted. I felt the price offered by Chrysalis was a good one and it would allow us to exit with substantial profits. I was certainly not going to be delivering profits of that level any time soon. Yet, if we didn't accept this offer, the board had to realise that they would have to invest further, perhaps another couple of hundred million pounds, to even compete against a stronger market. Added to that, prices were at the top of the market and if they bought more radio stations now they would have to hold on to them for at least a decade before they could see a return for that investment. The board decided to sell to Chrysalis, provided they could be persuaded to up their bid. Why we were asking for more money was unclear and no reason was forthcoming. Chrysalis flatly refused. The deal was dead and the board was now committed to building up the business through acquisition, as by then there were very few new licences to go for.

Some months later, we decided to turn the tables and put a reverse bid in for Chrysalis. We offered around one hundred and seventy million pounds but they wanted £225 million. Yet again, the marriage was blown apart at the altar. Phil Riley and I knew this was the best deal for both parties but our allegiance was to our respective boards. We were engaged but we could never find a way to conduct the marriage ceremony that suited both parties. So, faced with a future where I had to grow the company, I was determined to make things happen. The best-known radioman at the time was Ralph Bernard. He'd done more deals and had more experience of building up a radio group than any other and was a formidable force to deal with. He was either the chair or a director of most UK-wide radio bodies. I liked him a lot, we were fierce competitors though that didn't mean we couldn't get on. I'm lucky enough to get on with just about everyone in radio (well, before this book was published, anyway).

Ralph had been the boss of GWR Radio Group, while David Mansfield headed up Capital Radio Group. Together they'd formed one big company, GCap. After a few months of internal war games, Ralph Bernard came out on top as the new CEO. He was the leader of the largest radio group in the country and his opinion mattered even more than it did before.

Included in this newly formed group were the two stations I'd launched in the nineties, Century Radio North West and Century Radio North East. I had agreed with the GMG board that we would try to buy them.

Dealing with Ralph Bernard was like juggling with jelly. Just when you thought you had the deal in your hands, it would slip out of your grasp. To this day, I've never met a more skilled negotiator. After some weeks of courting, he agreed to sell us both stations for a total of sixty million pounds. A staggering amount, but the same figure that was paid to Border TV all those years previously. I'd warned the board, valuations were through the roof.

I was constantly going through the deal with Ralph but there were always a number of complications to work out. The worst was that he didn't want to lose the revenue he was getting in commission from selling national adverts to the two Century stations. He wanted the national sales at the two Century stations to remain with GCap. Second, he wanted an assurance that we wouldn't transfer the national sales contract to Chrysalis in the near future. Thirdly, Ralph also wanted our regional sales contract. This part was a deal breaker. I refused this but to keep the deal alive I agreed Ralph could have the national sales contract. I did not want to give all our national advertising to GCap because we already had a perfectly good deal for national advertising from Chrysalis but sometimes you just have to lose a little to win a lot. Ralph knew GMG Radio could not operate for too long with two different agencies supplying our national advertising and eventually we would have to end the Chrysalis contract and go with GCap as the national advertising agency for our entire network of stations.

However, with Ralph there was always something else. He would often email around midnight and we'd have a quick chat if I was still up. He'd say, 'John, you have the deal, well done, but ...'

There was always a 'but'.

'If I could just ask you to do one tiny alteration ...'

And so it went on like this for months. I explained to the board how frustrating it was but I was getting a world-class lesson in the art of negotiation.

Eventually, in 2006, we got to the point of doing the deal. We shook hands. In fact, in those days your word was often more important than the paperwork. I once did a deal in similar circumstances with Chris Evans for him to present The Sony Radio Academy Awards for The Radio Academy. I told Chris we had a deal and asked if he wanted any paperwork. He replied that my word was good enough, although I did later send him an email. I love to work with people like that very much. However, as this was a deal for sixty million pounds, paperwork was indeed very much required.

Ralph called me to explain that there was a slight issue. He had not yet had time to go around his key shareholders to tell them why he was selling two perfectly good, profitable radio stations so could we keep it quiet until then? As his company was a plc, if the news broke in the Press he would have to deny it or confirm it. If he denied it, then under the rules he could not do the deal again for at least six months. Clearly we didn't want this to happen and were happy to keep a lid on it for a couple of weeks.

'Okay, 'I said. 'It won't come from us.' The circle of people in our group who knew about the deal had been kept very tight.

A week later I had to tell my own boss, Carolyn McCall, that the Press had got hold of the story.

'What?' she demanded. 'Who the hell has got hold of it?'

'Er, The Guardian.'

'THE GUARDIAN!!!' she exploded.

'Yes, The Guardian, so could you go over there and do something about it please. If they go to print with that story we're doomed.' Our own bloody paper had the story and they could blow it for us. Now here's the thing. Even though Carolyn was the Chief Executive of Guardian Media Group, under the terms of the Scott Trust, she was barred from interfering with any of the editorial issues of the news-paper. She could ask, but she certainly couldn't insist. Carolyn made a call and brilliantly got the paper to hold off publishing for twenty-four hours but that was it. I called Ralph and told him the problem and we agreed to get the deal done that day. He would ring his shareholders.

Along with Andrew Zelouf and Stuart Kilby, plus GMG's team of solicitors, we turned up at GCap's lawyers' offices at two o'clock in the afternoon. We didn't finish until ten o'clock the next day. Sadly, when Eddie dropped me off in the car, I forgot to tell him it would be a long night. In the absence of instructions, he just sat there. At four in the morning, when I popped out for some air and a short walk, I noticed he was still sitting in the car. Oops. His words were choice to say the least and I sent him back to the flat for a kip.

Throughout the whole of this deal no one from GCap once came near us. They did everything on the phone. We'd already done some of the due diligence required but nevertheless, as the buyer, the onus was on us to make sure we knew exactly what we were purchasing. We also had to ensure the paperwork was correct even though I had owned both of these stations before. I was a little miffed no one from GCap was actually in the lawyers' office to help us through our questions. At two o'clock in the morning, a key point came up regarding the national sales contract. As part of the deal I had arranged with GCap a level of guarantee that would protect us in the future. The reason for this, I argued to Ralph, was that once he had sold this business to us, his team might not work as hard for the station as they might have done if they'd owned it. We needed some protection considering the level of revenue our national sales were generating. The deal was that we would get ninety per cent of the stations' sales target, no matter what. If they failed to sell enough airtime, they had to compensate us for that loss. This focused their minds and allowed us some breathing space. We needed to agree a clause to this effect but there was no one in front of us to do so. GCap's lawyers said they could not contact anyone because the people responsible were in bed and they didn't have their home numbers. I wasn't having this. I had their home numbers and would start with the commercial director and if he could not agree it, I'd ring Ralph at home.

At just after two o'clock in the morning, I called them up and got an agreement on the clause. If I was awake then they would be too! Around dawn, we were nearly there when I received a call from our Chairman, Paul Myners. He told me doing a deal at this kind of speed was always risky as we might overlook something.

'If you feel under pressure, John, walk away from the deal,' he said. 'The board will support you. There's no pressure to complete from this end.'

How good was that? It was the mark of a great chairman. Back out if you can't get the right deal. It empowered executives and underlined his skill.

Around ten o'clock we did the deal, I hadn't slept for nearly forty-eight hours. There's no doubt it was a thrilling day. I made the announcement but to be honest I was actually less emotional than the others in my team about getting my old stations back. I just saw it as the right deal at the right time for GMG. It was a bonus to have the Century stations back in my hands but by then it was just another business deal to me.

Shortly before our purchase was officially announced, I called Phil to tell him. I knew what this might mean to Chrysalis. The two stations we both wanted were now in our hands and worse still, the sales contract would soon have to be taken away from Chrysalis and put into the hands of GCap. This might just be the end of Chrysalis and both Phil and I knew it. I felt for him despite my success in getting the stations I wanted.

Sure enough, the following year Chrysalis was put up for sale.

Chapter Eighteen

THEY CALLED IT
HED KANDI

Richard Wheatly ran Jazz FM and was doing a great job with it. GMG were already shareholders in the station and an opportunity came up to buy it outright, but not at any cost. Richard had cleverly turned Jazz into both a radio and record company, using the radio station's output to promote Jazz CDs, which he sold online. At the same time he'd developed a new brand called Hed Kandi, which specialised in dance music. Jazz FM's two radio stations, in London and Manchester, were unprofitable but together with the record sales, which were profitable, it worked as a business.

A neat trick.

It was 2002 and our Chief Executive, Bob Phillis was confident a deal could be done to buy Jazz FM but at the last minute the price was going up, which wasn't unusual, so we had to make up our minds. To me the big opportunity we'd get from buying Jazz FM was that we could turn the radio station into a national brand, provided we won the newly-advertised regional radio licence for the West Midlands. This was the third regional licence to be advertised by the regulator. Considering there is only so much revenue you can take from a region, it was going to be tough for whoever won. To succeed you would have to be different.

*

I felt our application for Jazz FM could offer the listener real choice. I had informed the board that we should acquire these stations but to wait and see if we could win the licence for Birmingham to decide what to do with them. If we won in the West Midlands, then we could keep the Jazz FM brand intact. I put an application together that would turn Jazz FM from an unprofitable two-station enterprise into a three station near-network that would reach around seventeen million adults. Best of all, it would provide real choice on the dial. It made sense and, in one of my many meetings with OFCOM, I told the regulator this was not something we were going to do lightly. GMG was committed to the future of Jazz FM but we needed scale. They knew that, they understood that and they even had an inside track on the numbers to prove it. Every radio station submits their revenue numbers to the regulator each quarter, so they were acutely aware of our financial position and that of the whole industry. They, too, could see there was no future without scale.

My application proposed that if they awarded us the West Midlands licence then the chance of profitability greatly increased. We would guarantee to keep Jazz FM going.

Instead of giving us the West Midlands, they chose to award the licence to Kerrang Radio. This was the moment Jazz died as a radio station on FM in this country, as the regulator knew that to succeed we would have to change it into something else. I was livid and told them so. I also wrote to a number of MPs who were members of the Jazz Appreciation Society, informing them they that had the regulator they deserved. Perhaps I was just being emotional!

*

People moan about a lack of choice on the dial. The problem lies not just with the regulator but with the gravy train society we have encouraged. The regulator insisted applications were evidence led but they failed to add any common sense into some of their decisions. Hundreds of groups were applying for licences, not because they wanted to run radio stations or that they wanted to provide a service, but simply because it was the fastest route to Millionaires' Row. If you could get your MP to write and ask why your town didn't have a radio station, then OFCOM would do their best to get you one but there was simply not enough advertising around for all of these stations to exist. Even though I'd won and lost a number of times, I was always adult enough to admit either the winner had a better application or there was sufficient room for more than just one obvious gap in the market. That was fine and you take that on the chin but the loss of Jazz FM was hard to take.

*

We were left with no choice but to plough ahead with Plan B and immediately applied to change Jazz FM North West into Smooth FM from March the following year. Pleasingly, Smooth is widely regarded as an enormous success with better programming, flexibility of format, increased marketing, a focused approach and some great radio talent. Some of the jocks I later employed in Manchester included my old pal from Red Rose, Derek Webster and, believe it or not, Dave Lincoln. We hired Clear Marketing and they came up with a magnificent TV commercial that was the right advert at the right time. Over the years, the station has never had a better advertising campaign.

One of the downsides of being owned by Guardian Media Group, and there are not many, was that The Guardian newspaper was truly independent. The day after we launched Smooth, the paper ran a very critical review of our output. You can expect some negative comments but when the criticism was published by our own group paper it hit the staff hard. They found it very difficult to understand how someone from the GMG family could be so negative about one of their own. I sent a stern note to Alan Rushbridger, Editor of The Guardian, and he replied saying he allowed his journalists freedom of expression. Later on I was called by Bob Phillis and reminded that it was not wise to try and interfere with the editorial of the newspaper and, in future, I had to go through him. I wasn't interfering I was complaining but these problems were minor compared to the support and encouragement everyone in the group offered the radio team.

*

London, however, was the complete reverse of Manchester. The board was not keen for us to convert Jazz FM in the capital into Smooth FM until they were able to properly evaluate the success of the North West. This was all part of the fun of working with a big group and so there was an eighteen-month delay before we were finally given the go-ahead. The commercial radio market in the capital is very competitive, and with Magic FM as a direct rival, the challenge was that much greater. There's no point in offering excuses, under my time in the group we just couldn't make it happen and today, three years after leaving the company, the audience for Smooth London remains much lower than when we first bought it. Yet, and this is the irony, the station generates much more money than before due to the scale of being a national brand. I could bloody scream when I think what we could have done with Jazz FM.

——— 10 second break ———

Want a lift, son?

Bosses at a national radio station wanted to rid themselves of a colleague in the programming department. But how to do it without it costing them any money? The chap in question was a rather large-framed individual, so the management issued a memo to all the staff that said, in future, the lift would be turned off to save electricity. The man they wanted to move on worked on the third floor and was not happy. After four days of being forced to climb the stairs, he handed in his resignation. As soon as he'd departed, the station bosses switched the lift back on.

We were always having discussions about our format with OFCOM, and came in for a lot of stick from the regulator about the kind of music we were playing on Jazz FM in London. After OFCOM's decision not to award us the West Midlands licence, we widened the range of music the station played, even though we knew we were chancing our arm. The regulator argued that we were close to being out of format and if we didn't sort it quickly a fine would follow. I disagreed on the music and, at one point, I told OFCOM that while they were the regulator, they were not experts in the format and were not always right. I even threatened to bring the might of GMG's legal team into the debate and challenge their views aggressively.

I was always open to a debate but it had to be meaningful. One day, OFCOM asked me how I would describe jazz music. I told them that to me jazz was anything with a trumpet.

'What, anything with a trumpet?' the regulator said, incredulously. 'Are you joking?'

'Well, you started it,' I replied and kept that stance up for a while, as it wasn't actually dismissed out of hand. I recall asking one of our producers to put some trumpets into songs to see what they sounded like.

'We might be able to play them,' I said.

So he spent a couple of days mixing the sound of trumpets into the hits of stars like Phil Collins. It was madness, of course, but the longer we could put forward a view, the longer the regulators talked about it. It kept us out of trouble for months.

The smartest person the regulator employed was Martin Campbell but he was sidelined by those above him, for no other reason in my view than he was often quite reasonable and knew more about the world of radio than any of the rest of them. The problem, the regulator told us, was that the sort of people who liked jazz were also the sort who could write great letters and, better still, they knew which letterbox to put them through for maximum effect.

*

When I took over Jazz FM it was clear to me that Richard Wheatly had put together a fascinating business plan. The radio stations were losing about a million a year, yet the record sales side of his operation was making slightly more, so as a whole it worked. The trouble was the record business was starting to erode and Richard was selling out at the right time. By now we had turned the North West around but I had to tackle the non-radio part. The issue for me was that it was hard to understand. Also, GMG were not so keen on selling records and after a while they wanted me to sell on this part of the business to someone who specialised in this sector. We had hired an MD for this music division but it was bloody hard work to be honest. Their ethos was very different from my team in radio and, while I tried my best to ensure they were all included, it was obvious they didn't want to be part of our operation. They were in the record business, and radio was something else. They were becoming a distraction to the main event.

Part of the record sales side of Jazz FM was a record label called Hed Kandi. It was one of the rare times my own kids got excited about something I ran.

At a management meeting one day, Chief Executive Bob Phillis and Finance Director Nick Castro asked about one of the Hed Kandi party nights that the record department ran. Even now, I find it hard to explain but at the time it went like this. The team organised Hed Kandi evenings and would take something like £15,000 on the door. People flocked to these evenings because they were more than just an event playing dance music, they were a total experience. The door takings were then distributed to the evening's entertainers, including DJs, jugglers, flame-throwers and street performers. Any cash that was left over was brought into the office on the Monday morning, often in a brown paper bag. What was left from the fifteen grand takings might be as low as five thousand pounds. That was our profit but we had no way of checking the figures because so much cash was handed out over the weekend. I didn't like it and neither did my finance team. We would have had to run the whole night ourselves to get a grip, I explained, and GMG certainly didn't want us to get into that.

In the end I was told, 'John, just sell the thing and get what you can for it.'

There was interest in a management buy-out but we got a call from a competitive record company who were also interested in buying the operation. We hadn't put it about for sale but once management try to find investors, there are often no secrets. The record company could move fast and had the cash whereas the management buy-out would be slow and not guaranteed. However, I wanted to give the management every opportunity and set aside a window for them. All was going to plan, when I suddenly received a call from The Ministry of Sound. I met their CEO, Lohan Presencer, for breakfast and he asked if Hed Kandi was for sale. I told him it was but any offer would have to start with a three in front of it, although he was such a sharp operator he had a pretty good idea what it was worth. Lohan said he wanted the Hed Kandi label, its catalogue of songs and was prepared to buy it quickly for cash. He tabled me an offer that was roughly the same as we had on the table although it was miles better than the management buyout proposal. This was Tuesday morning and I told Lohan that if he wanted to buy it, Ministry of Sound had to do the deal that week. I was not going to delay the sale, it was first past the post. If he wanted to grab this opportunity then he had to move fast. Lohan left saying he'd be in touch. A couple of hours later he called and confirmed his offer provided we could guarantee exclusivity to complete the deal and see some figures. I really liked Ministry of Sound and Lohan in particular plus I would rather have sold it to him than a major record label where the product might be lost. I told him that the accounts were in our Leeds radio HQ so if he wanted to see them he had to jump on a train to Yorkshire which he promptly did and he then re-confirmed his offer.

I pulled in Andrew Zelouf, our internal deal maker and finance brain. I called Ministry of Sound and told Lohan that he had two days to complete the paperwork. We called in the lawyers and set to work. Selling a radio station or any company demands your focus and attention and you have to be absolutely sure of exactly what you're buying. The buyer wanted the music catalogue and that, in reality, was all they were after although they knew they would have to take the staff. They certainly didn't need the building. All GMG had to do was ensure we could prove we owned the music we said we owned under Hed Kandi and its associated brands and labels. We decided to provide guarantees on all of this, as the paperwork was not as good as it should have been for a purchaser because of the short timescale. All was going well and we met on the Thursday afternoon to sign the contract. With me in the boardroom that afternoon was Andrew Zelouf, our lawyers Davenport Lyons, Lohan Presencer from Ministry of Sound, their respective lawyers and one other, who I think was their chairman. Going through the paperwork we hit a hurdle. When doing a deal like this there is often an agreement on the level of claims the buying company can come back to the seller on, if they subsequently find something is not what we said it was. Ministry of Sound were buying Hed Kandi on just two days of due diligence. Despite a high level of care, they might have missed something. We were assuring the buyer that we held the rights for the parts of the business we were selling. If this turned out not to be the case the buyer could ask to be compensated. This is normal practice and the debate then is on the level of claims. The proposal from us on the table was that we would only look into any single claim of twenty-five thousand pounds or more and even then the buyer had to have a basket of claims totalling at least £100,000 before they could come back to us at all. Ministry of Sound wanted a much smaller figure, each claim being just five thousand pounds and the basket total of £25,000. The discussion was going nowhere. We were both set in our stance. It was a typical hold up in a deal and my job was to find a way around it. Also, I wanted to get back home to the North East that night if I could, so this impasse was starting to irritate me somewhat.

'Look,' I said. 'How about this as an idea? Let's see how flexible you are on the rest of the contract. If we get to the end and there are no other issues then I will in turn be more flexible on this particular issue. If, however, I find that this is just one of a number of issues that might hold up the deal then I won't be keen to do something on this point.'

'Okay,' they said. 'That's a good compromise.' So we rattled through the rest of the contract with ease. In the end, there was only one issue left on the table and I said that I was still minded to keep to my stance. They were buying a brilliant company with a strong music catalogue. Who knew what gems were in our vaults. They were paying a fair price but not a great price and in that case they had to take more of the risk. Furthermore, we were giving warranties on just about everything of importance so what was the problem? I could see this was not going to be acceptable. They were not having any of it. In their place I wouldn't have done so either considering I'd promised to be willing to compromise. Lohan is a smart operator who knows his business, so much so their company today is one of the best there is, a real credit to the guy and his team. I liked him but on all deals you have to lose a little to win a lot.

We were at a basket of claims of £25,000 per claim and £100,000 in total before they could come back to us. They were at £5,000 a claim and a basket of just £25,000. We were miles apart but I had a suggestion.

'How about we arm-wrestle for it?' I said, taking off my jacket and rolling up my sleeve.

Utter silence.

Andrew Zelouf insisted on an urgent meeting outside the room. I went out to be told I was absolutely mad. I couldn't risk the Scott Trust's money on an arm-wrestling match, he shouted.

'Are you suggesting I could lose this Andrew?'

'It's not about winning or losing, John,' he protested. 'It's a gamble and you can't gamble our money like this.'

'Okay, calm down, I'm only joking,' I said. 'I had to break the tension, so let's see how they are now.'

We went back and I announced that my internal lawyer had advised me that I couldn't undertake the challenge.

There was relief around the room. Then I threw in, 'But our lawyers could. Why don't we do it through them?'

Robert Charlton, our external lawyer, went white. Then their legal advisor asked, 'John would you be happy to agree to £10,000 a claim and a basket at £50,000?'

'Great, that's good enough for me.'

We did the deal. As it was now a little late, I decided to stay the night in London and travel up to the North East the next morning.

It's just as well I did.

Travelling out of London the next morning, I received a call from Bob Phillis's PA. He wanted to see me urgently and I had to come into the office. I turned around. When I arrived, I could sense a little tension in the room.

'Sit down, John,' said Bob. 'Now, please tell me that a main board director of GMG plc did not try and gamble a hundred thousand pounds of our money on an arm wrestling match. Please tell me it's not true.'

'Err. Well Bob, that's not exactly true at all,' I replied. 'The gap was much smaller than that and, in any case, it was just a bluff.'

'Well it wasn't a bluff that Andrew agreed with. He nearly had a heart attack.'

'Bob, that risk was small and in any case I needed to close the deal and get home.' I said. 'The deal is done, we have the cash transferred and we've got rid of a problem child. I thought you were going to shower me with chocolate and champagne but I take it this is a bollocking.'

'Correct,' he said. 'Don't ever do that again. Now well done, have a great weekend.'

And as I stood up to leave, Bob said, 'By the way, that's the most amusing tale I've heard for a long time.'

I loved that man!

Chapter Nineteen

A SMOOTH FINISH

After buying Century from GCap we wanted to increase the Smooth Radio footprint across the UK. This involved buying out Saga Radio, which was run by Ron Coles but owned entirely by Britain's biggest specialist company for the over-fifties. I felt a bit sorry for Ron because as far as I could see he was never given the appropriate budget to really do something quite unique with the radio stations, despite being owned by a company that had substantial funds.

I'd met Saga's management some months previously and I told them I'd be up for a discussion if they were interested in selling. I suspected Saga Radio would be on the market sooner rather than later because they were about to sell their overall business and the last thing they wanted was a loss-making company on their books eating away at their sale value. What they needed to do was to sell it beforehand and take the cash into the parent company accounts.

Saga Group put their four radio stations, covering the East Midlands, West Midlands, North East and Glasgow, on the market in 2006 and, as we were in the lead position, we acquired them in December that year, re-launching the whole group as Smooth Radio in March, 2007. There was no way we were going to pay top dollar for these four stations unless we had a fairly good indication from the regulator that we could make some changes to the format. The network we had included two stations that were once Jazz FM, plus these four stations from Saga and now we wanted them all to be called Smooth but with the same format. It was not an easy task. Ahead of the deal we approached OFCOM and were given the appropriate warm noises that, this time, our efforts to secure changes might be acceptable. I think they would rather we'd bought these stations than anyone else because at least we were more likely than other groups to try and keep the older listenership. We put together an application, backed up by research, to make the best case possible. To be fair to the regulator, they were helpful and offered good advice but it still had to go to the content board for approval. For that, we had to wait.

*

While we were never going to keep the Saga radio brand I had a problem with the name Smooth Radio. I came up with Smooth simply as a shorthand way of suggesting to listeners what we played. It suggested tuneful melodic songs and that, by and large, is what it is. We would certainly never play rock music.

However, now I had six stations instead of just the two, we would have to embark on a very expensive marketing campaign running into millions. If we were going to change the name, it was now or never. Magic FM in London used to be called Melody Radio and, althought it was no longer in use anywhere in the UK, it was still a name owned by EMAP. I approached Dee Ford to see if I could acquire it from her as it was a much more suitable description than Smooth but she wouldn't agree to it. I threatened to go ahead anyway just to see if they really would to go to court to defend their ownership but after a couple of sharp letters between us I decided to back off. I wasn't going to fall out with someone I've known for years, and respected, over a name.

Instead, I offered anyone in my group a 'Brucy Bonus' as I called it if they could suggest a better name than Smooth. This sort of thing always gets people involved and I was genuinely interested in finding something different. Despite a number of great suggestions, we just couldn't come up with a better one. Part of the problem was that when a name was suggested that might just work we couldn't get the appropriate domain name and in a world where everything is digital, that was essential. It was either already taken by someone else or it was not an exact fit. You can't just launch a name on FM and not worry about the Internet. The world is much closer and connected these days so it would be foolish to go ahead unless you had approval and ownership on all platforms. In the end, we kept the name and ploughed on. While I didn't get involved in the day to day programming or running of a station, I did, as you might imagine, ensure my view of life was heard. Having a strong personality helps plus as the leader of the business, this means people do have a duty to listen.

──────────── **30 second break...** ────────────

Vending Machine

A major UK radio station was given a gift of a vending machine stuffed full of chocolate and crisps and all the things that last two minutes on your lips and a lifetime on the hips. The staff paid for the contents and the station didn't make a profit but it didn't cost the management anything either.

The MD of the station received a call from the vending company who were thinking of pulling the machine because it was losing money. The problem was that while all the chocolate bars and crisps were being eaten, not enough cash was going in the machine.

The baffled radio station MD asked the vending machine owner to give him a few days so he could set up a secret video camera and wait to see what happened.

After a couple of days he pulled the video and started racing through the contents until something caught his eye. What he saw surprised him. The breakfast host, a man taking home a six-figure salary would arrive at 5.30 am when no one was around. He lay on the ground, pushed the wire from a coat hanger inside the machine and hooked out a hoard of goodies that he would then eat during his the show or take home.

Unbelievable.

This guy was paid a fortune but here he was nicking bars of chocolate, worth fifty pence each.

The MD faced a dilemma. This jock was brilliant on the air and there was no way the station wanted to fire him. They just needed to stop the theft.

They called him in and asked if he knew why the vending machine was losing cash. He completely refused to acknowledge any wrongdoing.

'It wasn't me,' he said adamantly. He crapped himself when shown the video. He'd been caught red-handed and now he was very red faced. He sought forgiveness and the management certainly didn't want to lose their star jock. Neither could they publicly rebuke him to the rest of the staff because they would all think he was a knob, even though he was.

Their solution to the problem was ingenious.

It just so happened that the monthly staff meeting was the next day, where the MD said the breakfast presenter wanted to make an announcement.

The star jock told the team how proud he was of their continued help with his show. He was popular because of how much work the team and, indeed the station, put in to make it successful. As a small treat, everything out of the vending machine for the whole of the following month was complimentary and he would pick up the bill. The staff thought he was a hero, the vending machine company did their best revenue ever and the jock simply paid up and shut up.

Sometimes, things work out just fine.

*

We toured the stations we purchased as one management team. I suppose I would say this but I believe the team we had at GMG was the best in the business. They were not only good at their job; they were also passionate about what they did.

Some people believe that when they buy a business everything the company did before you took it over was wrong. I always thought there were some things every group or station did well and what we wanted to do was take all the good bits they were doing and integrate it within our own larger group. Why wouldn't you want to do that? There is no point in re-inventing the wheel and in any case, there were things in our own group that could always be improved upon. GMG Radio today is a collection of what we were originally, plus the people we inherited along the way and, a mixture of systems we found that were better than our own. Although having said that, one area we never compromised on was the ethos of how people should be treated. My message to Jill Johnston, our HR Director, was that we should treat people the way we would want to be treated ourselves. Fairly and quickly. However, some employees take things too far and either lie or try to accuse you of underhanded practice. I always made it clear we would go straight to court in those circumstances and, in my time, we never lost a case we took all the way.

One case in particular involved a presenter called Adrian Allen. He was working for us on the late night phone-in show at Real Radio in Wales and accused us of offering him a 'verbal' contract that did not materialise. This was the first we knew about it and when a contract was not forthcoming, he threatened to take us to court in the hope that we would simply pay out. I called the PD who told me that he'd never offered any such thing. The claim was all false, he said. I actually liked Adrian and admired him as a broadcaster but you cannot let someone make a claim against you when it is not true. He initiated legal proceedings and, as it was not in the small claims court, I was advised by our company lawyers to make him an offer. It was going to cost us around twenty thousand pounds in lawyers' fees and management time just to get to court. I was livid. I just can't accept giving people money to go away when we are in the right.

However, under pressure from our advisors, we made him an offer and, lo and behold, he refused it. I was never more delighted because to be honest I wanted my day in court. I wanted to be there with my team to explain our position. I may be naive, but I cannot abide giving in and always believe the court will work out who is right or wrong. My own lawyers told me to up the offer even further, just a little. GMG told me it was good advice. With gritted teeth, I moved upwards in order to save both legal costs and management time but yet again it was refused. That was it and I told Adrian's lawyer there was no way I was going to settle on the steps of the courtroom. I took great pride in the way we operated and I was not going to allow someone to say we operated in any other way. Of course, we got it wrong sometimes but in those instances we put it right wherever possible. If he was going to force me to go all the way to Adrian's home town of Nottingham for a day in court, I would relish it.

Over dinner the night before, our barrister worried me a little. She told me that the case was not exactly about who was right or wrong, but more about who the court believed to be right or wrong.

Adrian spent the whole of the next morning in the witness box. It was unfortunate that he sweated very heavily and did not come over as someone as cool and collected as he appears on the air. When my team were put on the stand they performed as I'd expected, with authority, reason and gave a simple but correct explanation that this was just someone having a go because we were a billion pound company. The judge concluded by saying our evidence was thoroughly believable, in particular that of our Programme Director John Simons. We won the case one hundred per cent and were even awarded costs. You could not get a more concrete result.

Getting costs awarded and getting the costs from the individual is another matter entirely but, for me, it was the right decision and was a note to all those who fancied their chances that we were prepared to go all the way to defend ourselves. Sometimes you have to be seen to be doing what is right, regardless of the cost.

*

Employment laws in Britain really worry me. Everyone needs protection but it seems we have lost the balance between the employer and the employee. Today, running a business is so complicated and so wrapped up in red tape that the only winners are lawyers. I support the view of Lord Sugar when he says the law needs to be looked at again.

Take references. If you give someone a poor reference these days, and the employee finds out, they can sue you for preventing them getting a job. Why would anyone want to give a former employee a bad reference if they didn't deserve it? I resolved this in the end. Ninety-nine per cent of my employees loved working for GMG. Sometimes we got it wrong and when we did I liked to think we acted honourably.

When a new employer asked for a reference for an ex-employee I wasn't happy with, I simply wrote back saying that I was not prepared to give one for that person. In my book that is much more offensive but legally you are in a much stronger position. It is a shame the law drives us to that point. Anyone can be fired if you are prepared to pay what we call 'the sack tax', although I have often heard it called the Nose Clause. This is the term used where the manager wakes up and decides they don't like the shape of an employee's nose any more and wants to fire them for no other reason than that. In that case, you simply have to pay out what is due.

The reality of course is that when a manager wants to move someone on, they have usually lost trust or respect for that individual. Not always, but mostly. Managers can easily come up with five reasons to keep someone or five reasons to fire them. It is their choice but it's one of the key reasons why I always insist that you hire people you like first and their talent comes a close second. If you like someone, you are very often keen to work with them to ensure they sort themselves out and become a great employee. If you don't like them personally you'll often find a reason to let them go far too quickly. The stark reality of business is that it is hugely expensive to hire people, train them up, get them involved, spend the time and effort in ensuring they can be as good as they can be. Then to lose them because you made a bad hire is hugely destructive to your overall business. Hiring the right people for the right job is an enormous skill and a huge risk.

Despite the odd people issue I was enjoying life enormously. We were winning and there's nothing like it for raising the spirit of everyone around you. I have always liked rock music and was on the lookout for a station where I could play rock songs all day. The opportunity came when we managed to buy failing Q96 in Paisley for a relatively small sum and turned it into Rock Radio. The station got itself into a spot of trouble after complaints that it was promoting itself as a Glasgow station, which it clearly wasn't. Naturally, their competitors complained. The truth is that Q96 was just another victim of a time when the regulator handed out licences in hugely competitive markets when there was never any chance of them being profitable. A commercial station that is not a commercial success, or has no chance of doing so, is nothing more than vanity broadcasting. The marketing idea for Rock Radio was created by The Bridge Agency in Glasgow and it was brilliant work. We launched the station on a shoestring after moving it into the Real Radio building in Glasgow, sharing all the backroom costs. Apart from wanting to start a rock station, it was also protectionism of sorts, as I certainly didn't it to fall into the hands of anyone else. Q96 had a fantastic signal and you could hear it all over Glasgow so the last thing we wanted was someone to acquire it on the cheap and start to compete against us by playing the hits of the past four decades. When we changed the music format, it sounded unique, very different to anything else on the dial. The problem with rock music, or any other narrow forms of broadcasting, is that the listeners who love it, really love it and they know their music, too. It was always a fine balance between being commercial enough to succeed and providing an output that rock fans would be proud to call their own. In the end we achieved that goal but it confirmed that a stand-alone business like this would never work. Spot advertising, where commercials are played across the day, was hard to find, despite our success with Real Radio. You simply had to belong to a larger organisation and share resources.

Later on, when a radio station in Manchester was advertised, I decided to put in for it with a similar rock format but the audience research, conducted by QuestionAir led by the truly gifted Rachel Steel, showed that there was more than just one gap in the market. All I wanted to do was run a rock station but it was evident we would never win it if I ploughed ahead with that strategy. The two biggest gaps uncovered by the research were rock music and a speech format of some kind. Manchester is a very difficult market to find a gap where you could offer real choice on the dial and become successful. The Greater Manchester area is littered with radio disasters. One such failure was a station called Fortune. How wrong can you be? It reminded me of another station in Winchester called Win FM, which did anything but! In 2005, when another licence was being advertised for Manchester we put together an application for an all-talk based station. This was the home of the Manchester Evening News, the regional hub for GMG with hundreds of staff, but despite some creative ways in which we could share news and journalists, there was simply no chance of us ever making a commercial return. I told the GMG board and I sensed they breathed more easily after I made that decision. I even got a call from the regulator who told me how disappointed they were that we were pulling out but I explained that the risk was just too great. In the end, that particular licence was awarded to XFM. You had to think differently if you wanted to win something but there is no point in being so different that you commit commercial suicide. Mind you, I was called 'brave', which is just another name for idiot when, some years earlier in the East Midlands, I had this crazy idea to apply for a licence that would fund itself from just sponsorship and promotional airtime. My train of thought was that there were just too many stations competing for too little commercial spot airtime so I ran the numbers and we thought it might just work. I recall the regulator asking a lot of searching questions about this. I thought there was a chance when it turned out there was no chance whatsoever. However, this time I thought we had found a gap worth chasing so I made the decision to go with a rock-talk format. It was slightly grasping at straws but I believed if we could get entertaining jocks on the air at breakfast and drivetime who could do entertaining 'talk' rather than just waffle then it just might work. I also knew that the regulator would know that the two gaps in the market were the same as we had identified. Let's do both I said to the team so we put in an application under the name Rock-Talk that was just a mixture of the two.

I had been telling the executive team at GMG that we needed to develop our succession plan. As part of the process, John Simons had advertised for a deputy. We decided to hold the interviews in a Leeds hotel but I had completely forgotten that it was also the day of the Manchester Licence award. If we were successful, the call would come on my mobile at 4.30pm but to be honest, even though I am always positive, I was not feeling it that day. When the last of the candidates came in we were already running behind schedule. I told him that I was expecting or should that be hoping to receive a call bang on 4.30pm and apologised if I had to take it but nevertheless he should just carry on and present his case to us for the job. At 4.28pm my mobile started to ring with the words OFCOM coming up on the screen. The poor chap was in full flow but I was shouting to Simo, 'it's OFCOM'.

'Well, answer the bloody phone, man!' he screamed. I did and the Manchester licence was ours. It was such a shock that Simo and I jumped up and started hugging each other, completely forgetting this guy in front of us. We had to ask him to stop and come back and see us the following week as there was no way we would be able to concentrate from that point. To be fair, he was happy to do so and in any case, John Simons later employed him in another position. His name was Mark Matthews, a man I had worked with years before at Red Rose.

I immediately called up Nick Castro at GMG. Normally Nick enjoyed days like this but instead of congratulating us, he said, 'Oh no. That's another load of costs coming our way then!'

He didn't mean to say it the way it came out, he was trying his hand at comedy but Nick was always keen on radio and we later shared a drink together by way of a celebration. What we had now though was something quite unique. In Manchester we had Century Radio, Smooth Radio and Rock Radio all from one building, all with one management team and every chance to make it work commercially. I knew Rock Radio was always going to struggle, but it was an opportunity.

Dee Ford, the MD of Bauer Radio called me asking for clarity on what we were going to call the station as she felt there was a risk of confusion with regard to their Lancashire station named Rock FM and our similar named Manchester based Rock Radio. There was less risk with Rock-Talk but that name was just for the application. Despite the fact that these were two very different stations, playing very different types of music in two different areas, Bauer were nervous that listeners in minor cross-over areas, where they could pick up both stations, might tick the RAJAR box for our station when they were listening to theirs. I could see their point but I thought it was a mute one to be honest. The cross over for our respective transmissions was only slight but the problem was not so much the issue of our FM service but on the wider North West DAB regional multiplex. That covered the whole of their Rock FM area and she wanted assurances that we would not go on that service and cause confusion to listeners who might wonder which station they were tuned into. Considering the cost of going on the regional DAB was a near six figure sum and that this station would take at least five years to be break-even at best, I was happy to agree to this request for as long as we continued to use the Rock Radio name. In any case, five years is a long time for anyone in the media, not to mention radio. Today it's called Real XS.

We ploughed on and I hired the same advertising agency for the launch of the Manchester station as I had in Glasgow. They arrived with their creative ideas and, even though I was pressed for time, meetings like this are always something I enjoyed going to. In any case, I was so opinionated about marketing that nothing was approved unless I had seen it. The agency started their presentation and I said nothing. At the end I exploded and told them straight that this was the most dire, lazy, last minute creative idea I had seen for some time. They were taking me for some sort of mug and had somehow mistakenly believed that just because I had loved the Glasgow campaign that it was fine to just wander down the M6 with the same idea and spin it for Manchester. I was fuming and barked that if this was the best they could do they should just say so and I would get someone else. The whole of the room fell silent. What is more they knew I had caught them out. I ordered them to come back with something better within a week. To be fair to them, they did just that. The new campaign was miles better and much more on target for the Manchester audience. I rang up Alan Clarke, the MD of The Bridge agency and congratulated them on their attitude, professionalism and desire to put things right. As such, we had both won. I have a simply philosophy about business. If I am paying a professional fee then I expect a professional service. I pay on time provided the supplier delivers on time and on budget. What more can anyone want from a business relationship? When asked, I give clear instructions. I value debate, I love people to stand their ground but once a decision is made I expect professionals to get on with it with a smile on their face. It's only radio!

Chapter Twenty

A HORSE WITH NO NAME

Travelling over the Pennines on the M62, the phone rang in my car. I rarely answered any calls that said 'withheld' but for some reason I took this one. The caller asked if he was speaking to John Myers and wanted to know if I was able to talk confidentially. Even though my brother, Eddie, was driving me, I confirmed this was the case.

He told me his name, I'd never heard of him, and he asked if it would be possible to meet to discuss a personal matter. I said possibly, depending on what that personal matter might be. He was unable to give me any further details but it would be something to my benefit. I was absolutely happy at GMG, the board had sanctioned the purchase of both Century Radio stations and we had also just bought out Saga Radio, which included the West Midlands station we wanted. Those purchases had cost the company more than one hundred million pounds. There was no way I was going to be tempted by another job. I told him that if this was a job offer that involved me leaving GMG, I was definitely not interested and there was no future in a possible meeting. He didn't confirm it either way so I closed the discussion and thanked him for calling. It was impossible for me to move from GMG.

I thought no more about it until a week later when he called again. This time he said it was really important and all he wanted was fifteen minutes of my time. After that if I was still not interested, he wouldn't call again. I had no idea what this was about but I agreed to meet with him, more out of courtesy than anything else. However, I reiterated that if this was simply a job offer then it would be a pretty fruitless exercise.

We met at my London lawyers, Davenport Lyons, who very kindly gave me the use one of their private meeting rooms. The man quickly got to the point. He had a proposal but it was being made on one condition. If the offer or the proposal was not acceptable then he wanted assurances that his client's name would not be made public. Furthermore, for this particular meeting, he would not be telling me the client's name unless I wished to take it forward. I agreed to this request and, for that reason, I won't even reveal his name now.

While I have always maintained that confidentiality, I can talk about the actual proposal itself, which was quite unusual to say the least. He explained that his client wished to enter into the UK commercial radio sector. However, while he had the cash, he didn't have anyone who could run it and that's where I came in. I was a little disappointed to be honest. I'd told him twice that I was not interested in a job, although he was at pains to point out this was not just a job, it was a partnership that came with a significant slice of the company. Of course, I would be paid a very attractive package well in excess of my current arrangement but the real benefit was the future value of my shares. It could result in many millions. Anyone reading this would think this was madness.

'Let's assume I am interested enough to take this further,' I said. 'What's the plan?'

He explained there was plenty of cash available but very few good people to run radio stations. His team had earmarked a radio group that he felt was underperforming and was available to purchase. As most of the radio groups in the UK were plcs, anyone could buy them for the right amount of money. Before going ahead and doing that, they had to know I was secure. He then used a great sales line, 'If we can't bring you into our acquisition team, we might not enter the UK radio market at all.'

I pondered for a moment and was then quite honest with him. First of all, I was flattered. Who isn't when they get a job offer but this was quite ridiculous. I was the CEO of a major radio group that I had started eight years previously. I'd hired most of the executive team personally and many were both friends and work colleagues. On top of this, I was liked and respected at GMG and I loved working with them. While cash is always a motivator at some point, a couple of hundred grand extra was never going to be my motivating factor.

I said, 'Plus, you have nothing, absolutely nothing at this point in time. Acquiring companies, especially public ones, is fraught with difficulties.'

I then asked him to consider his proposal from my own perspective. Here I was meeting with a man I'd never seen before, who was telling me a very wealthy client, who he would not name, was insisting in getting into radio. They planned to acquire underperforming assets, turn them around and sell them on within five years, hopefully less.

'Is that correct?' I asked.

'Yes,' he replied but I was missing the important point that I would be a co-shareholder in those stations and not just a member of staff. While I understood that, only a fool would take this discussion forward. It was like backing a horse with no name.

He then said something I was not expecting, 'If we could demonstrate the seriousness of our proposal and find a way to remove any doubt about our intentions, would that be worthy of another meeting?'

I said it might but I was unsure how they could achieve that, based on our conversation. I also said that I did not wish to have another meeting without knowing the identity of the mystery backer. We parted on friendly terms but it was a strange meeting to say the least.

Late the following day, he called again. He believed he would be able to give me the comfort I required, plus reveal who his client was. This was just weird. My diary was already full, not to mention I considered continuing the discussion to be a complete waste of my time. We'd also just sent the regulator our proposal for changing the format for Smooth in London. Word was that it would go through this time, confidence was high and the team was clearly on a roll. Meeting with this chap would be foolish and yet I wanted to know who the buyer was. The only gap I had in the diary was an hour the following Tuesday afternoon, again in Manchester. When I arrived at Manchester's most fashionable hotel, The Lowry, he was already waiting and this time he'd brought a colleague who turned out to be his legal adviser. The man I had met previously was dressed in a smart, expensive yet casual style I often see in London that smacks of a confidence that comes from being loaded. The legal adviser was tall, slim, Savile Row suited with the shiniest shoes I'd ever seen. What I noticed most was that he carried a smart leather brief case with his initials on it. Flash git, I thought. The bar was empty, we found a corner table and straight away the man I had met in London revealed the identity of the mystery investor. I knew immediately they had the money. No doubt about that. They wanted to know how I felt and was I willing to continue talking? They were confident about their ability to gain the assets but were concerned about the terms of my present contract and any restrictions it contained. As they'd been upfront with me, I told them the facts. I had twelve-months rolling notice plus a period of exclusivity that meant I couldn't compete in any area in the UK where GMG had a radio station. In effect, if GMG wanted to play hardball, they could keep me out of the game for eighteen months, although you always hope to negotiate that down. They were not surprised and asked how litigious the group were. 'Very,' I told them. Guardian Media dealt straight but competed hard. I liked that about them. Furthermore, and this was essential to say, this was a contract I'd readily agreed to sign. It was a fair contract considering the investment GMG were making in radio and I would not wish to be seen to be breaking it or not standing by the terms of that contract.

'If they sacked me I would expect them to pay it up,' I said, 'and if I resigned, I would honour the exit terms I'd agreed.'

'That's what we thought you'd say,' he said.

Then the lawyer, who had not said a word until that point, jumped in. 'Mr Myers, here is our proposal. We'd like you to resign now so your notice period would start to kick in.'

'What, you must be joking,' I replied. 'You don't have any radio assets, you only have a dream. In fact, some people would call this a complete fantasy.'

'John, we can't buy a radio group that might cost us up to half a billion pounds and then have to wait up to eighteen months for you to turn up for work,' the lawyer replied. 'We'd be losing far too much value. We need to start your notice period ticking now.'

'Well that's not going to happen,' I said, laughing.

There was a pause and we all just looked at each other.

'We understand that you will not walk away from all that you have developed without some level of guarantee,' the first man said. 'We cannot tell you about our specific target except that the turnover will be in excess of a hundred million pounds.'

This meant they were talking about a much bigger group than I was currently running.

'We need you to depart from GMG now to either help us with that bid or to be able to run it as soon as we acquire the assets,' the lawyer reiterated.

'I understand that,' I said, 'but why would I?'

What came from his lips next stopped me in my tracks, 'Mr Myers, we will pay you a signing on fee of one million pounds.'

Silence. I was trying to compute what he had said.

'I'm sorry, did you say a million?'

'Yes that's right.'

Yikes, that got my attention. I sat there for what must have been a minute before bouncing back to reality.

'I'm sorry, I don't understand. You're offering me a million for leaving GMG? You know that as soon as I resign to go somewhere else they will put me on gardening leave for a year. They will be fuming that I've left them at this critical time and, believe me, they will hold me to every last restriction they can. I'd do the same if was in their place.'

'Yes, we understand that but we are serious and here are our terms: we will pay one million pounds into your lawyer's escrow account. We agree that if we don't acquire an asset of the size we have discussed within twelve months from the date of your signature, you can have the money. Your lawyer will hold the cash. However, we also want some commitment from you, too. If we do manage to acquire these assets, you have to use that million pounds to buy shares in the new venture, obviously at a discounted rate.'

That is quite normal in this type of deal. What is *not* normal is to have walk-away money if nothing happens. This was staggering. In all my business life I'd never heard of a deal like this. I had to clarify the position again.

'I'm sorry but I really need to be clear on this. I've never heard of you before but I have heard of your client. You want to buy some radio assets but, at present, you have nothing. You're asking me to leave GMG Radio, a company I've built up from zero, in order to run a business you presently don't have. If you do get those assets, I have to use that cash to buy shares in the venture, albeit at a discounted rate. If you don't buy any radio assets within twelve months of my signature, I get to keep the whole million pounds with no strings attached whatsoever. In short, you might very well be giving me a million quid just to sit at home for a year.'

'Yes,' they replied in unison. 'That's the deal.'

Bloody hell. What's the catch? I kept asking myself. The deal was plain and simple.

'We want an answer by the end of the week and your signature and resignation lodged with GMG within ten days,' said the lawyer. 'We can't wait any longer than that.'

*

I cancelled my next meeting and returned home. This was something I had to tell Linda face to face. When I told her the deal we both sat there flabbergasted. I shared this with just two very close friends. Both of them said it was such a crazy deal that I would be absolutely mad to pass up the opportunity. It was a genuine, one hundred-carat win-win deal. I couldn't lose. My friends asked me to remove from my brain any emotion whatsoever with regard to GMG. This was just business and brilliant business it was too. It was hard to fathom for a lad from Carlisle, born and bred on the turnip tops of life in Cumbria. I'd left school without a single qualification to my name and now here I was with an offer that was quite remarkable. I couldn't sleep and I certainly couldn't concentrate.

On the Monday morning, Linda said, 'Just do what you think is right. This offer may never come up again. If the lawyer confirms all the details then it's a very big decision. Whatever you decide is fine by me.'

I left the house still not knowing what to do, but I did agree to meet with the two men again in London. At that meeting, I accepted the deal. It was just too good to turn down and, even though I knew emotionally this would be devastating to both my team and myself, I had to do it. GMG Radio was more family than work and I loved it. But I was determined I wouldn't actually sign the papers until I had told my boss I was going. They were never going to be able to compete with this and that was not the intention in any case. I just needed to tell them face to face. This was not going to be a happy meeting and I lost a few days sleep before walking into Carolyn McCall's office. She was shocked and I practically broke down as I told her I was going. We'd known each other for ten years so I told her why and hoped that, even though she'd be fuming, she would understand. To my astonishment, Carolyn did not get upset or angry. In fact, she was amazing.

'John, this is a fantastic deal,' she said. 'You're right to accept the offer. Anyone would do the same and all of the board would, of course, understand that. It's a million pounds, for God's sake. Let me ask you is it just the money? Are you happy at GMG? Is there anything else or any other reason why you would want to leave us?' I said not at all, it was just that the offer was so good and it was one I had to accept.

Then Carolyn said, 'I'd like you to give me one day to see what I can do at GMG.'

I assured her I was not asking for that. It was why I'd brought my resignation in writing to that meeting. In my experience, people who resign without having written a letter don't want to go. I was going. Carolyn knew that was not the case and said so. Even so, she said that considering all that GMG had done for me over the past eight years, it would be good if I could wait twenty-four hours before signing for the other party so she could make a few calls. It would probably come to nothing but that was her choice. I agreed but thought there was no chance. Why would they?

The following morning, Carolyn called and said the board were happy to match that offer. I could have fallen off my seat.

'What, you're going to give me a million to stay?'

'Yes, we are,' she said. 'We're prepared to do that but with a few conditions.' GMG would pay me a bonus of £250,000 immediately and the rest would be paid over three years in equal measure. If I left the company I would also lose the remaining cash, depending on when I quit. In short, I was being hooked into the company for three more years. That was it.

I was now in a very different position. It meant I could keep the job I loved, remain at GMG and would get the cash in any case - the best of all worlds. Carolyn said the paperwork could not be sorted for at least a week, as it had to be signed off by the board although the chairman, Lord Myners, was in full agreement. We did the deal on a handshake and I called the other parties to ask for a meeting the following day.

Again we met in The Lowry in Manchester. They had brought along all the paperwork as they assumed I was signing but sadly I had to let them down. They were stunned but the lawyer told me he was not surprised. I met Lord Myners at his home the following week to apologise for putting him and the board through this.

'John, someone put you in a very difficult position out of your control,' he said. 'It was an amazing offer and we either matched it or lost you. We decided to pay. It was not a long conversation.' Who would have thought it?

I was now forty-seven years old and things were going well. GMG signed all the paperwork in due course and we were making great progress within the radio division. Carolyn had been on at me for some time to find a deputy for the business. She felt that the radio division was too exposed and GMG were pushing for a much more visible succession plan. Since the new deal had been put in place the pressure to find someone was becoming more urgent. One day, Carolyn's PA called and arranged a meet at a hotel in Edinburgh. This was strange, so I knew something was up. At that meeting, Carolyn made it clear that the board had supported me throughout my time at GMG. They wanted her to ensure that a proper succession plan was in place and she thought I was stalling. She was right. I was. Her message was that I had to sort it out; it was not open to discussion. GMG would help me if required. I could tell this was serious, although not totally unexpected. I really liked Carolyn a lot and there was no way I was going to go to war with her on this topic. I readily agreed, provided I could choose my own deputy. We hugged, laughed about other things, worked through some other stuff and I headed home. Once I have agreed to do something I like to get on with it. I would sort this as quickly as possible.

Stuart Taylor had already been appointed as my Commercial Director and MD of Smooth London. I later appointed him as my Deputy CEO of the whole radio group but it was not a decision that went down well with the senior management team. They thought Carolyn was trying to make amends for the fact that a couple of years earlier he had been passed over as MD of the Guardian. This was not correct. We had gone through a proper process, hired a good recruitment company and, to be fair, Stuart performed well at the board. In addition, I was smart enough to know that when you're told by members of the board how much they liked Stuart and what a visionary he was, it would have been foolish to pick someone else, unless they were brilliant. Some time later, I was having breakfast with Mark Dodson at The Lowry hotel in Manchester when I suddenly collapsed without warning. Paramedics who were called thought I'd had a stroke of some kind and

I was immediately taken to hospital. I was off work and banned from driving for around three months as specialists tried to figure out the problem. In the end, they couldn't figure it out and decide to label the episode as 'unexplained'. It was a warning, though, and I was told to slow down. Working eighty-hour weeks, travelling the country non-stop and being overweight were certainly not helping my health. At the same time, I'd always held a lifelong desire to retire at the age of fifty and it was becoming more evident that I'd have the opportunity to make that dream happen. I was more than financially secure and my fiftieth birthday coincided with exactly ten years at GMG. It was the ideal time to go, and this health warning was just the jolt I needed, plus I had told GMG this was my plan when I first started the company in 1999. I met with Carolyn and gave her the news. I would work my one-year notice period, support Stuart and make sure he had traction in the exec team. That turned out to be much more difficult than I thought. In a year's time I would be on my way. Carolyn agreed and said she sensed it coming. However, there was a problem. What were we to do with the final two payments of my million pounds? I was entitled to the third section of my pay-off, as I was leaving by agreement. However, I told her that I felt bad about leaving when I had not completed the whole three years. Even though the agreement allowed for it to be paid, I would reduce the next payment by a hundred thousand pounds. We signed this off and the only thing I asked for was that they treated the exec team fairly when the end-of-year bonuses came due. It was pure luck that I had found myself in that wonderful position. GMG had always been good to me and I really wanted to leave on pleasant terms. They were absolutely the best company I have ever worked for in my life. As it turned out, I actually departed one month earlier than planned in order to accept an invitation from the Labour Government to deliver The Myers Report on the future of Local Radio.

Chapter Twenty-One

STARBUCKS AND THE BBC

While seeing out the last few weeks of my notice period, I met with Tim Davie, boss of all things radio at the BBC. He was unlucky to take over just as the row exploded over the debacle we now know as the Ross-Brand affair, which landed the BBC with a £150,000 fine from OFCOM.

Comedian Russell Brand and TV presenter Jonathan Ross, who both had magical weekend shows on Radio 2, left a series of voice messages on the answerphone of Andrew Sachs, the actor who played Manuel in the TV sitcom Fawlty Towers. Those voicemail messages, which included lewd comments about Sachs' granddaughter, the model Georgina Baillie, were broadcast in Brand's pre-recorded show in October, 2008, and led to a record number of complaints. Both Brand and Lesley Douglas, Controller of Radio 2, resigned from the BBC. Ross was suspended without pay. The whole sorry episode is highlighted in Jeremy Vine's autobiography, *It's All News To Me*, and I understand the paperback version will have more juicy details that have not been published to date. Of course, everyone had a view on the scandal and my own was that it was not just the fault of the talent, although they needed some stern words. All talent push the boat and test just how far they can go. It's what makes people like this interesting. They do things that most sane people would never do. It's why they attract an audience. The episode was a dire case of mismanagement at both the producer and senior level. It was a hell of a baptism of fire for Tim, who successfully ensured BBC Radio sailed their way through it, although not without some tight turns.

Lesley Douglas falling on her sword was a big loss to the BBC. She was perhaps the best in the business at the time in terms of programming. Both she and her predecessor, Jim Moir, are responsible for the biggest turn-around of a radio station I have ever known. Lesley rightly has a huge reputation in radio. I got on with her very well and still do. While Lesley moved into the music business, Tim began the process of finding her replacement. We met at the coffee bar opposite Broadcasting House, which staff at the BBC nicknamed Studio Six. Tim asked if I was interested in the role. He was certainly not offering me the job but who wouldn't want to be considered. This was the biggest radio station in Europe, with the best talent and a budget to die for. The problem was, I was heading on a long trip around the world as well as seeing out my notice at GMG. Furthermore, I would be losing out on a significant slice of my exit payment if the Radio 2 job did actually come my way.

To any programmer anywhere in the UK, this is the plum radio job. I explained that I certainly wasn't prepared to put my hat in the ring just to make up the numbers and if he did want me to apply formally, then I wouldn't be able to do it. However, I was available for a cup of tea with people if they wanted to meet up. I've always disliked the way the BBC go about recruiting people but it's the way they work. Any organisation taking public money needs at least to be seen to be doing the right thing. I've always taken the view that if you know who you want, just get on and hire them. This was not the way the BBC operated. Even those putting in for the job of Director General have to formally apply.

A couple of days later I was asked to 'come and have a coffee' with Tim and Alan Yentob, the BBC's Creative Director responsible for overseeing creative output on television, radio and the Corporation's interactive services. I went along thinking that I'm so bloody outspoken, this would be a short meeting but it was quite the opposite. For over an hour we discussed radio, life, Radio 2, Ross-Brand, the network, management and how I'd run the station. I liked Alan, he's a bit of a programming genius and some of the things he's done are quite remarkable. In any case, I suspected he just wanted to make sure this commercial radioman was not a nutter. There are certainly a few of those around!

--------------- **10 second break...** ---------------

Presenter: Alan Brazil.   Station: TalkSPORT.

'Our talking point this morning is George Best, his liver transplant and the booze culture in football. Don't forget, the best caller wins a crate of John Smith's.'

*

I heard nothing for a few days until Tim called to ask if I would like to meet Mark Byford, the Deputy Director General. Now, this was getting serious. I asked him straight if this was a real possibility but Tim is a manager, a politician and too darned smart to be caught out by such an obvious question. I did some digging around and was left in no doubt that I was a serious contender. I later discovered the choice for the job of Controller of Radio 2 was between me and Bob Shennan, who was someone I knew well and a nice guy to boot. Bob was an experienced exec who had earned his spurs as Controller of 5 live so was not just a safe pair of hands. He also came with a great reputation, was liked and respected and could do the job brilliantly. Personally, I always believed he was the favourite but here I was on a shortlist of two, although that was never formally confirmed. The Press were desperate to know who was on the list and my name started being bandied about as a potential candidate. I had to deny it completely or announce it and tell GMG. One afternoon, I got a call from someone high up in HR at the BBC.

'John, you need to formally apply for this role before you see Mark,' she said.

Well, I wasn't going to do that, so I told her if that was a condition, I wouldn't be attending. However, I did think it was time to come clean with Carolyn about where this might go. That night I sent her a note asking to meet up and said the BBC were asking me to apply for the Radio 2 job. I was asking her permission to do so; bearing in mind this was a complete one hundred and eighty degree turn from my previous position. GMG would do one of two things, I thought. They'd either say this is an amazing job, your life's desire or they would go into a right old frazzle about it. I soon got a reply from her PA simply saying 'nine o'clock tomorrow'.

I turned up at GMG the next morning and could immediately tell there was something in the air. I noticed Nick Castro had a little smile across his face. I knew Nick well enough to know he was thinking, Myers you are about to head into an interesting meeting.

I exchanged the usual hugs and smiles with Carolyn but then she got serious.

'John, we're quite shocked. You're supposed to be leaving to tour the world, you told us that after you wanted time off. Now, I receive this email telling me that you might apply to be the new boss of commercial radio's biggest competitor.' She continued, 'We have a commercial deal with you on your exit, John, and a moral one. If you want to go for this role, it would be quite difficult to explain your change of mind, especially considering where we are in radio today. If you're saying you might very well be joining the very people who are, in your words, our biggest competitors we will have to act accordingly. We will certainly not pay you your exit agreement and we'll review your contract to ensure that any restrictions to your employment with the BBC would be enforced.' That was it in a nutshell. Direct, straight to the point, informative, honest and without emotion.

'Carolyn, I didn't send you that note expecting you to say anything different,' I said. 'If we go along this route then I now fully understand the position.'

I left her office thinking I would have done exactly the same. I'm not sure I would have done it as well as her, mind you, but that's Carolyn, a class act even when the message is a difficult one. On the other hand, when I set all of this into motion, there was no Ross-Brand scandal going on, and absolutely no possibility of a job at Radio 2. Certainly, I had never considered for a moment that my own name might be right up there for consideration. A colleague of mine told me I'd been mad to even tell GMG about this offer until I had the job in the bag. They might have been right but that's not how I worked. In any case, Dame Liz Forgan, chair of the Scott Trust, had close ties with the BBC from her time as the corporation's Managing Director of Network Radio and it would all have come out in the wash. Better to be upfront now. That said, it was fast becoming decision day.

I told HR at the BBC I would not be formally applying for the role but I would, should they need it, send them a note of my history in radio to date. As you can get this on Wikipedia, I was hardly giving them something they didn't already have. Plus, at this stage of the proceedings, if they needed a CV then they didn't need me. I recall someone once calling me for details of my career. I was very rude and said simply, 'The last thirty years is all spelt out for you on Wiki'. What a prat I was. Looking back that was just ego, not something to be proud of.

*

A couple of days later, I was asked to go along for a coffee with Deputy DG Mark Byford. It was agreed that I wouldn't need to apply after all. Mark was a sharp operator and the relaxed coffee in his office was well done. He knew a lot about me and therefore he focused more on how Radio 2 could evolve. Personally, I didn't think Radio 2 had a problem. They were in a fantastic position, the best of the best at what they did and in my opinion had already been beaten up far too much.

'All radio stations get themselves into trouble now and again, but that's no reason to blow the whole lot up.' I said. 'I would evolve the station slowly, not go in with a commitment to change.'

I already knew Terry Wogan was going from his hugely popular breakfast show to be replaced by Chris Evans, although this was not public knowledge at the time. This was a masterstroke but needed to be handled well. In any case, no station should aim to make more than one major change a year. Anything else would be just too damaging for the audience to accept. Mark and I got on well but it was clear I had to stand up or get off the pot, as the saying goes.

Tim wasn't in this meeting but the decision was always going to be his, I thought. Both Mark Byford and Alan Yentob had been involved just to check that I could be trusted. Once they confirmed that to be the case they were happy to let Tim go ahead. In truth, I was going along with this because I thought it would be interesting to see how far these talks went. Now I was at the final gate with only two horses in the running, Myers and Shennan. I was starting to get a little excited about it. The choice was a new broom versus someone they knew already and who had great BBC heritage. I was coming straight from commercial radio with a reputation for being a bit of a maverick at times. Could they really appoint an outsider? The next day Tim called me as I was driving along the central motorway in Newcastle. He told me that he was minded to go for Bob. I congratulated him and told him it was exactly the right decision. If he'd said that I was the winner, then I'd have jumped for joy but that was not the case. I pulled over for ten minutes right outside BBC Radio Newcastle's studios and was actually quite disappointed at what might have been and spent a few moments in thought. People make decisions and sometimes they work out and sometimes they don't. On this occasion, Tim got it absolutely right and I told him so over lunch one day. Radio 2 is in much better shape than ever before and the changes Bob has implemented, plus the management of Chris Evans into breakfast has been remarkable. I'm not sure I could have done it as well or any better. Mind you, if the job came up again I would be up for it, especially with what I know right now.

Tim was not finished with me, though. In a strange turn of events, I was asked to lift the drain covers at the BBC and report on what I found. I knew my first job as a sewer rat might come in handy. You couldn't make it up.

Sadly, I felt this episode soured my warm relationship with GMG. Although they have never said a word, you just get the vibe. The truth is you can't predict what life will throw your way. You can only be honest in dealing with what you have before you. How was I to know that, despite my original plan, Ross and Brand would throw themselves into a period of madness that changed radio in the UK? I would have kicked myself if I hadn't taken those meetings forward, despite the financial hit. In the end, it worked out best for everyone. However, GMG have not spoken to me at all since that last meeting. We had a nice farewell dinner and Carolyn herself remains a friend and a supporter of Team Myers. Indeed, I often smile when I see her face and her comments in the in-flight magazines of easyJet, where she is currently Chief Executive. Carolyn McCall is a motivator of people and that's the skill of a great leader. It does not reduce the sadness I feel about my departure from GMG. They still remain the best company I've ever worked for.

Chapter Twenty-Two

JOHN MYERS REPORTS FOR DIGITAL FM

Andrew Harrison was Chief Executive of The Radio Centre, the umbrella organisation that champions the aims and ambitions of all the commercial radio in the UK. He had been in discussions with the Department for Culture Media and Sport about the future of radio. The government was working through a plan for the forthcoming digital economy act and there was a report to be done about radio. Andrew suggested I might be someone who'd be available to help them. Soon after, I received a call from Lord Carter of Barnes, the one and only Stephen Carter, Minister for Communications, Technology and Broadcasting. We had known each other from his time as the founding CEO of OFCOM. He's as sharp as they come and for a politician was amazingly straightforward.

Stephen asked if I would be available to undertake an independent review of the rules surrounding local radio and content. He wanted it done rather quickly and, in doing so, I had to leave GMG a month earlier than planned to work on what became known as The Myers Report. I liked that, although it was clearly not a job you would do if you needed to be paid well. The money was a pittance compared to my daily rate but I really wanted to do it. It was new, I would learn something along the way and, furthermore, it was a chance to give something back to the industry I love.

A couple of days later my phone rang at 8.30 in the morning. It was Lord Carter. 'John, a slight issue,' he said. 'The feeling in government is that although this is your report, we should surround you with a bunch of people who can help and advise along the way to ensure you have a wide view and perspective.'

'Okay,' I said, hesitantly, 'as long as the final edit is my own.'

I would take advice from anyone but I wanted the report to be as thorough as possible and if others could help in the process that was a positive in my book.

'Who's would this bunch of people be?' I asked.

'No idea,' he replied. 'Just surround yourself with a broad section of the industry so that when you come up with your report you're not standing alone and there are others to back you up.'

I had a lot to learn and I liked that idea. This guy was smart. I quickly pulled the following people together to form my own A team:

Kip Meek, *Ingenious Media*
Helen Boaden, *BBC*
Peter Davis, *OFCOM*
Andrew Harrison, *Radio Centre*
John Mottram, *DCMS*
Jaqui Devereux, *Community Media Association*
Santha Rasaiah, *Newspaper Society*.

This was an impressive team by any measure with bags of experience and we met on two occasions. The report was submitted in time and published at the end of March 2009. I travelled the length and breath of the country talking to a large number of radio managers, owners and people with experience. I had a view but I needed input and some of that changed my thoughts completely. This report is freely available from the government's own website.

There was a lot to take in but the huge benefit of heading up a task like this is that you very quickly find out what is fact and what is fiction. So often something that was said as an off-the-cuff remark can somehow find its way to becoming a fact. This was fascinating work and I came across a number of files and paperwork that, even to this day, are confidential but that information provided me with a rounded view of life and helped shape the report I was putting forward. The key point for me that came out of my research was the complete failure over the years of the licensing process of both the former regulators and now OFCOM. There were good people in those organisations but some of their decisions were breathtakingly poor, especially in hindsight. Today, some regard me as a hero while others believe I'm closer to Darth Vader, for the way the industry has progressed recently. The truth is neither but it's worth reflecting on the position I found when I began investigating the radio industry.

In 2009, eighty per cent of all commercial radio stations in the UK were unprofitable. That is a remarkable statistic. Worse still, overall the industry was breaking even at best, in many cases because of the huge cost associated with servicing the debt to purchase these stations. Change was required but there was no point in moving forward without understanding the lessons of the past. This is not a chapter that is bashing the regulator for what they did. They could claim to be damned if they did and damned if they didn't but that was the life they chose. Believe me, I'm a fan of most of their achievements. I worked with them closely but, just like my own business, not everything was perfect. Not everything worked and often you wish you could turn back the clock to make a better decision.

I really believe what we have today in UK Radio is the result of the failure to award licences in a sober and educated frame of mind. The award committee of OFCOM, and before that the Radio Authority, must have had great boozy lunches before they made some of their decisions. That can be the only logical reason. The truth, and I know this may hurt the radio purists, is that the way the current radio owners are merging stations to form national brands is what should have happened in the first place. The industry has had to sort itself out to survive. There was a time when, the regulator had an option to either advertise a range of big regional radio services around the UK or award two national FM services that would have competed head-on against Radio 1 and Radio 2. They chose to do the former and while it is true I made my name and reputation in regional radio, the best decision would have been to award two or three national commercial stations instead. This they may claim might not have been an option at the time, although I suspect it was. The result is what we have today.

While my argument on regional versus national is open for debate, what is not in question is that a whole tier of very local radio licences were awarded in spades over a number of years, especially in the Nineties, and had a detrimental effect on the industry. Until then the really big stations like Metro, Clyde, Piccadilly and BRMB, which had managed to survive through the difficulties of the Seventies, were all profitable. They had big audiences and still managed to broadcast a range of specialist programming like jazz, big band and Country. These stations were also delivering a local service that made local stars of some of their presenters. As more and more local stations came on air, they started to eat away at the audiences of these really big local stations, which became less profitable. First thing to go were the expensive programmes they produced that had little audience appeal but were local through and through. It was content like this that made them stand out. The objective of awarding a mixture of regional and very local licences was to take audience away from the BBC and grow the commercial radio cake. The complete opposite happened. Commercial radio started to eat itself while the BBC grew ever larger, partly because they could continue to deliver really good content, paid for through our licence fee.

I highlighted in my report the bizarre way the regulator determined localness. They took the view that to be truly local you had to be actually sited within the broadcast area. However, there was nothing to say that you actually had to talk about the local area. You could broadcast all day, meet the minimum requirements of local news and information, but never once mention the place you broadcast to. This was nuts. What does a local listener want? A station that broadcasts local information but may be sited in another town or region? Or do they want a local station that is based in their town but does not mention that town at all? This had to change and by and large it has.

By 2009, commercial radio was in a bit of a state and was getting worse. The whole drive to digital radio meant that costs of transmission had jumped up enormously as DAB proved to be more expensive than FM. Money that should have been spent on content was being given to the company that controlled UK transmission, Arqiva. Each local licence was for a fixed term of around eight to twelve years. At the end of this period the licence was re-advertised. To prevent this, the industry as a whole, foolishly if you ask me, agreed to accept a rollover for another twelve years in return for agreeing to put themselves onto digital. The future of their FM service was then tied to their investment in digital. From the information presented to me, I could see and indeed I predicted that some fifty radio stations were about to go bust unless something happened quickly to help them. Of the two hundred and fifty plus commercial stations in the UK, it was clear to me that a number of these should never have been licensed in the first place and in turn they should be allowed to go bust. You can't polish a turd, as they say. Another group of stations had the chance to succeed if they could reduce their costs by merging and sharing a lot more of the back office. It would reduce localness but there was a chance of profitability. Others that were still profitable should continue to be locally led. Regional stations should be encouraged to go national so they can take on the national BBC stations more effectively while removing themselves from the local advertising market. That would free up smaller clients for the local stations left behind. I was trying to correct the mistakes of the past and, while it made sense, I was also absolutely sure it was not ideal. It was just the best of a bad job. This was by and large accepted by the Government, who uplifted my recommendations into the digital economy bill. The note I received from Lord Carter calling my report a brilliant piece of work is still close to my desk today.

You cannot just blame the regulator for the state commercial radio found itself in. The industry itself often hired complete muppets to run some of their stations. In the first month after taking day to day control of Radio Investments, the group that housed twenty-eight stations across the UK, I received a call from the regulator to say they'd just received a call from one of my managers who'd had an idea and was asking for permission to do it. Did I know about this they asked?

'Err, not at all. What's this great idea?'

'Well, they think that if they could dump the local news bulletin at 9 am and play music instead they'd keep more of their audience. He feels people tune out when the news is on.'

I was staggered. 'Which idiot proposed this idea?' I asked. They told me and I promptly gave the manager some very clear advice. The key one being that it was nothing short of idiotic to remove the one thing that makes a local station local. He didn't last that long after that, not because of this particular instance, but because he just did not get the value of localness at all.

Make no mistake we have some wonderful local radio stations. Take UKRD as a primary local radio player that is making profits, paying dividends and is run by someone who knows the business inside out. Local Radio can work, it does work and it will work but the framework must be clear and in place to allow that to happen.

Today, we have a new wave of local stations owned by large groups who offer a slice of localness that just fits the legal requirement of their licence terms. The regulator has to decide if that is acceptable. I think it is, if the total mix of stations within a particular area is sufficient to provide a choice of listening. To hear some people talk on the idea of localness, you would think that anything that is not produced locally has no benefit whatsoever to the local community a station may serve. Would you rather have great content delivered nationally or poor content delivered locally? There is some wonderful creative local content on the air every single day of the year in every single radio market in the UK but that does not mean there is no room for content that is produced elsewhere. Great content is great content no matter where it comes from.

Where I do think the regulator gets it wrong is on the penalties they issue when stations totally ignore the rules. We all fall over now and again so I am not talking about genuine errors, but some people just take it too far. The regulator needs to be much more aggressive in this instance. It is often said that being penalised by the regulator was like being attacked by a dog with no teeth. The worst you could get was a nasty suck.

30-second break.

Indian Take-away.

In the early days of commercial radio most stations aired a range of specialist programmes in the early evening, like big bands, classical and country music. Some programmes were in a foreign language. The presenter of the weekly Hindi programme started life at the station on a bicycle but by the end of his first year, the PD noticed he had swapped this for a Mercedes. The local university was called in to translate the whole of the past month's Hindi programmes into English. When the four scripts arrived on his desk, the PD's eyes nearly popped out. The presenter had been running about twenty live commercial reads an hour for his mates and breaking just about every broadcasting rule in the book. He was making a fortune, but as the boss couldn't understand a word that was being broadcast, he'd been getting away with it for nearly a full year. It was only because the fool turned up in a Merc that it aroused the PD's suspicion. If he'd continued to arrive by bike, he would probably have made enough cash to build a house.

Chapter Twenty-Three

HELLO, I LOVE YOU, WON'T YOU TELL ME YOUR NAME?

It is natural to have some regrets, no matter what you do or how successful you become. I've yet to hear a parent who doesn't moan about the lack of time they've had with their children when they were young. I agree with that, where did all the years go? You look around and suddenly they go from children, to teenagers, to adults and leave home. Choosing photos for this book, I've had to look though boxes of pictures and it was a time tunnel of fun, laughter, worry and shock.

As soon as my digital report was complete, Linda and I toured the world. We are together because we love each other, yet we have spent so much time apart over the years. We not only have a great marriage we also have a great partnership. To be suddenly thrown together twenty-four hours a day can be a jolt. Luckily for me, it just underlined what I'd been missing. I kept saying, 'Hello. I love you, won't you tell me your name?' The words to a Doors song only those of a certain age will recall.

I like to be busy, but when on holiday I just potter around, not doing anything really. It's the total reverse of my normal day. I was surprised at how cheap it was to travel if you go around the world rather than going somewhere specific and coming straight back. As long as you do the circle, so to speak, it is amazingly economic. When we returned after three months, people always wanted to know which was our favourite destination? That was easy, the south island of New Zealand and the warmth and pace of life in Hawaii takes some beating. We liked the other destinations, too, especially the train trip from Cape Town to Johannesburg but there is something extra special about the first two.

Back home, I started to feel a little unloved. I was used to receiving around two hundred emails a day, now I was lucky to get one. I became grateful to those people who enquired if I wanted any penis enlargement pills. I nearly replied to a chap in Nigeria who had sadly lost his father and had to transfer a hundred million pounds into my bank account. It got so bad, that at one stage, I even emailed myself just to check if my computer was working.

I kept thinking, I can't just play golf all day. Surely there is something else I can do? You do start to worry when the phone no longer rings, too. You start asking yourself questions about the people who you've worked with for so many years. Do they care about you now? Out of sight, out of mind they say. They do care, of course, and are always happy to see you but the reality is that they have their own lives to lead. There is a new boss, God save the new King. It took some getting used to I can tell you.

*

I received a call from Bob Shennan, who not only ran Radio 2 and 6Music but was also chair of the Radio Academy. The Academy is a cross-industry body that is there to support the whole of radio. It also runs the Sony Radio Academy Awards, The Radio Festival and a number of nationwide initiatives to celebrate, promote and educate people about the medium itself. Above all, it is a charity. I thought Bob might want to talk to me about doing a weekly show, although even I must admit that was a long shot. Instead, he wanted to know if I would consider working for the Radio Academy for a while, as it was being re-energised and needed a leader. This was the right idea at the right time. For nearly three decades, the Sony Radio Academy awards had been led by Alan Zafer who'd done an excellent job. In fact, it's fair to say the awards would never have begun without him but, while I was away touring the world, the industry had decided to remove this role from Alan and bring it inside The Academy. This new role meant that I would be the Chair of the Sony Awards and Chair of The Radio Festival. Both appealed to me and, as I had time on my hands and it was just two days a week, it fitted perfectly. I promised them a year and so, with a great management team led by Mandy O'Connor, we set to work. Both the events I ran really raised the bar considerably and showcased what a brilliant industry we have. In any field of competition, tensions can run high. The Academy sat in the middle of the BBC and commercial radio and, at times, it was difficult to keep everyone onside and on track. I actually quite liked that and, because I knew everyone well, could convince both sides that working together for the good of all was the best route forward. I might try to solve the Syrian crisis next.

*

The commercial radio industry has gone through some changes over the past decade. Because of buy outs, sell outs, mergers and failures we now have a completely different mix of owners, Chief Executives and strategies than when I was part of that mix as CEO of GMG Radio. Is it any better now? I have no idea, it is just different. People moan about the demise of local radio, and I can understand that, but far too often a rosy-coloured view of the past leads to the wrong conclusion. If you look at the reality with a coldness of thought, the past was not that great. It was just our time and that's what made it special. I am saddened at the loss of a number of truly local stations that we once had but we still continue to have some wonderful local radio today.

The old model was doomed the moment more licences were awarded on top of each other. People made what they thought were the right decisions at the time. In every business, in every walk of life, it is only with the benefit of hindsight can that be reviewed properly.

I don't blame anyone, no one purposely got it wrong but life is about decisions.

*

I was travelling along the M4 when I received a phone call from Lord Carter, the Minister for Broadcasting. I was actually on my way to a meeting with him and a whole collection of radio bosses at his office in the Department of Culture Media and Sport. The meeting had been called because the commercial radio industry claimed it could no longer go on paying for double transmission costs and quite right too. At the meeting would be representatives from OFCOM, Bauer Radio, Global, The Radio Centre, DCMS, my old company GMG and more.

Lord Carter wanted to know what he was letting himself in for. He already had a good idea but wanted an inside track before he walked in. I told him the truth. He was going to be asked to give commercial radio a break. The industry was now a loss-leader, we were at a crisis point, my report had clearly showed him that eighty per cent of the industry was unprofitable, DAB was costing a bloody fortune, that there was not a lot of confidence in the digital future he was driving us to. Widespread opinion in the industry was that commercial radio needed more freedom to do what we thought was right. He was amazed that commercial radio even believed they could survive without a digital plan. The whole world was going digital; the money was leaving analogue and not coming back. In his opinion, if the plan was to stay on FM, then we were planning to lose.

At the end of our conversation he said, 'Thank you. It's also what I've heard from another source. Can you do me a favour?' he asked. 'When the meeting starts, please don't say anything. I will be very direct and to the point, it is not an attack on you, so don't rise to it.'

It was a measure of the man that he continued to be upfront and honest, although I had no idea whatsoever what he was going to say.

We arrived at his office to plead poverty and get some help. We all filed in and sat around a huge table. Stephen Carter arrived with three others riding shotgun. That always seems to happen in government meetings. One to record what he said, another to record what we said and another to advise him. Stephen started off by asking Andrew Harrison to explain succinctly why the Radio Centre had asked for this meeting. This is a perfect way for any chairman to start because it means you have to focus. Also, it's a reminder to be sure everyone knows why they are having the meeting in the first place. Whenever I have a meeting with someone and ask why they're there and what they want to achieve, you'd be amazed at how few have really thought about it and are able to give a one-minute overview. As I knew I wasn't going to speak, I focused on taking notes, which I still have today. Andrew is a sharp operator and was able to provide a clear outline. Stephen then asked OFCOM for a short and considered response on why the Radio Centre's request was not acceptable. He was already ahead of the game, of course, as in a previous life he'd been the person who set up OFCOM. The regulator was also succinct. Then Stephen offered up a master class of tone, focus and directness that took even me by surprise. Here are my notes of what he said:

Here is what I think you are saying to me. You have all bought radio licences at the top of the market. I assume you all did your due diligence when buying these licences and would have noticed that they came with an obligation to be on a digital platform. Not one of you called me and asked if you were paying too much for these businesses and why should you? That is your business. Not one of you called me and wanted a debate about those obligations. And why should you, there's enough brainpower around this room to make up your own minds. No, what you did was make a business decision. You bought a business right at the top end of the price range and the cost of doing that is the cost of servicing any bank debt that, if it was not there, could instead be used for programming, content, news and being on another platform. I didn't tell you to buy those radio businesses, I didn't tell you to take the actions you did, you did this yourselves. Now, as I understand it, here you are before me bleating on about the cost of running commercial radio, the lack of freedom, and the hurdles you have to overcome and that so many stations are under threat of going bust. Well, I'm sitting here thinking about an alternative solution. Why don't I just ignore your concerns? We live in a commercial world where the markets decide. We may have to support some UK-wide structures because they are invaluable to the UK citizen but radio is not that. I might think it's a good idea to let you all go bust. I will then simply re-advertise your stations and any new owner would not have the huge weight of their banks debt to service. This would mean that any new successful applicant could provide and promise each area a radio station that was able to deliver a larger amount of local content and be local twenty-four hours a day. Now, I might consider your proposal if you were offering me something that would be of some benefit to the regions that so many of the MPs represent. However, what you are asking me to do is to stand up in Parliament and tell the Members that I have agreed to reduce the number of local programmes that their radio stations provide, I have agreed to reduce the amount of local news each of their stations can provide and I have reduced choice. In return, I am giving them a big fat zero. I'm not offering a new UK-wide news station, for example, that might compete with the BBC and Sky. I'm not offering Parliament anything that they would consider to be a win. Why would I do that? Why would I agree to all of this when it would appear that I'm doing all the giving and not getting anything in return?

Silence. Not a word from around the table.

Eventually Andrew Harrison and Ashley Tabor, head of Global Radio, recovered their composure and fought their corner but the reality was the industry had to give something credible and sustainable in order to get the changes they wanted in other areas. It was why the Radio Centre was there, to act for all the commercial radio groups. So they went away and returned with a plan and from that came a range of consultations and agreements between government, the regulator and the industry itself. Part of that includes the new memorandum of understanding that was published in 2012. It sets out a plan for digital but it continues to support the FM infrastructure.

*

The reality of course is that if we were to build the radio landscape of the future, we would never start from where we are today. In fact, in the mid-Noughties I got a few radio industry chief executives together and said, 'We all have great radio companies but in part the regulator has awarded a number of stations to the wrong groups in the wrong areas. Why don't we all put them on the table and work out which of our groups should own what? We'll still have to work within the rules but we'll have stronger businesses and a much better radio landscape.' Nice idea. We tried but the one thing that always kills a deal is ego. We all have them, mine is no smaller than anyone else's, so in the end we just gave up. No one could ever agree on price, either.

*

There is nothing wrong with DAB if people want to be on DAB. It is just another platform but being told you must be on DAB to continue to broadcast on FM is totally wrong, in my view. The biggest issue is not so much the technology but the price of being on it. If access to the DAB platform was guaranteed and was the same price as FM then the demand would be huge. The reality is that the current cost of being on FM for a small station might be as low as £20,000 a year but if they had to also transmit the very same station on DAB, the cost of that may be closer to £100k per annum plus the cost of being on FM. Considering most small or mid-size stations are barely profitable, that's just not feasible, especially when the reality is that FM will never be turned off, certainly in my lifetime. There is absolutely nothing wrong with FM; it is a sustainable, wonderful and efficient delivery system that works. As long as any radio station has to put their programmes on both FM and DAB the cost of running both means content suffers. You have to run a station with fewer people and do more networking just to survive.

There is also a lot of debate about brands and the growth of big names while local names, such as Trent FM, have been changed to, say, Capital FM. I don't see what the fuss is about to be honest. People change, companies change, names change, strategies change, get over it. The growth of the Internet means the choice of radio stations we can

tune into has exploded. We will soon be connected up to wi-fi, even on
the bus. You can choose what you like when you like. The platform will
become more and more irrelevant over time but right now, AM, FM
and DAB is what we have, especially in cars. If the government really
wants a digital future, they have to pay for it themselves. In doing that,
I would also take back some of the freedom the regulators gave radio
stations to do what they liked and ensure news, content and local
information is cemented into the rules on licences. That won't stop
brands being brands and it won't stop the really great radio operators
being great but it will be something the government can get back for
their investment in taking the industry to a digital future. The industry
itself will then be able to surge forward.

As I keep saying, in the end only one thing matters. Content.
Everything else is a sideshow.

Chapter Twenty-Four

CLOSE, BUT NO CIGAR

Part of my exit deal when I left GMG was that I was contracted to do fifty days a year consultancy for them. This is quite normal when a senior exec leaves a business on good terms, as it allows for a smooth transition, and it would give the new CEO, Stuart Taylor, an opportunity should he wish to call on me for any advice. For months before my departure, I had been under pressure from the executive team to re-brand the Century stations as Real Radio. Century North East had lost its football coverage and research was showing that the station needed an urgent overhall, audience levels and revenues were falling but, rightly or wrongly, I wouldn't agree to it. In my view, the risks of a name change alongside launching Smooth Radio in the North East around the same time, were far too high. There were, of course, difficulties networking the same show across stations that had a different name. I understood it would be cleaner to have one name across them all but I was reluctant. When the seal of authority switched from me to Stuart Taylor, around January 2009, he promptly gave permission for the two Century stations, in the North East and North West, to become Real Radio. That's fine by me. Managers have to make decisions and he was making one that he felt was correct. He was the new leader. But in my opinion the plan was deeply flawed from the start, largely due to a lack of an adequate marketing spend to ensure the message got through to listeners. When you do something like this you have to tell the audience, then tell them again, and then smack them hard with it a few more times after that. Century had sixteen years of history, particularly in the North East, so you can't expect listeners to 'just get it' on one showing of a poster or a television commercial. My central position was that without the right budget for a re-brand, you shouldn't be doing it.

On top of this, the creative for the switch was not good but even I would agree that this is always subjective. Even though I was supposed to be their paid consultant, I cannot recall ever being asked for my advice on this particular topic, despite having created the whole group a decade earlier. I knew the reason why, of course. They no longer had to.

To work through my consultancy days I often presented the breakfast show on various Smooth stations across the UK. I loved doing the shows. It was like going back to my roots, the very reason I got into radio in the first place. The only reason I ever got into management was to do what I felt was right on the air. I was constantly frustrated by those above me who were always frightened to take chances, often stopping me from doing things that I thought were good. Therefore, the only way I could do what I wanted was to control the station. I guess it was a means to an end.

The reaction from listeners was positive and it didn't cost any of the stations a bean either as I was already being paid by GMG head office. Very soon, I became the regular stand-in for any breakfast show host who had a holiday. It is great being the person who fills in as you are not under pressure about the quarterly listening figures from RAJAR. You just go in, do your thing and depart. The trick is to keep the listeners happy and entertained but not enough to ruin it for the main presenter when he or she returns.

Because of the recommendations in my digital report to the Government, Smooth had an opportunity to move forward as one big network by broadcasting the same programming across the West Midlands, East Midlands, the North West, the North East and London. Scotland was the exception, as they had to continue providing local programming at least for seven hours of the day. To do this, GMG had to find a national platform such as Digital One, the DAB network. I knew that Simo was looking at a number of options for the breakfast show and the budget was tight but he asked if I would be interested. I was thrilled. It was perfect for me; I'd launched the Smooth brand because I wanted a station that slotted into the gap I'd identified in the market. This was proving to be the case. To jump from being the CEO of the whole group to being the breakfast show presenter on a brand I had created was wonderful. It was, in effect, going full circle and the fee was not my driver here. There was a lingering problem, though. I was acutely aware that, for any new boss, having the old one still around was difficult. Such was the force of my personality that everyone knew when I was in the building. I am larger than life so I deliberately tried to tone it down. I made a huge effort to come in, do my shows and leave almost immediately, never going upstairs to see anyone unless I was specifically asked to do so. It seemed to be working, although I still sensed an uncomfortable feeling. The contract had been sent to my lawyers and we were working through the clauses but I still had a gut feeling that Stuart Taylor was not happy. He never said anything but at a dinner in Newcastle I tackled the issue face to face with him. Even though the deal was practically agreed, I suggested to Stuart that if he was in any way uncomfortable about me doing the breakfast show he only had to say so. This discussion would remain between us and I would simply say that I had changed my mind and decided not to do it. That would protect everyone. Stuart insisted he was absolutely fine with it all.

The contract contained a clause that I simply couldn't agree with. It was a generic clause that was in place for all presenters however, in my case I felt it had to be removed. It centred on GMG having to agree to any of my outside work. My view was that I was an exception on this point as no other presenter I know had been the CEO of a large media organisation for the past decade. I was working with other groups at the time on a wide range of issues that were not presenter or output related so I was hardly going to give someone a say over all of this, just to present a breakfast show. I was happy to work exclusively for GMG on the air but as the programme itself would be a smaller percentage of my overall income, there had to be some movement with regard to this particular clause. As I never attended any current management meetings at GMG Radio, the only time I knew what they were up to was when I received an email at the same time as the rest of the staff. Where was the possible conflict?

As I said, this was a standard clause but without its removal, there was only one decision I could make. Discussions came to a halt but Stuart and I talked on the telephone once more as I tried to explain my position. He was pleasant, and professional as he always is, but he felt that it was important to have something in writing that said I needed their express permission. This was a deal breaker for me.

I called my lawyer and he agreed this was a tough one but he also felt it could be worked out if there was a willingness from both sides. By then my gut feeling was telling me a clean break was required. Sometimes when you pause for thought what seemed like a great idea at the time turns out to be not that great after all.

The opportunity to be the first national breakfast show presenter for Smooth radio therefore disappeared. I was quite disappointed to be honest, as I really wanted to do it, but bitter experience has taught me that emotion comes before a fall. If I have learned only one thing over thirty years in business it is to ensure you have to have the contract right at the start and both parties are comfortable. For whatever reason, we were not at this point. In the end, GMG opted for Simon Bates to present breakfast on the station at, I might add, significantly more cost than I was charging. Although, even I have to admit, he is a significantly better jock. As events would prove, it turned out to be the right decision one for both parties.

There was a big positive from this episode. I managed to get my golf handicap down to nine and very soon I was heading to the BBC.

Chapter Twenty-Five

LIFTING THE DRAIN COVERS AT THE BBC

The BBC was getting grief about their costs and the Radio Centre, led by Andrew Harrison, were asking awkward questions. Tim Davie had an open style but he knew that if he didn't get someone from the outside to have a look at radio's costs, the BBC Trust might just do the job for him. It was better to be pro-active than to have it forced upon you, he thought. I don't know of any other organisation that would invite someone in from the outside to snoop around, produce a report on what they were doing wrong and then publish that report widely for everyone to attack them over its contents.

Some might call it brave management, or even madness, but as a public service the BBC were obliged to do just that. They needed someone who would review their operations while having no ulterior agenda to bash the BBC. I suspect it was a very short list and hence I was asked if I'd like to do it. The brief was an interesting one in that they wanted me to spend a few weeks wandering around Radio 1, Radio 2, 6Music and 1Xtra just seeing what the stations did, how they did it and suggest ways in which they could deliver their service in a more cost effective way. My experience of working at just about every level in UK radio meant that I could do this with ease but I suspected

I'd be walking into a hornets' nest. I'd be as popular as Gary Glitter standing outside a school gate.

Tim was excellent. He never once told me where I could or couldn't go. In fact, he said if I came across a roadblock to just call him and he'd get it shifted. Tim was genuinely looking for savings and anything I could suggest would be helpful. This did not mean, of course, that he would or could agree to the savings I was suggesting but he knew he'd be given an honest assessment.

Once again, I seemed to be in the right place in the right time with the right amount of freedom to do this job. I thought it was ironic that I was deemed unacceptable for the position of Radio 2 Controller yet now I was asked to review what many Controllers were doing. While I was given unlimited and appropriate access, one area that was out of bounds was any information regarding talent costs. I was not given any access to the detail of how much the presenters were being paid, the one thing all the media were desperately keen to find out. To be honest, I was delighted. If I had been able to give a view on the salaries of the BBC's stars, everything else in my report would have gone unread, that would have been the headline no matter what I else said. That said, I could sort of work it out from the information I was given but as that was never part of my brief, it was not something I commented on. Other than that, I was given an access-all-areas pass.

The Myers report would take me about two months in total but before I could start, Tim needed to inform his controllers and I was both a little embarrassed and worried that they might reject me out of hand. I told Tim that if anyone had any difficulty, I was happy not to proceed at all. It was important to me that I was not entering a 'difficult' environment and he appreciated the offer. He called me back a few days later and said my fear was unfounded and indeed the Controllers were delighted for me to go in. They respected and liked me personally and, on top of that, they were confident I was not a BBC basher and would give them a fair shout. Most of all, they were proud of what they were delivering and why not, they are at the top of their game. They also hoped that once I saw how it was all put together and was able to deliver a fair report, it might stop the industry constantly having a go. All they asked was that I kept them in the loop as to what I found along the way. That seemed reasonable enough to me, so I found myself inside Radio 2 for the first few weeks. My first meeting with Bob Shennan was fruitful in that he was genuinely interested in finding savings. If I could find a more productive way for them to work, saving cash or working within a different structure he was up for it. He also wanted to use some of those savings elsewhere to create a more compelling output. God, I thought, if this station gets any bigger some of their competition may have to close down. The Myers Report was published in May, 2011, and is freely available online for those who want to read it.

I really meant it when I said that the whole team at the BBC is impressive. Quite honestly, many are the best in the business and I was given fantastic access to the studios and respective teams. I sat in with every single show on daytime and a large number across the weekends. I wanted to see how they did it and what roles the people played around them.

No matter what your experience is of working in the outside world, once you are in the BBC you kind of go native. Things that once looked ridiculous start to become reasonable. You look at trees so often you start to become one.

One of the things that really surprised me was the way in which old-fashioned, unionised ways of working were still in operation. Alan Dedicoat is a much-loved character. Over breakfast he told me how he came in early, did an hour then Moira Stewart took over and he came back on air to finish the morning. It was a staggering admission of how the world has gone mad. Here was someone who knew his craft inside out, but at the same time he was admitting to working what was effectively two minutes an hour. Alan is much more talented than this suggests and is equally just as well known for being 'the voice of the balls' on the lottery programme. The central newsroom based in White City provided the news to Radio 2. He and the other announcers read it out. He does, of course, lead a team of fifteen announcers so perhaps he might regard this as a misguided remark but nevertheless, it was a surprise to me.

The man has a voice to die for, one that is finely tuned to be easy on the ear while allowing you to digest the information. He is as much a part of the output of Radio 2 as Steve Wright. In my view, he's a performer and should be treated as one instead of being sidelined to news or continuity duties. It was a management issue to resolve and they had failed for years to tackle the problem of this bizarre way of reading the news on Britain's biggest stations. It underlined part of the problem within the BBC.

One weekend, I was sitting on my own in the Radio 2 production office when suddenly from behind me a piano burst into life and a wonderful voice began to sing. I turned around to discover Michael Ball preparing for his Radio 2 show and then an hour later the same thing happened again when Tony Christie used it to prepare for a moment in the studio. Later, Elton John arrived in reception. He had sent one of his pianos to the station as a gift and turned up to play a couple of tunes on it. What a mad and exciting working environment this must be, I thought.

*

The team at Radio 2 certainly know their audience. Over time the station has evolved and the audience has moved with it. I found it interesting to watch how a national station kicks subjects around for discussion. There was no greater evidence of this than when I watched the Jeremy Vine lunchtime programme go out. I came in early to see how the team worked the agenda of the day alongside what to include and, more importantly, what to ignore. They had a mini-debate themselves beforehand and I liked the way that they were not afraid to be popular or alternatively tackle quite difficult subjects, especially those that might not sit that comfortably within a lunchtime format. Jeremy is a skilled interviewer, of course, and he has a knack of asking the right question in the right way. It is one reason his audience continues to grow. He often re-tweets negative comments about himself which underlines that he knows you need both types of people to make the show a success. Interestingly, I was due to interview Jeremy at a Radio Academy event in Bristol so I tweeted about this and asked if anyone had any thoughts on what I should ask him. I was immediately contacted by a man who absolutely hates Jeremy's Radio 2 show. In fact, he hates it so much he listens every single day and writes down all the things he doesn't like and then sends his list to the BBC complaints department demanding answers. Why does Jeremy cut listeners off, why is he so rude, why does he not listen more? This love-in with the JV show has gone on for years. The listener even has a website to air his grievances, although I suspect he secretly loves everything Jeremy does.

All stations attract people who love to hate a show, it is just part of the deal when you start broadcasting. Sadly, I've never attracted nutters just kind people who send me cakes and stuff to eat. Seriously, I would turn up some days and people would be sitting in reception with tins packed full of home cooking. However, they were never eaten because on my first day in radio I was warned to NEVER, repeat NEVER, eat anything brought in by listeners. You don't know what they've put in to those home-made products, especially the cakes!

*

A lovely fruitcake I did sit in with one morning was Chris Evans. Now here is an exceptional talent surrounded by great production and support staff, headed by a wonderful producer called Helen Thomas. She's a potential Controller if ever I've met one. I noted seven people on this show. On the face of it that might seem a lot but this was the biggest radio station in the country with nearly fifteen million listeners a week. I noticed that when Chris was on, he received about three thousand text messages, around a thousand emails and the phones lines were constantly jammed. Yet, on air I rarely heard him plugging for anything. It was just an example of the public trying to connect with the show. The power of radio in action before my eyes!

Chris has a way of approaching his role that I've seen before from top performers. He rarely got into the studio too early because he likes to jump on air and wake up the nation with a certain style and attitude. He doesn't want to lose the momentum. He likes the blinds open so he can watch the sun rise along with his listeners. I liked that and understood exactly why he did it. Even though he had regular catch ups about his show with his producer, Helen, and Bob Shennan, he also critiqued his own show along the way. He knew if the show was good or bad that day, but like all performers you can't see the whole thing in the round. What he thought was a bad show was often a good one and vice versa. The mark of a great performer is never being happy about your own performance. You always think you can do better. The search for excellence is what makes people better than others. To take over from the huge star that was Terry Wogan and deliver a bigger audience is some achievement especially when everyone, including me, expected it to go down initially.

*

The most expensive show on the Radio 2 network is Friday night is Music Night. It's expensive because it uses the BBC Concert Orchestra and the show is recorded weeks in advance with a live audience at a location, usually somewhere around London. The show is produced by one of the BBC's best, Anthony Cherry, or Lord Cherry as he is affectionately known. He invited me to a recording of the show, so I decided to take my wife, Linda, along for a night out. It's not often I can say I'm the youngest in the audience but, boy, I was by some distance. It was not lost on me that this was the most expensive show on the network, yet not a single person in the audience paid for their TV licence as every one of them was over seventy! When you get to this age you get your TV licence free as a reward for surviving that long. Well done them.

The BBC produces this show brilliantly and you could argue this is exactly the area where we want the BBC to be, offering programmes that are never going to be delivered by the commercial sector. Another reason for the cost explosion at Friday Night is Music Night is that the producers often have to have musical scores re-written for the artist they are using that week. For example, if Elaine Page can only sing in the key of C and the music dots are written in F then you have to change the music for the whole orchestra to accommodate her range. It's this attention to detail that often goes unnoticed.

Another part of Radio 2 that fascinated me was their choice of music. This is the biggest music and entertainment radio station certainly in Britain and probably in Europe. Commercial radio spends a fortune in ensuring they play the right songs at the right time. It is heavily researched and there is no way a presenter on commercial radio today could ever choose their own song to play. That would be a sackable offence unless, of course, they'd asked beforehand. Yet, here at Radio 2 they had such a relaxed approach to their music. I watched as experienced presenters and producers just went into the music system and played what they felt was right. Even to me there were some wild choices. Chris Evans launched his breakfast show one day with The Sweet and *Blockbuster*. My God, I hadn't heard that for decades - but this is why Radio 2 is so different. Of course, there was a head of music in Jeff Smith, a very experienced and well-liked individual, but people, on the face of it, could choose to play what they wanted when they wanted. I was quite taken aback by this approach and you can hear an amazing range of music on this station. I once told someone very high up in commercial radio that Radio 2's success is based on playing the songs that commercial radio rejects. If you compared the music on this station versus that of commercial radio, the cross-over at the time I did the analysis was something like eight per cent. Commercial radio could play the sort of songs Radio 2 play if they wanted to, but they chose not to. Of course, a radio station is all about the total mix of the output and it's fair to say commercial radio is a different beast, but it's an interesting debate. I attended the music playlist meeting at Radio 2. This is where they select a few songs each week that producers have to play in between their free choices. As I sat there, Gary Bones, an experienced hand, said that Radio 2 shouldn't play a certain song because it was 'too commercial', as in commercial radio. I said nothing. Another song was played and again he said the same thing. I was now starting to get irritated. The third time he said it, I couldn't help asking what he meant by that. His answer was an interesting one and gave me some food for thought. His view was that the song in question would be played a lot by commercial radio. When commercial radio likes a certain song they add it to their A list, a category where songs can often be played over ten times a day. These can then be regarded as a 'commercial radio success story' and, as such, it was the duty of the BBC to offer an alternative listen. However, if the song was a hit, I suggested, people liked it so were Radio 2 not going to be accused of taking an active stance not to play a popular song just because commercial radio played it so much? That seemed a strange decision to me. Not at all, he replied, they would still play it but not as often as some other songs that were more acceptable to their own audience. It highlighted to me the huge difficulty of working within a music format. Music is so diverse. What I like, you might not and vice versa but you can't argue with the success Radio 2 were having. It was just another point of view and I pondered on that for some time. I came to the conclusion he was probably right.

A few days later, I was due to sit in with Chris Moyles. I didn't think I'd met Chris but I was a fan. The day before I was due into the studio, I received a call from his boss Andy Parfitt. Andy is the man who over the years has changed the face of Radio 1. Along with Jim Moir and Lesley Douglas, his record will take some beating. He is also a skilled politician and was able to protect the network from the BBC suits who often wondered what those 'young uns' were up to in their own building, Yalding House. Over coffee, he surprised me.

'John, can I take you back to 1993?'

'Err, okay, Andy. Go on then.'

'In 1993 you were running a radio station in Carlisle called CFM.'

'That's right. One of my favourite times,' I recalled.

'Well, you had an application from a young presenter called Chris Moyles.'

I laughed, 'Oh really, well fancy that.'

'Yes, John,' he smiled. 'Better still, you hired him.'

'Great, that's good news for tomorrow then,' I said.

'Yes, well, great in one sense. You're actually featured in his book I think.'

'Am I?'

'Yes, he talks about you but doesn't actually name you, I believe.'

'Go on, tell me more. There must be a point to this conversation surely?'

'You gave him a job and then, just before you launched on the air, he called you to say that he wasn't going to come after all and you apparently gave him the biggest bollocking of his life.'

'Oh really. Well, let me tell you this Andy, I can't remember that moment at all but I would have to admit it *does* sound like me! He's going to apologise then tomorrow, is that it?'

'I doubt it, John. I'm told he has never forgotten that bollocking and he's never forgotten you. So tomorrow when you come in to watch the show go out, I can't really predict what might happen and he may very well put you on the show live and have this out with you.'

I started laughing. 'This is great, Andy. Look, I'm a huge fan of Moyles. I love his show, he makes speech radio come alive so don't worry about me. Also, I've spent my whole life on the air so if he takes me on that'll just make great radio for everyone. I'll give as good as I get. However, more importantly what you're saying is this: Chris Moyles applies for a job for a station where I was the boss. I was good enough to give him that job and yet with just a couple of weeks to go when all the marketing had been done, other people had been told no and the station line up was complete, he rings and tells me he's not coming.'

'I think so,' said Andy.

'Yes, you're probably right. In those days I could respond with a temper and he probably did get a bollocking, but, to be honest, I can't recall if it's a true story or not. That said, what you are also saying is that Moyles is *not* taking the opportunity after all these years to apologise in person for promising to come and then not coming at all and creating me a ton of work at the last minute. Instead, all he remembers is that bollocking.'

'Yes, John, that's probably it,' he replied.

'Don't worry Andy. I love the show, I really like him and I rate him highly. I won't get in the way and I can handle myself.'

'That's great, John, but I might just come in to the studio nonetheless.'

I turned up the following morning at 7.40 am. I only needed to watch an hour to see who was involved, so this was early enough. As I came around the corner, Chris was outside having a cigarette in between a couple of records. It's well known at the station that Chris only plays a couple records to have a fag break. If he didn't want one, I think he wouldn't play any records at all.

As we met each other outside I said, 'Hi Chris, John Myers. I hope you don't mind me coming into the studio this morning?'

He looked at me and said, 'Well, I do actually, John, but there's not much I can do about it is there?'

That's a nice welcome. You're absolutely right about that Chris, I thought. There is fuck all you can do about it and I legged it downstairs. Chris gets some bad Press yet he's a great jock. He talks about stuff that others couldn't do or would not dare, even if they had the knowledge. Radio is about engagement and Chris knows how to engage, you can see this by his audience figures and the way his audience react to him. Sometimes I listen to the show and there is nothing really going on and then there is a great moment of genius. That's what separates great presenters from run of the mill. You might not like his act, but you can't deny he is good at it. As I sat in the production studio watching the show go out through the glass, I glanced at the texts coming in. Evans had about three thousand a show from an audience that typed in sentences with full stops, offering Chris great content if he wanted to use it. On this show, the tech-op leant over and told me the daily text figure is a staggering 42,000. I was shocked and when I looked at some of the contents most were four or even three words. Of course, a few just contained two words! That was his audience. This was how they wanted to connect. This was someone who communicated. As I watched these texts come in, I couldn't help myself smiling at the profit a commercial station would be gaining from these numbers at eleven pence a time. The BBC doesn't charge at all. I could have cried!

To be honest, I have no recollection of that moment in 1993 yet there is every possibility it's true.

*

Recently Chris has decided to move away from the breakfast show and why not? He has nothing more to prove. His marathon breakfast show for Comic Relief raised around three million pounds, although he had to do more than fifty hours of live radio to achieve that. I was amazed he failed to even get a nomination for this huge effort at the following Sony Radio Academy Awards, but even though I'm chairman of that organisation, it is the judges who make the decision.

What this all proved was that Chris can do the breakfast show standing on his head, his audience numbers were impressive and, despite the call to bring the age of listeners down, he will be a tough act for anyone to follow. That point is interesting, though. The drive for Radio 1 to bring down the age of their listeners is driven by commercial radio. One of the big problems with having a 'personality' on air is that demographics go out of the window when you add someone to the line up with humour or a strong personality. People don't listen to the radio and say, 'I'm forty and there's no way I should be listening to this programme'. Humour has no age restrictions. Everyone I know believes they are at least ten years younger than their actual body age. Why should we act our age in any case? We should act how we feel and if we feel like listening to Moyles, Kiss, Capital or Smooth then go right ahead. You never hear a commercial station complaining in public they have too many listeners, regardless of their age profile.

The biggest problem I found at the BBC was not so much the operation of the networks but the detail behind that. The BBC are so big and so complicated that their finance systems are hard to penetrate. Their web of internal recharges and cross-budgeting systems are so complicated that it is practically impossible to work out what the true cost really is. It's like knitting fog. You can try but you will simply lose a day out of your life that you won't get back.

There is always going to be a debate about the cost of this organisation. Yet, I am a fan. That does not mean I think they have a perfect model or that changes and savings cannot be made.

Can they work cheaper? Of course they can.

Can they work with fewer staff? Absolutely.

Do they provide a service the British public is proud to call its own? Every single time!

Can they work sharper and more productively? You don't need me to tell you that.

The area of my report that got the most coverage came from just one sentence. I didn't even comment on it as I knew just including it in the report would probably set off a chain of events. How true that was. The deal with Tim Davie was that I could not mention any figures that were not in the public domain. That seemed fair enough and I proceeded on that basis. In the course of researching the report, I was invited over to the offices of Newsbeat, the newsroom that services both Radio 1 and 1Xtra. It was technically out of my remit, I hadn't asked to go to Newsbeat but I was invited. The unit is run by one of the country's greatest radio news editors, Rod McKenzie. Not only is he experienced he is also a gifted newsreader himself. As he showed me around his team, I was struck by the fact that there were absolutely no empty seats. In commercial radio this is not good news. We like to see empty seats. I used to often go and see my Sales Director for a catch up and if I looked out of the window and saw lots of empty seats, it meant the staff were out selling. That pleased me. A row of bums sitting in seats means less revenue coming in. They should be in front of clients.

Here in Newsbeat the room was packed. I asked Rod how many people worked in his department and was genuinly shocked when he told me fifty-two, plus some technical support. I wrote that down in my diary at the time as it was such a big figure although I had no idea if I was looking at that many right at that moment. Radio 1 ran ninety-second news bulletins on the half hour, plus a fifteen minute bulletin twice a day. It was brilliantly produced, I watched one of these bulletins go out and you cannot doubt the excellence of the staff. That was not the point though. They had fifty-two people to do all of this. I left Rod's office and a short while later I sent him an email asking if he could confirm those numbers again. He did just that, so I put it into my report.

A couple of weeks later I presented my draft to Tim Davie and he said, 'Hey John. We agreed that we wouldn't put in any numbers. 'You're right,' I said, 'but these are publicly available figures and, what's more, Rod McKenzie highlights that he does all this wonderful work for the network with fifty-two staff on his own website. So it's publicly available.'

Tim had to agree that it stayed in the report. When my report was published soon after, there was nothing genuinely headline grabbing in it but then the Press spotted the line that Newsbeat had fifty-two journalists and it all exploded. A twitter hash tag started called newsbeat52 and the media had their story. The Media Show with Steve Hewlett on Radio 4 really went to town and Tim Davie was called to account live on the air. My God, I thought, the BBC really know how to kick themselves in the balls. Tim went on the show and managed to defend Steve's attack quite well but it was a difficult time. I was asked what I thought as I hadn't actually commented on that particular point until then but I did say it was 'a surprise' to say the least. Steve Hewlett was aghast, he just couldn't understand why Newsbeat had more staff than Panorama. Neither could those on the top floor.

To be honest, I was both pleased and not so pleased by this point being the focus of it all. On the plus side, it got a lot more people to read it all and I am pleased with the reaction, especially from within the BBC who thought I had nailed it (mostly). On the negative side the Press focused just on this point when even I would defend their stance that Newsbeat do a lot more than just produce their bulletins. They also do a lot of international reporting and features but it was too late, the number was the number and it was embarrassing to the BBC. The reality is that delivering news to a young audience, who often have the attention span of a fruit bat, is hugely difficult. Eventually it all calmed down and Newsbeat had to agree to reduce this figure from fifty-two to thirty-seven. As of today, the BBC have taken up about seventy per cent of my recommendations and it set me up nicely for my report into BBC Local Radio.

Chapter Twenty-Six

FORTY UNUSUAL SUSPECTS

I received an email inviting me to lunch with the BBC's Director General, Mark Thompson. Very nice I thought, I'd certainly go to that. It was not a one-to-one lunch as such but rather a select gathering of around six people from across the industry, plus a small army from the BBC. I'm always amused at the number of people who can accompany Mark. I don't know whether that's to protect him from us or to protect us from him. I've known Mark, since he was executive producer in Trouble at the Top, the documentary that filmed the launch of Century in the North West some thirteen years previously. He has a sharp intellect and is far more impressive in small gatherings than he comes across to the media at large. For some reason, he has always been unloved by the cameras but, make no mistake, he's as bright as a pin and when a review of his time as head of the BBC is written it will be a positive report.

Looking out of the window from Broadcasting House, along Regent Street, we quickly chatted about local radio. In return for signing off on a licence fee settlement with Government, the BBC started a process called DQF, Delivering Quality First, under which the goal was to find savings across the board. Their considered report on how they were going to achieve this had just been published and overall, there were no major surprises with the exception that DQF appeared unfair to BBC Local Radio who had been singled out for larger than expected budget cuts. A rumbling of discontent was gaining momentum and was clearly not going to go away. Later, I received a call from Radio 4 asking if I would appear on the breakfast show to discuss the cuts. I was happy to do it but called up David Holdsworth, who was in charge of the BBC's English regions, to make sure he had no objections to my appearance on the Today programme. On the face of it, the BBC were asking for a reduction of £15m from a budget of £115m. To my eyes, that seemed very easy to achieve and the next day I told them so. The Today programme also interviewed a freelance writer from The Guardian who was moaning that local radio in Merseyside couldn't manage to do what they did, and in the manner in which they did it, if these cuts went ahead. I told him to sober up. It was madness to think BBC Local Radio could not make fifteen million pounds of cuts from a budget that would still have £100million left.

At the lunch, the DG was kind enough to tell me he was impressed by my report into the national music services so I suggested that perhaps, if it would help him internally, I could have a look at their local problem, too. He jumped at the chance and before long I was in discussions with their strategy team on the way forward. We had not agreed anything, as I wanted to put this on hold for a short while. I was chairing the prestigious Radio Festival in Salford the following week where Mark Thompson had agreed to step up to the podium and explain his thinking around the overall DQF review. We all knew he would have to explain DQF's effect on radio in more detail. It was the first time the Radio Festival had sold out and we were all ears as Steve Hewlett, host of Radio 4's Media Show, interviewed the DG and started to dissect the speech Mark had given. I had said nothing to anyone about my discussions with Mark and his team, but this did not stop the DG announcing to the UK media that it was practically a done deal. To be fair to Mark, he was slightly pressed into this as Steve Hewlett asked him why, if he was getting all this stick about the proposed cuts for local radio, wasn't he asking someone like me to review the network and come back with a proposal. I had done that for their national stations so why not do the same for the local operation? I thought Mark might just bounce this right back with a bland answer but instead he announced they were going to do just that. Bingo. The news was out and suddenly the Press was hounding me around the hall for a comment. I could have done without this as being Chair of the event meant I had to focus on the festival, not on the work I was potentially doing. A statement was called for and BBC Local Radio quickly issued one as it grew to become the hot story of the festival. I felt for David Holdsworth who had better things to do than field questions over this. He was besieged by his own network of local stations asking what the hell was going on? His task was not helped by the fact that on my personal blog through my myersmedia website I had recently penned a couple of articles about BBC Local Radio and how it could be improved. Quite rightly, some of the staff wanted to know how I could be chosen to form an independent view when, on the face of it, I had already formed one and found the whole lot of them guilty of having too much cash and not enough vision.

A slight exaggeration, of course, but even I have to admit it added a little fuel to the fire.

I did smile as I was now sitting in a good negotiating position because we had not yet agreed a fee ahead of agreeing this project with David Holdsworth. In any event I saved them any embarrassment by agreeing a lesser fee for this job than I did for the network stations, even though this was going to include a lot more hassle and travelling.

I was a little annoyed with myself for lambasting local radio during my interview on Radio 4 the week before. At the time I was under the impression that the fifteen million pounds of savings had to come from the total budget of £115m, yet when I got into the detail at the start of my review, I found out this was not the case. Instead, £15m was being slashed from an operational budget of £71m. This was a totally different story to the one I had first been given and changed my perspective of the ambition set by DQF.

In this review, David Holdsworth had a much tighter brief than the one Tim Davie had given me. David was determined I wouldn't wander into areas that were not within my remit, which is a shame because I could have done another twenty pages just on their programming ethos and presentation style. There was so much that I wanted to say to help improve what local radio did but a deal is a deal. I'd agreed to this tight brief and therefore I had to hold to my side of it.

David Holdsworth is a very experienced executive and has worked in local radio for most of his life yet yet he was open to ideas. Following my comments about Newsbeat on Radio 1, his boss Helen Boaden, the head of news, was anxious that I be given a shorter lead. Mind you, as the review went along no one ever stopped me going anywhere I wanted. All doors were open and I have to say everyone was very accommodating. This is so very BBC. You just wouldn't get anyone from commercial radio inviting someone in to review their operations, paying them to do it and then making that report public for the world to read. That's what a public service does, though, and it's quite unique.

*

There is a lot of truth in the well-trodden phrase that turnover is vanity while profit is sanity. There is no future in a business where the costs are greater than the profit line. When I was at GMG, if the audience figures went down but the revenue remained up no one was too concerned. However, if the reverse happened and audience figures rose but revenue went down that was a problem. I used to say to the programming team that they could dream, create, invent and have as much fun and success as they wanted, but one of us had to be sober. Someone has to have a handle on costs. There was no future in producing a product we couldn't sell. The clue to what we did was in the title, commercial radio. My Finance Director at GMG, Stuart Kilby, was perhaps the best finance executive I have ever worked with. He loved numbers but he also loved radio. He came to work because he loved what we did and he made a difference. He really wanted to help provide the structure for programmes to build audiences. People like that make a business successful. Best of all though, I loved his ability to say 'no' more times than he said 'yes'. We had a unique bond. The team quickly learned that in order to get me to say 'yes', they first had to convince Stuart Kilby. He was my right arm and if Stuart didn't agree then it was an uphill struggle to get me on side, too. We were a team. Whenever someone came up with an idea, I would glance over to Stuart and if he was shaking his head, I would defer judgment so that I could look at the project in detail. Sometimes I went ahead regardless, that's what a leader does but I could count on one hand the number of times I moved forward without him.

*

In BBC Local Radio they don't have a P&L as such, they only have the L part or perhaps it should be defined as the cost line. In addition, the finance screen was just as foggy as the one I found in the Corporation's national radio networks. The numbers were smaller but still just as difficult to work out. This was overcome a little when Strategy provided a man from their department, Terence Derbyshire, to ride shotgun with me. He was smart and could batter down a few doors to get the answers I was searching for. He also had contacts internally that I didn't and that helped enormously. I travelled to nine local stations, from Brighton to Cumbria, just snooping around, talking to staff, seeing what they did and how they did it. I really did think that this would be a nightmare, like walking into a nest of vipers, and at one stage, I nearly pulled out. Thank God I didn't. It was quite the reverse and as soon as I arrived at a station they were keen to show off what they did and the professionalism that was there for all to see. Bottom line, I was genuinely surprised and impressed. I had a view of local radio from my past history and it was wrong to have formed that opinion without looking inside what it was like today. My report, therefore, was actually very different from the one I thought I'd be writing. It shows the importance of an open mind. It underlined to me once again not to pre-judge things. I was continually learning and, in the end, I offered up quite a glowing review of the staff in particular.

*

Having reviewed the national services and now, quite soon after, the local operation, it was abundantly clear that there was a huge imbalance between the two. National seemed to get all the attention, while local radio staff very often were working in quite poor working conditions compared to commercial radio. I would never allow any of my stations to work with equipment that simply failed to do the job. It's a matter of pride to me. Never ask anyone to do a job that you wouldn't do or to work in a building that you wouldn't be prepared to work in yourself. I have kept to that belief all my life.

I surprised myself by going against the proposed budget cuts as much as I did but the report itself was really difficult to do. I had final edit, but everyone was very nervous about what I was saying. I've done eight reviews for different worldwide organisations and this was the most problematic. Too many people wanted a say in the final outcome and I was pretty unmoveable, to be honest. David Holdsworth held the ace card and handled the situation perfectly by saying that an issue I'd commented on was outside my agreed brief and, while interesting, could not to go into the report. He was right even though it was frustrating. At the same time I was not sure how Mark Thompson and his team would appreciate my findings as I would be saying publicly that they had got it all wrong. In the end, my savings proposal suggested a top whack of nine million pounds, down from their proposed £15m, but that they could find another £2m, which I believed they'd missed from their own review. This extra saving could come from sharing top-flight station managers, or Editors as they are called.

*

BBC Local Radio has forty managers looking after stations. These managers are on an average basic salary of about £65–70K a year plus BBC salary top ups and the employment costs of pensions, medical cover etc. This meant that the actual cost to each station was much closer to £100,000. In my opinion, in the right areas, a manager could very easily look after two stations. In a number of interviews with the TV and Press afterwards I kept saying this. David was dead against it, as his long experience told him it would not work. He argued that BBC Local Radio needed strong editorial control and that had to be done station by station. I disagreed and wanted my view included in the final report. To his credit, he never asked for me to change my stance, but told me he would disagree in public as loudly as I would be promoting the need for change. We agreed to disagree.

My report recommended changing the BBC Local Radio management structure and this, in turn, became the headline in the press: 'Myers says sack the managers' or 'Myers says cut managers not staff'. Nevertheless, there is no doubt whatsoever of the value of BBC Local Radio. It is a huge piece of gold that far too often goes unloved and under appreciated by the Corporation. Perhaps now, after all the stink of cut backs, this will change. I hope so as it is a powerful reason why listeners pay their licence fee.

*

Mind you, there were some wonderful moments along the way. As I was sitting in studios around the country watching local radio shows go out it was evident there was some nervousness about me suddenly turning up a bit like the Hotel Inspector. I always made a point of ignoring stuff that was outside my brief, as best I could. However, I did over hear one person moaning that there was no fruit basket in the studio that morning as management had cancelled the order that day in case I found it to be excessive. On another occasion, I watched as a producer had a conference call with their manager just so that she could get approval for a phone-in topic they wanted to run. Barmy, I thought, you make someone a producer and they aren't allowed to make basic decisions like this on their own.

However, my best moment came after the Myers Report was published. It was released around 10am and by two o'clock I had more than sixty-five emails from BBC staff praising the report. I was so chuffed by this, as it was totally unexpected. There were comments like: 'At last, someone has said what we've always wanted to say.'

'Well done, John, you've nailed it.'

As I scrolled down these emails, one stood out. It said:

Dear John,

    You're a cunt.

      BBC Employee

*

It made my day and I laughed at that for hours. I tried to reply but all I got was a bounce back saying address not recognised. It had been sent from a fake account but I loved it so much I printed the email off and keep it in my office along with other letters from nutters. This was special.

The next day, David Holdsworth called and revealed that, as luck would have it, the BBC Local Radio conference was being held the following week in Salford.

'As you've said that half the managers should be fired, I wonder if you might come along and explain yourself?' David asked.

'How long is the slot?' I inquired.

'About thirty minutes.'

'Not long enough,' I replied. 'I'd need at least an hour.'

'Okay, you're on,' he said.

The following week I stood there in front of all forty managers. I was first on and relishing it. What an opportunity to tell them things that were not in the report. I opened up with the story of how, on the day the report came out, I'd received sixty-five emails from staff saying how much they had appreciated the contents. 'They are also,' I told them, 'in total agreement with my findings that fifty per cent of you should be fired!'

There was a loud gasp in the room. Between you and me, I'd made that bit up but it was a good line. I then told them about the one email I received that simply said I was a cunt.

'There are only forty suspects for that email and you're all in front of me,' I said. 'Would the guilty person please stand up? You made my day, please take a bow!'

Nothing, just silence and a few smiles, but I'd broken the ice and we had a wonderful debate about what they did and how they did it. What I am asked to do in these reports is simply give a view based on my experience and a lifetime in radio. Nothing else. My view is no more important than their own view, it is just perhaps an honest assessment from a different perspective. It was a great meeting and underlined to me the depth of talent across the management board of local radio.

*

My biggest concern with BBC Local Radio is not the actual network itself but the way in which they sometimes communicate with their audience. Even though they would argue that seven million listeners a week is a great figure, I think it is quite disappointing as it could, and should, be over ten million with a little fine tuning. The content is often superb, they have all the tools but they can occasionally adopt a tone that suggests I am lying in a hospital bed or need to be talked to slowly or have things explained to me in too much detail. This is so wrong. The local radio audience were brought up in the rock 'n' roll years. We like change, we were part of the generation that had free love and flowers in our hair. Presentation techniques could change I said, even by just a little. It would have an enormous effect on their listening numbers. When you consider the huge demise of local commercial radio, the opportunity for BBC Local Radio is enormous. I should state right now that this is not a universal problem, some stations are indeed excellent with gifted presenters in their line up but there needs to be more personalities within the mix and those who can articulate their world in an interesting way. Too often we have great voices on the air who are not great presenters. I will keep saying this until I am blue in the face. Content is important but so too is how you say it.

I will give them this tip for free. News is important, local information is essential but programmes need to be presented by people we love, with a personality that is magnetic and appealing. Just one of these presenters in the line up is all that it takes. Listeners go where they are invited and stay where they are entertained and informed. How difficult can it be?

Chapter Twenty-Seven

THE APPRENTICE

The best talent is not a broadcaster on any radio station I know. Instead the greatest talent has not yet been discovered. It is the audience who always have the funniest lines, who know more about a story than we ever will and are much more intelligent than any so called professional we can put in front of a microphone. These people make radio stations come alive and it is our job to ensure they can tell their story or amusing tale. To enable us to do that we need to experience life at the coalface of radio and take advantage of any training offered.

In my early days I read just about every self-help book going and came to the conclusion that 99% are a complete waste of time. Biographies are much more interesting in my view. One that I would recommend comes from a guy called Victor Kiam. '*I was so impressed, I bought the company*!' That's a great read and so is anything by the great American motivator Zig Ziglar, guru in the area of motivation and sales. His motto '*See you at the top*' is inspirational stuff.

Beware, though, as there are some genuine nutters about. I've attended courses where someone will stand up and tell you that you can be unbeatable, you can change the world, you can be the greatest if you really want it. The reality is that if you dropped down with a heart attack right now, no matter how great I've convinced myself I am, there is no way I can do open heart surgery on you right there and then. Instead, what they are suggesting is that a positive frame of mind can work wonders. Negativity is a killer and I absolutely 100% agree with that. If you believe you can't then you won't. If you believe you can, then you probably will and that's why confidence works. It is the whole basis of these self-help books so don't buy any. I have saved you a fortune. Just surround yourself with those who have the same passion for life and opportunities.

*

It may be my age, but I believe too many people want things given to them right now instead of being prepared to work their socks off to get it themselves. It's all part of this instant stardom world we live in. Incredibly, some of those who do eventually make it big, blow it by becoming difficult to work with. They believe their own feelings matter more than those of anyone else when they simply don't. Difficult people nearly always come unstuck. I know someone who has upset so many people along the way that when he lost his job, no one wanted to catch him on the way down. It was a hard landing.

When I became a boss, I was often stunned by how little some people would do in order to get my attention, to seek out a job. I was on the phone nearly every day to potential employers but my phone rarely rang. On the rare occasion it did I was stunned by how many have zero people skills or knew how to prepare for an interview. Some just couldn't even communicate properly. Schools and colleges need to do better and prepare their students for practical interview techniques. They do all the academic work but they don't do the practical. I interviewed a young lad for a job one day who told me how badly he wanted to work at my radio station, how he'd work hard and do anything to get into it. Fantastic, I thought.

I asked him two questions: What frequency do we broadcast on? Silence. He didn't have a clue.

Who is our late night presenter? Silence. No idea. No prep, no interest, no job. Goodbye.

*

A young lady from Newcastle holds the record for the shortest time I've ever given anyone in an interview. The receptionist is perhaps the most important person I can hire. Their attitude reflects the station's attitude. Get it wrong here and you are so out of business. Reception is the first contact point for listeners and clients, and what's more, they have to make people pleased to be in the building. Receptionists have to be proud advocates of what we do and engage those around them in conversation. This was an important job at Century Radio, so I was personally doing the hiring. I'd made a point of ensuring that we kept all the interviewees in reception for at least ten minutes so they had a chance to talk to the current receptionist and find out what the role involved.

I went down to reception, met this candidate and took her to my office, where my PA, Joanne, asked the young lady if she'd like a coffee. In the five minutes it took Joanne to walk back upstairs with the drinks, I was walking this girl out of the building. What is the point in continuing with an interview just for the sake of it, if you've already made up your mind she isn't going to get the job? It's a waste time for both of us. I asked the young lady why she'd applied. She told me that the job sounded great and she had always wanted to work for a radio station. (Not *my* radio station, I noticed).

'What do you think a receptionist's job entails?' I asked.

'Err, not really sure but I'm a quick learner.'

'Did you not speak to the receptionist downstairs about the role while you were waiting?'

'Not really,' she said. 'I like to keep myself to myself if I can and not bother anyone.'

'Hmm, what do you know about this radio station?'

'Nothing really, I listen to Metro radio (our rivals) but my mam told me about this job and I thought it would be great and it's close to where I live.'

'Look,' I said. 'I've asked you four simple questions. You've not listened to the station; in fact by all accounts you never listened at all. You've not shown any initiative whatsoever by talking to the receptionist about the job while you were sat in front of her and, furthermore, you have not done any research or have any idea what a receptionist does.'

'Sorry, no.'

'On top of that you're chewing gum!' I said! I'm sure you are busy so why don't we leave it there.'

I walked her out to the door, but that didn't stop her asking if I'd sign a photo for her mam!

*

I once asked a director from one of the biggest HR firms in the country why people lose out at an interview. Her answer was very revealing. She told me how often people do brilliantly in the interview but blow it on the one-minute walk to the lift or the front door. They think it's all done, they've got through it but let their guard down on this short walk and say the most stupid things. The interview is never over until you are outside the door, she said. How true that is.

*

Perhaps the greatest triumph I can recall was when a young lad came to us at Century. He was just a teenager but he loved news. In fact he slept, ate, dreamt and worshiped it. He was a news junkie. We gave him a job. He had been through all the usual college courses and had his legal training but that was it. He was now learning in the field. He often went out of the office to record interviews, but we noticed that he was not the quickest of reporters in coming back to the studio with his audio. We had a chat with him and discovered he did not have a driving licence. He was just 16. He didn't want to tell us in case he blew the job, so he used to go out on reporting assignments by jumping on public transport or even paying for a taxi out of his own money. He just wanted to do the job. How can you not love someone like that?

On top of that he is a thoroughly nice guy. We supported him and made sure he passed his driving test. His name is James Rea and over a decade or so he rose through the company to become group head of news. Right now, he runs LBC in London and the news network for the largest commercial radio group in the UK. He got that job because he wanted it more than he wanted anything else. Desire, commitment, attitude right there in a nutshell.

The reason great talent does not always get the job they deserve is because they just won't do whatever it takes to get the job. They don't want it badly enough. Yes, you can be unlucky but in my book the only time to use that phrase is on a golf course.

Chapter Twenty-Eight

AND FINALLY...

What fun these three decades in radio have been. I started off trying to find a way to make easy money but I ended up working longer hours than I ever thought possible. I wanted to experience everything radio had to offer and I have beeen lucky enough to do that and more. As I write the closing sections of this book I wonder what radio will be like over the next thirty years. At the time of writing it would appear that GMG Radio, the company I launched in 1999 will become part of the larger Global Radio Group, subject to regulatory approval. We have fewer owners, bigger groups, less diversity and reduced localness than a decade ago. Is this progress? Are the radio stations we have today much more professional in sound than a decade ago? Of course they are, although I doubt they are as much fun. You can't stop the world from changing and there is no doubt that radio has to progress in order to survive. The world is a much different place, certainly digitally these days. The competition just gets harder, yet while 92 per cent of the population tune into this wonderful medium of ours every week loyalty to our radio stations is falling away. I fear this is because we are losing the art of hiring engaging personalities. A decade ago you could name twenty local radio stars today you can count them on one hand. Music radio is also an art. Make no mistake, the programmer today is just as vital to a station's success as one that works with the best talent. They are just very different roles and like most things in life, a balance is required but a radio station without a personality is always one that sounds incomplete to me. Perhaps that's my age but I can get music from anywhere, what I can't get is the creative link through a skilled performer that makes me want to listen more. Radio purists want the ideal station but it doesn't exist anymore. In fact, I very much doubt that the time I experienced in radio will ever return and neither should it. That was the past and the future appears to be all about brands, but the best ideas, the greatest creative thought and those with a gut feel for how radio really works will always win the day. Looking back, the doors that opened before me took me into a wonderland that has made me what I am. In life you become a mixture of the people you meet, the values you hold dear and the experiences you encounter. This is the real YOU.

I learned more about management and how to deal with people from observing the world around me rather than from any book or course I went on. The way I've been managed personally in the past was the best learning experience of my life. Mostly, it taught me what **not** to do, although the most positive learning curve came from working with Bob Phillis and Nick Castro at GMG. Bob, sadly no longer with us, was someone I loved, respected and admired greatly. Nick taught me the value of distancing yourself from emotion, to stand back and ask yourself what is the right thing to do. He was, and is, majestic. GMG taught me about ethics and standing by what you believe in. I learned that winning is infectious, that most people want you to succeed and that a deal was always possible if you are prepared to accept that the other party has to achieve their goals, too. Winning at all costs is rarely good business. I learned about myself. I know what I can and can't do and the importance of surrounding yourself with people who are much better at things than you are. Most of all I learned that content is everything.

*

I hope this book reveals a journey and one where I have matured along the way. I have made tons of mistakes but they were honest ones that came from walking forward into the unknown, sometimes without a safety net. I started off being a little crazy, determined to plough my own furrow. In my early years I was controlling, I had to know what everyone was doing. Over time that changed. I've learned from experience that there is more than one way to make things happen. I caught on to the fact that, more often than not, other people had better ideas than my own. If I could pick something in me that is unique, it would be my ability to spot a great idea the moment I hear it. I would hear twenty ideas a week from programming. Eighteen were mad, but two would be sensational. It was knowing which two that made the difference. The key was allowing my team to make it happen. My job was to lead them to success and then get out of the way. The best companies in the world are only the best because of the people they employ.

Everything in life is an experience to behold, even when things don't go to plan and believe me, there have been many times when my personal confidence simply evaporated. My Christian values helped me through these times and they have remained with me since my days as an altar boy at Christ the King church in Carlisle. I've concluded you don't have to go to church to be a believer in doing good, but you do have to act with kindness whenever you can. My dad used to say, 'It's nice to be nice, son.' That is right, it costs nothing and is a trait worth having.

I like to watch people, examine how they do things and wonder why? I have an inquisitive mind and take the view that you never stop learning. What I have come to realise is that weak people surround themselves with those who won't challenge their authority or their vision. Even though I will strongly hold my ground, I want to be challenged. I would say to my team that I don't have the monopoly on being right but at some stage I will have the monopoly on telling you I'm right. That's what a leader does. They make decisions from experience and after reviewing all the information to hand. I have worked with so many managers who can't bring themselves to make a decision. They are paralysed by a fear of getting it wrong. Fear is such a barrier to progress that it can often bring a business to its knees. Few things are more frustrating than working for an idiot who has been promoted above their competence. It's not their fault, it's the person who hired them who should be flogged. It is a sad fact of life that too many great people have lost their jobs in radio due to nothing more than being managed by a complete buffoon. Perhaps the worst trait in management today is indecision. It is the cancer that will slowly and surely kill any business. I insisted that whenever there was bad news to convey to staff it was important for station managers to do it themselves. If it was a Group decision, I would do it myself. If you stand up and explain the reasoning and can openly show why you have reached the decision you have made, the staff appreciate it. They might not like the content of what you are saying but they always appreciate it was you who said it. Another rule of good management is to insist on 'bad news early'. I can wait for great news but bad news is always more important. The sooner I hear it the greater the chance I have to solve the problem. I would tell my team no matter how bad the message tell me quickly. I might just be able to turn that around. We all have to deal with news that is not pleasant at times but someone who keeps bad news to themselves until the very last moment deserves neither my respect nor gratitude.

*

Working with young people especially is such a thrill. They teach me things that I never thought possible. You have to constantly challenge what we have today. Only young people with inquisitive minds can do that do that and they provide a window into a world that old farts like me can learn something from. They see things differently from many of us. I like to be around positive, inspirational people and keep away from those who are negative and destructive. Those who say they can't often find themselves to be one hundred per cent correct. I keep trying to retire and play golf, but after a while someone excites me with a thought and bang, off I go again.

There's only one thing I have that the young ones don't and that's experience. It is this experience that allows a new generation to shortcut failure. It is why, thankfully, people want to keep working with me. I remind everyone I meet, that no matter how talented they are, no matter how intelligent they might be, no one ever wants to work or be around people they don't like. You have to love people, love life and have a zest for knowledge to get on. I find it inspiring to empower those around me to be the best at what they can be as it is such a warm and emotional feeling. Motivation is essential but so too is the right support and understanding. Leadership is the key to the future of any business. Show me a poor leader and I will show you a failing business or one that will never reach its full potential.

*

As I finish this book my life is past the half way mark, in golfing terms I guess I'm walking down the thirteenth fairway and in my world it's a sunny day. I am keen to do other things, to learn new experiences and to enjoy new challenges.

I started off writing this book as a personal record of three decades in media. It's been a pleasure to write but, more importantly, it's been a joy to experience all that it entailed. My senior executive team became personal friends especially John Simons, Stuart Kilby, Jill Johnston, Joanne Riordan, Shaun Bowron and Billy Anderson but there are so many more I can equally put into the same box. They were the reason we became a family at GMG Radio, yet even they would admit it involved so many other people too, far too many to mention here. Going forward I remain involved in radio as Chair of the Sony Radio Academy Awards. I spend a few days a year as a Visiting Professor at the University of Cumbria and within Sunderland University, I proudly chair my local hospital radio station, Radio Tyneside, and a new venture called Teamrock, led by my good friend Billy Anderson.

*

The constant challenge in my life is my weight. It goes up and down like a bride's nightie. I've been overweight since I was eighteen and it is the only thing I have never tackled successfully. I pity those who say they are overweight because they have a medical problem, ninety-nine per cent of the time it is a complete lie. They are overweight because they eat too much and don't do enough exercise. That is absolutely the reason here. I don't drink and I don't smoke, but I love my grub. I have months of being totally in control and can lose five stone at a time. I treat it like a project. Yet when I come off it, the weight crawls back on just as fast. This is just my nature, everything to excess. Everything full on. I am just not trying hard enough. I don't really want it badly enough. It's like golf, I can never beat it.

*

Best of all, I am blessed to have a wonderful family. My brothers and sisters have always been supportive, especially my brother Eddie. My own kids keep me young and make me burst with pride. My son is the bright new tomorrow of radio and is far more advanced and further ahead of the game than I was at his age. What a talent and what a lovely man he's become. He'll do brilliantly as he is as driven as me and I'm excited just to watch him at work. My daughter lives in the real world, equally lovable and inspiring, full of fun yet with a steely grit and determination that is impressive. I am very lucky especially now that I now have the joy of two wonderful grandkids in my life. It is a credit to Kerry that Marcus and Mia have turned out so well in a world where that can be more difficult to achieve than ever. As any grandparent will tell you, they turn you into jelly. I love that and make no apologies for being an easy touch in their hands. Through it all, my lovely wife Linda is the real success story. She hates the limelight but without her by my side, this life would never have happened and this book would never have been written.

I have received many awards in my time. Every one meant a great deal and it is a reminder that I haven't done that badly. I really like that and it means a lot. More recently, I was awarded a fellowship by the University of Cumbria for what they tell me is an outstanding contribution to the medium of radio. Considering I left school without a single qualification this is lovely reward for the years I've spent in the University of Life itself. My acceptance speech was something I had to ponder on quite a lot and I have included it at the back of this book. It offers a little advice to all those starting out in life.

Being awarded this honour is an opportunity to give something back to those who want to experience just a little of what I've enjoyed. I have no hesitation in saying that radio is the greatest medium in the world – bar none. The golden generation are those who can teach and inspire people to be all that they can be. To encourage a new generation to succeed but more importantly to get them enthused about the wonderful world of radio is exciting. This does not mean I have become serious all of a sudden. Quite the reverse! In the words of Paul Simon, I'm *still crazy after all these years.*

✳

Thank you so much for finding the time to read my story, I hope it's not been a disappointment. I've certainly enjoyed writing it.

If you can, please feel free to let me know what you think via book@myersmedia.co.uk.

EPILOGUE

One of the proudest days of my life was when I was invited to become an Honorary Fellow of Cumbria University in recognition of my thirty years in the media. Here is the speech I gave to students at Carlisle Cathedral in July 2012:

Being awarded a Fellowship from Cumbria University is a huge thrill and I have to tell you that when I first received the invitation I assumed it was some sort of prank. Someone was getting their own back for those all those years when I pulled their legs while working in TV and radio in this area.

I've had such a wonderful and engaging life in the media, and radio in particular, that it would be ridiculous to suggest it's been anything other than pure enjoyment. I've never wanted to work in any other profession and got out of bed eager to get to work and, in fact, still do. Everyone here today knows about hard work and commitment and, from what I've just seen, I can sense the anticipation of a good night to follow in celebration of all that you have achieved.

As I stand here it's a trifle embarrassing to reveal that I left school some thirty-seven years ago this very week without a single qualification to my name. It's not something I'm proud of but that's just how it was at the time. Yet, for some reason, that's never held me back or indeed hindered my progress. Instead, my own education came through life itself and the joy of working with people who loved what they did and wanted me to be as good as them, if not better. Today, education is more important than ever and there are times where I do wonder what might have been if only I'd been inspired by someone who knew how to get the best out of me as a teenager. If you only have one natural gift, I hope it's the one where you have the ability to inspire others to be the best they can be. Too many people will tell you what you can't do. Just ignore them.

My own success has been driven from an inner belief in my own ability, driven by a love of people and a zest for life itself. Education, while important can only take you so far. What you've achieved over the past few years would suggest you've learned how to learn and you possess the ability to focus and to work hard. This is an impressive start and, as such, it will open doors. As you walk through them, your own passion for what you believe in and the way you engage with society will determine your future. It is what you do from this point that will actually shape the person you will become.

I strongly believe that you can be ANYTHING you want to be in life if you just allow yourself to dream a little. What I would give to be in your position today knowing the opportunities that are soon to come your way. There are no boundaries any more. The days are gone when the right family, the right background or the right amount of money was important. What matters now is how you conduct yourself going forward. I've employed thousands of people over the years. I've hired those with the best education to those with no education whatsoever. For 25 years I've been in the business of hiring talent, the very best talent I could find, but I've NEVER hired them at any cost. Instead, I hired people first and talent second. I was recently asked at an employment conference what it took to get a job these days. So many people have degrees, so many are chasing the same roles so what makes someone stand out? Simply put, you do have to ensure you give yourself the best possible chance to be employed but I come across so many who fail to impress me due to a complete lack of basic people skills. I'm told by those who've gone before me that it is normal practice, indeed it's expected, for me to offer you some advice as you set out on the road ahead. My own pearls of wisdom are not written down in any book I know of, but they come from years of practical experience. In my book, there are four basic ground rules to getting hired:

I've never hired anyone in my life with a weak handshake. If you can't get that right at the start, what chance do you have? If you don't have a firm handshake, get one!

Very few employers I know ever hire someone they don't like. You can be the brightest person in this wonderful cathedral today but if the person who's hiring you doesn't like you, you simply won't get the job. Learn some basic people skills, get used to meeting people, and smile.

Be courteous and annoyingly persistent. I'm always more impressed by those who don't give up.

Fourth, and perhaps the most important of all. You have to have integrity and honesty and be happy to wear that as a badge of honour.

Considering the media is in the dock right now that might appear to be a little patronising, but I believe the reverse is true. This industry has a huge number of people who work in it each and every day who perform brilliantly and professionally for the benefit of the greater good. In any case, in life you set your own standards and that is why I love radio. It is, in my view, the most respected and trusted medium on the planet.

The best companies in the world are only the best because of the people they employ. It's as simple as that. I was once asked why some of the companies I have run have won so many awards for excellence. It was an easy answer to give. I employ great people with amazing talent and then I get out of the way. Another asked me what I most feared? That was also easy to reply to. The best talent in my company walked out of the building at the end of every single day and I just hoped they wanted to come back the very next day to do it all again. The best employers know that. The worst don't care. As you take your talents to the market, I suggest you set your own standards and absolutely refuse to work for anyone without morals or for a company without a strong commitment to the people they employ. Better still, start your own business. Become an entrepreneur and set the world alight with your brilliance. In a world where we've seen more technical progress in the past 20 years than there's been over the last century, we've all come to realise that there's no such thing as a local skills market any more. Your amazing talent will be in demand around the world. You've learned skills that I don't have but I would certainly want. News is instant, content has no boundaries and people travel further today in the pursuit of their goals than ever before. Your talent has been given to you for a purpose. It's not to be kept locked up. Instead, you've a duty to share it with everyone around you. This means you must seize every single opportunity that comes your way and, of course, this might just mean working at the other end of the world. Relax. It's actually a very small place. We can be anywhere in 24 hours. You have the opportunity and, in fact, a duty to make this world a better place for everyone and to go about it with a great big smile on your face.

Wherever you go in life you'll have moments of madness. This is good. Madness is good. Crazy is better. Life is for living and all it does is make you a more rounded person. Failure is also good. In fact, I suggest, those who've never failed have never lived. The greatest leaders of our time have failed more than once on their route to success. It's the fastest way to learn so never be ashamed to fail, just remember why it happened, learn from your mistakes dust yourself down and keep on going. If you're faced with challenges, always take the more interesting route.

Thank you again for this wonderful honour. I'm a Carlisle lad, born and bred on the turnip tops of this very county. I'm proud of the area and indeed the people who've made this city what it is today. There are so many people who've helped me over the years and it would be remiss of me not to thank my own family for their love and support, not to mention keeping me grounded whenever there's been a moment when I forget myself! However, if there is an award for total commitment and dedication then it should be given to my wonderful wife, Linda, for allowing me to be the best I can be. There's absolutely no doubt that everything good in my life has come through this wonderful and inspirational woman. I've been very blessed indeed.

As I look around you and see your smiling faces and the joy of this day please take a moment to congratulate the people closest to you for the way in which they have led you to this point. Believe me, and I speak for all parents here, YES, you were more trouble that we had imagined and YES, there were moments when we held our breath, but we wouldn't have missed a single day of being part of your life. Being with you and watching you grow to this day has been at the centre of our own lives too.

Chancellor, this recognition is one I will cherish. Therefore, it is with enormous pride and gratitude that I accept this honour of a Fellowship, in the hope that I can continue to make both the city and its people proud. However, let me end by saying this. Today is not about me. It is about all of you. Please do the following:

Respect yourself.

Never fail to speak your mind

Work hard and enjoy life to the full.

Never, ever, be boring.

HERE'S A CORKER

The magic of radio…

Time to put a Cork in it

A CORK radio station was running a competition – words that weren't in the dictionary yet could still be used in a sentence that would make logical sense. The prize was a trip to Bali.

DJ: "96FM here, what's your name?"

Caller: "Hi, me name's Dave."

DJ: "Dave, what's your word?"

Caller: "Goan… spelt G-O-A-N, pronounced 'go-an'."

DJ: "… You are correct, Dave, 'goan' is not in the dictionary. Now, for a trip to Bali: What sentence can you use that word in that would make sense?"

Caller: "Goan f**k yourself!"

The DJ cut the caller short and took other calls, all unsuccessful until:

DJ: "96FM, what's your name?"

Caller: "Hi, me name's Jeff."

DJ: "Jeff, what's your word?"

Caller: "Smee… spelt S-M-E-E, pronounced 'smee'."

DJ: "… You are correct, Jeff, 'smee' is not in the dictionary. Now, for a trip to Bali: What sentence can you use that word in that would make sense?"

Caller: "Smee again! Goan f**k yourself!"

2 15 16 17 25 26

ROLL CREDITS

Written by John Myers
Edited by Mike Ridley
Amended by John Myers
Edited again by Mike Ridley, with a sigh
Another story remembered by John Myers
Edited by Mike Ridley
Lawyer requires some edits
Re-edited by Mike Ridley, with gritted teeth
Pictures supplied by Mrs Myers
Inserted by Brigitte Bell
Amended by John Myers
Jacket design by Clear Marketing
Loved by John Myers
Jacket words inserted by Mike Ridley
Checked by John Myers who…
Remembered yet another story
Told to 'sod off' by Mike Ridley
Finally sent to printers.
Went to pub…

ACKNOWLEDGEMENTS

You don't undertake a project like this on your own. You need to be inspired, led, helped and supported along the way. So many friends kept telling me to write my story and put down on paper some of the amazing tales I often tell at dinner parties. After travelling on a train one day with Jeremy Vine, he told me to 'just do it' and having done just that, he kindly agreed to do the foreword. Next stop was to call on the services of a dear friend, Mike Ridley.

We go back to the days of Radio Cumbria and Mike knows some of the tales I reveal from personal experience. He is also a sharp editor and possesses a lovely sense of humour, for which I am grateful. Without Mike, this tablet of words would never have reached your hands.

Of course, my lawyer and friend, Paul March from Clintons, did a wonderful job, offering suggestions and changes to reduce the risk of a writ!

And to everyone I have met in more than thirty years working in this wonderful industry, you have given me so much material. I am sorry I can't name you all. Maybe in Book Two?

Finally, I have written this book partly from my diaries that my wife has lovingly kept since 1988. I didn't even know she had them but they allowed me to recall some of the moments you have read about.

Most important, please remember this is just my recollection of events. I'm sure other people may recall it differently and, if they do, please be assured I am happy to be wrong. Their memory might be better than mine, so if anyone shouts, 'That wasn't how it was,' I ask you take their word for it, not mine. I deeply apologise for anything that may be offensive or just incorrect. It was done and said with heart-felt honesty and I recognise how the memory can play tricks.